The
Classic Guide
to
CRICKET

The
Classic Guide
to
CRICKET

W. G. Grace

AMBERLEY

This edition first published 2014

Amberley Publishing
The Hill, Stroud
Gloucestershire, GL5 4EP

www.amberley-books.com

British Library Cataloguing in Publication Data.
A catalogue record for this book is available from the British Library.

ISBN 978 1 4456 4038 9 (print)
ISBN 978 1 4456 4071 6 (ebook)

Typesetting and Origination by Amberley Publishing.
Printed in the UK.

Contents

Introduction

Cricket as an organised sport originated during the eighteenth and nineteenth centuries. The history of 'creckett' can be traced back to early sixteenth-century England and the Tudors – the first confirmed reference being in 1598 – it was at this time that the rules and structure of the game evolved, making it the national sport of England. Bowling evolved in the 1700s with the change to 'pitching' the ball rather than simply rolling it along the ground towards the batsman. This led, of course, to developments in bat design, and the evolution of the modern straight bat over the old hockey-style shape. The Marylbone Cricket Club (MCC) was formed in 1787, along with the opening of the Lord's Old Ground, and the club quickly became the custodian of the Laws of Cricket.

New laws were introduced towards the end of the eighteenth century, including leg before wicket (lbw), and the nineteenth century saw underarm bowling replaced by roundarm and overarm bowling. Organisation at county level later led to the official County Championship, and the expansion of the British Empire served to export the game, which became popular in many other countries, leading to international Test cricket.

Today, cricket is a worldwide, multi-billion-pound industry. The International Cricket Council (ICC) has 10 full members (Australia, Bangladesh, England, India, New Zealand, Pakistan, South Africa, Sri Lanka, West Indies and Zimbabwe), 37 associate members, and 60 affiliate members. The 2012 T20 Cricket World Cup was watched by over 1.5 billion people, and The Ashes, one of Test cricket's longest-running series (first tournament 1882/83) was watched by almost 10 million people in 2013. With recent controversial decisions and promises of review and innovation of the laws of the game in the future, now is the perfect time to look back on the early development of cricket, and one of its great pioneers.

The last two decades before the First World War have been called the 'Golden Age of Cricket', and the period produced some great players and memorable matches, especially as organised competition and county and Test level developed.

Often described as the greatest cricketer of all time, W. G. Grace began his impressive career in 1865, in the midst of some of the developments detailed above. As such, he is said to have been integral in revolutionising the sport. He played for a total 44 seasons, from 1865 to 1908, and during this time he captained England, Gloucestershire, the Gentlemen, MCC, the United,South of England eleven and several others. A right-handed bowler and batsman, he was extremely influential during this time, and many of his technical innovations left a long-lasting legacy. W. G. was also a qualified medical practitioner, and therefore only ever an 'amateur' cricketer, but it has been argued that he made more money from his cricketing than any professional cricketer. He played in 878 first-class cricket games, scored over 54,000 runs, held a batting average of 39.55, and his top score was 344.

W. G. Grace continued to play for several years after his retirement. He died on 23 October 1915, aged sixty-seven. The greatest cricketer of all time set down much of the history and knowledge he had accumulated over his long career in one of the very first 'manuals' of the sport in 1891 – *Cricket* by W. G. Grace. *The Classic Guide to Cricket* is a remastered version of this seminal work, including many contemporary illustrations.

The Editor

1

The History of Cricket
1300 to 1845

I cannot remember when I began to play cricket. Respect for the truth prevents me from saying I played the first year of my existence, but I have little hesitation in declaring that I handled bat and ball before the end of my second. My family was known as a cricketing family a quarter of a century before I was born. My brothers Henry, Alfred and E. M. were respectively 15, 8 and 7 years of age when I appeared, and though my mother did not lay claim to being considered a player, I am inclined to believe, judging by the light of later years, she knew how to play as well as any of them; she was certainly most enthusiastic, and ever ready with sound counsel and cheering words. And I know in her heart she hoped that I should be a credit to the family.

I have been told that I was an easy subject to teach; always willing to listen to words of wisdom, but rather casual in carrying them out, and looking as if I had a theory of my own about playing the game. Perhaps even at that age I realised the duty resting on every cricketer who desires to add a page or two to cricket history.

This much, then, may be safely accepted, that not a year has passed since 1850 in which I have not, in some form or other, played the game. That must be my justification for giving my experiences to the cricket-reading public.

But I have been asked to say something about the history of cricket; to touch upon the remote past, about which every writer has an opinion of his own, and upon which very few agree. Where wiser and more learned heads have failed I cannot be expected to succeed. I am a player pure and simple, and have been all my life more interested in the doings of players than in reading this and the other account of how the game began and where it was first played. I would rather read a hundred pages of Frederick Lillywhite's *Scores and Biographies* any day than half a dozen pages which try to prove it is absolutely untrue that the game had its origin in Rome, or Greece, or indeed anywhere but in England.

Club-ball was played in the thirteenth century, and the Revd J. Pycroft, author of *The Cricket Field*, and a friend of my own family, has little doubt of it being single-wicket cricket in its earliest form. He also quotes from Strutt, who wrote to this effect, fifty years later:

> In the Bodleian Library at Oxford is a Ms, No. 264, and dated 1344, in which a female figure is represented bowling a ball of the size of a cricket-ball to a man who is raising a bat to strike it; behind the bowler are figures, male and female, waiting to catch the ball. The game is called Club-ball, and the score is made by running and hitting as at Cricket.

A modern writer, who examined the MS also, takes exception to Strutt's assertion that some of the figures in the picture are females, and says: 'All the figures are monks, with their cowls up and down alternately.'

In 1477, 'hand-in-and-hand-out' was mentioned as a kind of cricket, and identical with Club-ball.

The word 'Cricket' is said to have been first used in the year 1550. John Parish, an innkeeper in Guildford, enclosed a piece of waste land that year, but was ordered to give it up in 1593. John Derrick, one of Queen Elizabeth's coroners for Surrey, aged fifty-nine, said: 'When he was a scholler in the free school of Guldeforde, he and severall of his fellowes did runne and play there at *crickett* and other plaies.' That has been accepted by writers generally on the authority of Russell, a local historian, who transcribed it from the old records of the borough of Guildford; but another and more careful reading has shown that Russell must have, innocently or intentionally, substituted *crickett* for *quoits*.

The seventeenth century was half through before the word was again heard of. Bishop Ken, in his thirteenth year, entered Winchester College in 1650, and Lisle Bowles, writing of him, says: 'On the fifth day our junior is found attempting to wield a *cricket* bat.' Eight years later Edward Phillips, John Milton's nephew, in his poem entitled

'Treatment of Ladies at Balls and Sports,' says: 'Would that my eyes had been beaten out of my head with a *cricket ball* the day before I saw thee.' In 1670 the British sailor added his testimony. The chaplain on board HMs *Assistance* wrote to the effect that while they were lying at Antioch, on May the 6th of that year, 'Krickett' and other games were played. This is his letter:

> This morning early at the least 40 of the English, with his worthy the Consull, rod out of the city about 4 miles to the Greene Platte, a fine valley by a river side, to recreate themselves with such pastimes and sports such as duck hunting, fishing, shooting, hand-ball and *Krickett*, and at 6 we returne all home in good order, but soundly tyred and werry.

What is considered as the beginning of the doublewicket game was played in Scotland in 1700 under the name of 'Cat and Dog' Dr Jamieson, in his Dictionary, 1722, says:

> This is a game for three players at least, who are furnished with clubs. They cut out two holes, each about a foot in diameter and seven inches in depth, and twenty-six feet apart; one man guards each hole with his club; these clubs are called Dogs. A piece of wood, about four inches long and one inch in diameter, called a Cat, is pitched by a third person from one hole towards the player at the other, who is to prevent the cat from getting into the hole. If it pitches in the hole the party who threw it takes his turn with the club. If the cat be struck, the club bearers change places, and each change of place counts one to the score, like *Club-ball*.

If we are to accept that as authentic, then small beginnings have had great developments, and something may be said in favour of English Tipcat as having made its mark on the game.

Strutt, in his *Sports and Pastimes*, quotes from Thomas D'Urfey's *Pills to Purge Melancholy* (1710):

> Her was the prettiest fellow
> At football and at Cricket.

Cricket. (*From a picture by F. Hayman*, RA, *belonging to the Marylebone Club.*)

In 1736 all doubt of the game being firmly established is at an end, for Horace Walpole on the 6th of May of that year, two years after he had left Eton, wrote:

An expedition against bargemen, or a match at *Cricket*, may be very pretty things to recollect; but, thank my stars, I can remember things that are very near as pretty.

And again, in 1749, he says:

I could tell you of Lord Mont ford's making *cricket matches*, and fetching up parsons by express from different partsof England to play on Richmond Green.

Clubs were now springing up rapidly, the most important of them being in the counties of Kent, Hampshire, Surrey, Sussex and Middlesex. Matches were of frequent occurrence, and according to several accounts large sums of money were staked on the result, and not unfrequently lawsuits followed. It said well for the popularity of the game that it fought through that stage and reached its present pure and healthy position in the hearts of the English people.

The oldest recorded score is:

KENT *v.* ALL-ENGLAND
Played in the Artillery Ground, London, 1746.

ALL-ENGLAND

1st Innings		2nd Innings	
Harris, b Hadswell	0	b Mills	4
Durgate, b Hadswell	3	b Hadswell	11
Newland, b Mills	0	b Hadswell	3
Cuddy, b Hadswell	0	c Danes	2
Green, b Mills	0	b Mills	5
Waymark, b Mills	7	b Hadswell	9
Bryan, st Kips	12	c Kips	7
Newland, not out	18	c Lord Sackville	15
Harris, b Hadswell	0	b Hadswell	1
Smith, c Bartrum	0	b Mills	8
Newland, b Mills	0	not out	5
Byes	0	Byes	0
Total	40	Total	70

KENT

1st Innings		2nd Innings	
Lord Sackville, c Waymark	5	b Harris	3
Long Robin, b Newland	7	b Newland	9
Mills, b Harris	0	c Newland	6
Hadswell, b Harris	0	not out	5
Cutbush, c Green	3	not out	7
Bartrum, b Newland	2	b Newland	0
Danes, b Newland	6	c Smith	0
Sawyer, c Waymark	0	b Newland	5
Kips, b Harris	12	b Harris	10
Mills, not out	7	b Newland	2
Romney, b Harris	11	c Harris	8
Byes	0	Byes	3
Total	53	Total	58

Kent winning by 1 wicket.

The Royal Academy Club in Marylebone Field. (*From a Picture by F. Hayman, RA, belonging to the Marylebone Club.*)

It will be seen that the match was closely contested, and the long-stopping exceptionally good. Only 3 byes were scored in the whole match, and those were in the last innings of Kent.

Up to 1700, and for some years after, the stumps were two in number, 1 foot high and 2 feet wide, surmounted with a bail. Between the stumps a hole was cut in the ground, large enough to contain the ball and the butt-end of the bat. In running, the striker was required to put his bat into the hole to score a notch; and the wicketkeeper had to place the ball in the hole before he could run the striker out. Wicketkeeper and bowler had many severe knocks on the hand from the bat; and the present mode of placing the bat inside the crease was substituted, and in force in the match I have given.

The following have been the changes in the size of the wicket:

1700 – Two stumps, 1 foot high, 2 feet wide.
1775 – Three stumps, one bail, 22 inches by 6.
1798 – Three stumps, one bail, 24 inches by 7.
1816 – Three stumps, one bail, 26 inches by 7.
1817 – Three stumps, two bails, 27 inches by 8.

There has been no change in the laws respecting the size of the wicket since 1817; but in the Gentlemen *v.* Players' match in 1837 the Players by arrangement had to defend wickets 36 ins. by 12 ins.

The distance between the wickets has been always 22 yards. All bowling was underhand, and of very indifferent quality; pace without length was the aim of everyone.

The strongest club at this stage of the game was undoubtedly the Hambledon Club, in Hampshire, holding a position somewhat similar to the MCC today. It was formed in the year 1750, and held its own against all comers until 1769. Meeting with many reverses that year, it was on the point of dissolution the year after: but in 1771 its supporters determined to make another effort; and against Surrey County, in September of that year, they were successful by the narrow majority of one run. The next ten years saw them add to their laurels. Out of fifty-one matches played against England during that time, they won twenty-nine. They have been immortalised in one of the earliest and most charming of all books published on the game – Nyren's *Cricketers' Tutor* – Nyren gives the names of the most eminent players when the club was at its best, and says of them: 'No eleven in England had any chance with these men, and I think they might have beaten any two-and-twenty.' The eleven were: David Harris, John Wells, – Purchase, William Beldham, John Small, jun., Harry Walker, Tom Walker, – Robinson, Noah Mann, – Scott, – Taylor.

Beldham and Harris were the great men of the team – Beldham as a batsman, Harris as a bowler. Of Beldham, Nyren says:

We used to call him 'Silver Billy'. He was a close-set, active man, standing about five feet eight inches and a half. No one within my recollection could stop a ball better, or make more brilliant hits all over the ground; besides this, he was so remarkably safe. I hardly ever

saw a man with a finer command of the bat, and he rapidly attained
to the extraordinary accomplishment of being the finest player that
has appeared within the latitude of more than half a century. One of
the most beautiful sights that can be imagined, and which would have
delighted an artist, was to see him make himself up to hit a ball. It was
the *beau ideal* of grace, animation, and concentrated energy.

Of Harris, he says:

> He was a muscular, bony man, standing about five feet nine and
> a half inches. It would be difficult, perhaps impossible, to convey
> in writing an accurate idea of the grand effect of Harris's bowling;
> they only who have played against him can fully appreciate it. First
> of all, he stood erect, like a soldier at drill; then, with a graceful
> curve of the arm, he raised the ball to his forehead, and drawing
> back his right foot, started off with his left His mode of delivering
> the ball was very singular. He would bring it from under the arm
> by a twist, and nearly as high as his armpit, and with his action
> *push* it, as it were, from him. He never stooped in the least in his
> delivery, but kept himself upright all the time. His balls were very
> little beholden to the ground when pitched: it was but a touch and
> up again; and woe be to the man who did not get in to block him,
> for they had such a peculiar curl that they would grind his fingers
> against the bat.

Harris may be considered the first bowler who knew the power of
a good-length ball. Until he appeared, daisy-cutters were about the
only balls bowled. Everyone knows the result of hitting at a ball on
the rise that is off the wicket; or how easy it is to get a batsman
out who can only play back. The two best batsmen; of that time,
Beldham and Lord Frederick Beauclerk, could play both back and
forward, and the display was considered of a very high order when
Harris was bowling against them.

Tom Walker was another of the Hambledon worthies, the coolest
fellow in existence. Patience and imperturbability were his chief
virtues; and he had the reputation of keeping up his wicket from
the beginning to the end of an innings, and playing his first ball as
he would play the last. Tom's appearance on a cricket-field would

startle the carefully dressed player of today. 'He was the driest and most rigid-limbed chap I ever knew,' says Nyren.

> His skin was like the rind of an old oak, and as sapless. I have seen his knuckles knocked handsomely about, from Harris's bowling, but never saw any blood upon his hands. You might just as well attempt to phlebotomise a mummy. He had a wilted, apple-john face; long, spider legs, as thick at the ancles as at the hips, and perfectly straight all the way down.

Tom was not satisfied with underhand bowling, and was the first to raise the arm above the level of the elbow; but he got no encouragement from the Hambledon Club, who decided it was throwing, and he had to give it up.

Nyren, while strong in the opinion that the Hambledon Club was head and shoulders above every other, was not blind to the merits of his opponents. He is great in praise of Lumpy – Stevens was his real name – a Surrey man. Lumpy could bowl the greatest number of length-balls in succession of any bowler he knew. He had a great reputation as a single-wicket player, but was completely and unexpectedly sat upon on a certain occasion. The match in which he was playing having been concluded early in the day,

> A long, raw-boned devil of a countryman came up, and offered to play any of the twenty-two at single-wicket for five pounds. Lumpy was persuaded to accept the challenge, but would not stake more than a pound; the rest was subscribed. The confident old bowler made the countryman go in first, for he thought to settle his business in a twink; but the fellow having an arm as long as a hop-pole, reached in at Lumpy's balls, bowl what length he might, slashed and thrashed away in the most ludicrous style, hitting his balls all over the field, and made an uncommon number of runs before he got rid of him. Lumpy was not much of a bat, and the countryman quickly upset his wicket with a fast daisycutter, and won very easily, amidst the uproarious laughter of those present. Lumpy swore he would never play another single-wicket match as long as he lived, and he did not.

Nyren's description of a match is as hearty and enthusiastic as his sketch of the players.

> Little Hambledon pitted against All-England was a proud thought for the Hampshire men. Defeat was glory in such a struggle; victory, indeed, made us only a little lower than the angels. Half the county would be present, and all their hearts were with us. And whenever a Hambledon man made a good hit, worth four or five runs, you would hear the deep mouths of the whole multitude baying away in pure Hampshire, 'Go hard! go hard! Tich and turn! tich and turn!'

We can shout today when occasion requires, but the players of the past seem to have had rather the best of us there.

The Hambledon Club played first on Broad-halfpenny Down, afterwards on Windmill Down, both close to the village of Hambledon. An old painting gives the eleven in their club costume of knee-breeches, stockings, buckles, shoes, and velvet caps. Lord Winchelsea's team some years later played in silverlaced hats.

Harris's introduction of good-length bowling caused the bat to be altered from the hockey shape to a straight form, and playing with a straight bat was now cultivated. There was no law in existence as to its size, and a player named White, of Reigate, appeared at a match with a bat larger than the wicket; but a rule was immediately passed regulating the size, and the Hambledon Club had an iron frame made through which every bat was passed before it was allowed to be used. Leg-guards now came into use, but they were very simply and imperfectly made. They consisted of two pieces of wood placed anglewise to protect the shins, and were anything but comfortable.

There were laws of a kind governing the game about the year 1700; but umpires had not the powers they possess now, and few matches were played without bickerings and quarrellings. Those of us who have had any experience of country cricket know that the umpires' decisions do not always receive the respect due to them, and that many a match has terminated in a dispute. That was not an uncommon ending to many a close match from 1700 to 1708. No man was ever justly out; many claimed to go in twice; catches were often disputed. The side going from home had the right of pitching the wickets, and a good general took care they were pitched to suit his own bowlers.

One maxim of Nyren's will show that each side was only too anxious to steal an advantage over the other in the preliminary arrangements. He says:

> In making a match you should be careful to stand on higher terms than you have an absolute occasion for, that you may the more easily obtain such as are necessary; keeping in mind the old adage, 'A match well made is half won.'

The following laws are the oldest published, and remained in force until the beginning of 1774:

THE GAME OF CRICKET, AS SETTLED BY YE CRICKET CLUB AT YE STAR AND GARTER IN PALL MALL.
The pitching ye first wicket is to be determined by ye cast of a piece of money when ye first wicket is pitched and ye popping crease cut, which must be exactly 3 foot 10 inches from ye wicket. Ye other wicket is to be pitched directly opposite, at 22 yards distance, and ye other popping crease cut 3 foot 10 inches before it. The bowling creases must be cut in a direct line from each. Stump. The stumps must be 22 inches long, and ye bail 6 inches. The ball must weigh between 5 and 6 ounces. When ye wickets are both pitched and all ye creases cut, the party that wins the toss-up may order which side shall go in first at his option.

LAWS FOR YE BOWLERS – 4 BALLS AND OVER.
The bowler must deliver ye ball with one foot behind the crease even with ye wicket, and when he has bowled one ball or more shall bowl to ye number 4 before he changes wickets, and he shall change but once in ye same innings. He may order ye player that is in at his wicket to stand on which side of it he pleases, at a reasonable distance. If he delivers ye ball with his hinder foot over ye bowling crease ye umpire shall call no ball, though she be struck or ye player is bowled out; which he shall do without being asked, and no person shall have any right to ask him.

LAWS FOR YE STRIKERS, OR THOSE THAT ARE IN.
If ye wicket be bowled down its out. If he strikes, or treads down,

or falls upon ye wicket in striking (but not in over running) its out. A stroke or nip over or under his batt or upon his hands (but not arms), if ye ball be held before she touches ye ground, though she be hugged to the body, its out. If in striking both his feet are over ye popping crease and his wicket put down, except his batt is down within, its out. If he runs out of his ground to hinder a catch, its out. If a ball is nipped up and he strikes her again wilfully before She comes to ye wicket, its out. If ye players have crossed each other, he that runs for ye wicket that is put down is out. If they are not crossed, he that returns is out, If in running a notch ye wicket is struck down by a throw before his foot, hand, or batt is over ye popping crease, or a stump hit by ye ball, though ye bail was down, its out. But if ye bail is down before, he that catches ye ball must strike a stump out of ye ground, ball in hand, then its out. If ye striker touches or takes up ye ball before she is lain quite still, unless asked by ye bowler or wicketkeeper, its out.

BATT, FOOT, OR HAND OVER YE CREASE.
When ye ball has been in hand by one of ye keeper or stopers and ye player has been at home, he may go where he pleases till ye next ball is bowled. If either of ye strikers is crossed in his running ground designedly, which design must be determined by the umpires. N.B. The umpires may order that notch to be scored. When ye ball is hit up either of ye strikers may hinder ye catch in his running ground, or if she is hit directly across ye wickets ye other player may place his body any where within ye swing of his batt so as to hinder ye bowler from catching her, but he must neither strike at her nor touch her with his hands. If a striker nips up a ball just before him he may fall before his wicket, or pop down his batt before shee comes to it, to save it. The bail hanging on one stump, though ye ball hit ye wicket, its not out.

LAWS FOR WICKET KEEPERS.
The wicket keeper shall stand at a reasonable distance behind ye wicket, and shall not move till ye ball is out of ye bowler's hands, and shall not by any noise incommode ye striker; and if his knees, foot, or head be over or before his wicket, though the ball strike it, it shall not be out.

LAWS FOR YE UMPIRES.

To allow 2 minutes for each man to come in when one is out, and 10 minutes between each hand to mark ye ball, that it may not be changed. They are sole judges of all outs and ins, of all fair and unfair play, of frivolous delays, of all hurts, whether real or pretended, and are discretionally to allow whatever time they think proper before ye game goes on again. In case of a real hurt to a striker, they are to allow another to come in, and the person hurt to come in again, but are not to allow a fresh man to play on either side on any account. They are sole judges of all hindrances, crossing ye players in running, and standing unfair to strike; and in case of hindrance may order a notch to be scored. They are not to order any man out unless appealed to by one of ye players. These laws are to ye umpires jointly. Each umpire is ye sole judge of all nips and catches, ins and outs, good or bad runs at his own wicket, and his determination shall be absolute; and he shall not be changed for another umpire without ye consent of both sides. When ye 4 balls are bowled he is to call over. These laws are separately. When both umpires shall call play 3 times 'tis at ye peril of giving ye game from them that refuse play.

'Notch' was the term used for a run in those days. Scorers generally were not sufficiently educated to enter in writing the runs as they were made, and the primitive form of cutting a notch in a piece of wood was resorted to. A deeper notch was made every tenth run. Rarely were individual innings recorded in other than first-class matches; and it is difficult to say when the important clubs began to keep complete and reliable results of their matches. The year 1774 left its mark upon the game. A committee of noblemen and gentlemen, from the counties of Kent, Hampshire, Surrey, Sussex, and Middlesex, met at the Star and Garter, Pall Mall, on the 25th February, and revised the Laws. Compared with those already given, they showed distinct progress, though falling short of the completeness and comprehensiveness of those in existence today. The great point gained was, that an authoritative body of players, chosen from the chief clubs in the kingdom, had spoken out, and their decisions were sure to be respected. Very few of them have stood the criticism of the 117 years that have elapsed since they were drawn up; but they were the outcome of the united wisdom of the best players of that time, and met the demands of the game for a good many years afterwards. The footnotes with regard to betting would not be tolerated today; but, if we are to accept the statements of different writers, that nearly every important match played then was for a sum of money varying from £50 to £1,000, we can see the need for them and understand why they were added.

The year 1775 saw the abolishment of placing the ball in the hole between the wickets, and the increase in the number of the stumps from two to three. At an important match that year, Lumpy, one of the best bowlers of the day, two or three times bowled balls which passed between the stumps. This was naturally considered hard upon Lumpy, and the third stump was added, and placed so that the ball could not pass between them without knocking the bail off. Two years later, 1777, what was considered a phenomenal score was made by James Aylward, for the Hambledon Club, against England. He scored 167 runs out of a total of 403. Individual performance and aggregate score were reckoned among the sensational doings; and it was thought that the former would stand as record for a century at least; as for the same individual exceeding it, no one dreamt of it. The same year saw the last match played on the Artillery Ground, Finsbury Square, the scene of many great and exciting contests for a considerable number of years.

The first recorded match of the White Conduit Club was played in 1785; and two years later the Marylebone Club was started. Farther on I have written more fully upon the rise and progress of the club, which has been looked upon as the authority upon all points of the game for more than a century. This much will suffice here: in 1779 a number of gentlemen among them Lord Winchelsea, Sir Horace Mann, Sir P. Burrell, Lord Strathaven, and others were in the habit of playing matches in the White Conduit Fields, and in the Artillery Ground, Finsbury. They formed the White Conduit Club the year after, and continued playing until some misunderstanding arose among the members. Thomas Lord, an attendant and enthusiastic player, was one of their bowlers, and he was instructed to look out for a ground, and promised support if he succeeded. By some writers Lord is given as a Scottish Jacobite; by others as a native of Yorkshire. It matters little to which country he belonged: he possessed the enterprising qualities which both Yorkshiremen and Scotchmen have the credit of; and in 1789 Lord's Cricket Ground, and the foundation of the MCC on the

A young cricketer.
(*From a Picture
ascribed to
Gainsborough,
belonging to the
Marylebone Club.*)

site of Dorset Square, were accomplished facts. Here he remained for some years, until driven out by encroaching builders, when he and the club moved, about the year 1811, to another ground, where South Bank, Regent's Park, now stands. The cutting of the Regent's Canal compelled him to move a second time; and 1814 saw him and the MCC established for good in St John's Wood Road. The MCC played matches in 1789, but there is no published record of their doings until the year after; and until 1791 a club match-book was not kept.

The year 1791 saw the dissolution of the Hambledon Club and the dispersion of its members over the counties of Surrey, Hampshire, Kent, and Middlesex.

Lord Frederick Beauclerk (height, 5 ft 9 ins; weight, 11 st. 12 lbs) played his first match at Lord's in the same year for the MCC *v.* Kent. He was in his eighteenth year, but gave no promise in that match of

Mr George
Osbaldeston.
(*From an old
print.*)

the skill which attracted the cricketing public a few years later, and which stamped him as the best amateur batsman of his day. He was a fair bowler, and kept up his form for nearly a quarter of a century.

Surrey, Kent, and MCC were now the crack clubs in England, and before the end of the eighteenth century they were in turn strong enough to play an eleven of All-England. County matches were of frequent occurrence: Surrey played Kent, Hampshire, and Middlesex; Kent and Middlesex played Essex; and Nottingham played Leicester.

The first twenty years of the nineteenth century introduced seven names which will live in the memories of cricketers as long as the game is played. To belong to the MCC even in those days was the aim of most players; to be considered good enough to play for or against it, was to stamp the player as belonging to the first flight. W. Lambert made his first appearance at Lord's in 1801, playing for Surrey *v.*

England; E. H. Budd in 1802, playing for Middlesex *v.* Surrey; George Osbaldeston in 1808, playing for MCC *v.* Middlesex; W. Ward in 1810, playing for England *v.* Surrey; Jas. Broadbridge in 1817, playing for Sussex *v.* Epsom; George Brown in 1818, playing in a single-wicket match; and Fuller Pilch in 1820, when only seventeen years of age, playing for Norfolk *v.* MCC

W. Lambert (height, 5 ft 10 ins; weight, 15 st.) was a good all-round player: first-class as a batsman, possessing tremendous hitting powers, a good bowler and wicketkeeper, and one of the best single wicket players of his time.

Mr Edward Hayward Butt (born at Great Missenden, Buckinghamshire; height, 5 ft 9 ins; weight, 12 st.) excelled as a batsman, but was good all round: he used a bat 3 Ibs. in weight, hit terrifically, and played cricket from his seventeenth year until his seventieth.

Mr George Osbaldeston (born 1786 or 1787; height, 5 ft 6 ins; weight, 10½ st.) was a splendid batsman; but made his mark more as a bowler, being considered the fastest who had yet appeared. His reputation as a single-wicket player was only second to Lambert's, and together they were equal to any pair in England. A good story is told of a single-wicket match made between Osbaldeston and Lambert on one side, and Lord Frederick Beauclerk and Howard on the other. It was a p. p. match for fifty guineas, and the result was thought to determine which was the strongest pair of that time. On the day of the match Osbaldeston was ill, and Lord Frederick was asked to postpone the match.

'No! Play or pay,' said his lordship.

'I won't forfeit,' said Osbaldeston. 'Lambert may beat you both; and if he does, he shall have the money.'

His lordship would not hear of it. 'Nonsense,' he said, 'you don't mean it.'

'Yes; play or pay, my lord. We are in earnest and shall claim the stakes.'

Score: Lambert – First innings, 56; second innings, 24; total, 80.
Lord Beauclerk and Howard – First innings, 24; second innings, 42; total, 66.

Fuller Pilch.

It was a great victory for Lambert, and he displayed excellent judgment. Wides did not count in those days; so he bowled them to his lordship until he lost his temper, and then catching him napping, bowled him with a straight ball. But Lambert will be remembered as being the first to score the century twice in a first-class match in the year 1817 which stood as a record for over fifty years.

Mr William Ward (born at Islington, London, 24th July, 1787; height, 6 ft 1 in.; weight, 14 st.) was a better batsman than bowler, and will be remembered for his great score of 278, when playing for the MCC against Norfolk, in 1820. He played with a bat 4 lbs in weight, and was one of the few who accommodated himself quickly to the change from underhand to round-arm bowling. Indeed, the change made little difference to him; and after it was introduced, he continued to score as freely as ever.

Jas. Broadbridge (height, 5 ft 10 ins; weight, 12 st.) could bat, but his name stands out as one of the two great bowlers of his time. Lillywhite and he were the two great exponents of round-arm bowling, and by their exceptional skill raised Sussex to a very high position in the cricketing world.

George Brown (born at Stoughton, Surrey, 27th April, 1783) is supposed to have been the fastest underhand bowler that ever played. He was so very fast that two longstops were needed for him, and nearly all the fieldsmen were placed behind the wicket. At Lord's a man once tried to stop the ball with his coat, but Brown bowled through it and killed a dog on the other side! Jackson, Tarrant, and Freeman, of later years, we can most of us remember, but Brown's pace at his best is said to have been faster than theirs. His height was 6 ft 3 ins; weight, about 16 st.

Fuller Pilch as a batsman, was head and shoulders above the others, and was undoudtedly the crack from 1820 to 1850. His height was 6 feet 0½ inches; and he possessed an exceptionally long reach, which he used to the fullest advantage. He played forward, and was thoroughly at home against all kinds of bowling. He was born at Horningtoft, Norfolk, 17th March, 1803, but migrated to Town Mailing in 1835, and by his personal skill raised Kent to the position of being able to play an eleven of England. He scored the century at least ten times in his career, which was considered a remarkable and exceptional performance then. He was past playing when I saw him first; but I can remember the pleasure it gave me when I met him at Canterbury, and we talked about the past, present, and future of the game. His star had set: mine was in the ascendant; but the light of battle was still on his face, and I could see what manner of man he had been.

Those were the players who made cricket history from 1800 to 1825; and I can quite believe they would give an excellent account of themselves today on our improved wickets against our best bowling.

Eton and Harrow played against each other at the beginning of the present century; but the earliest published score in existence is of the year 1805, when Eton won by an innings.

The Gentlemen and Players commenced in 1806; but then and for some years afterwards it was a case of the Players giving one or two of their best men, or playing against odds. The first match of that year the Gentlemen had Lambert and Beldham given them, and won; the second match Lambert only, which they won also. For years the Gentlemen struggled to make a fight, but all in vain. Various suggestions were made to make the match interesting and give them a chance of victory, but the results were still the same; and it became an accepted fact that if anyone desired to establish a reputation for prophecy, he could do it easily by naming the Players as certain winners in their match against the Gentlemen. Apathy began to pervade the ranks of the Gentlemen, and a collapse seemed inevitable. Here and there enthusiastic players kept advocating the claims of the match, Mr Ward among them. The year 1837, at his suggestion, the Players defended wickets 36 inches by 12; the Gentlemen, 27 inches by 8. The result was still unsatisfactory, the Gentlemen scoring 54 and 35 to the Players' single innings of 99. Like all innovators, Mr Ward got little thanks for his invention, and the match was dubbed the 'Barn-door Match,' or 'Ward's Folly.'

The year 1817 saw a great decline in the powers of Surrey. Considered good enough to play thirteen of England some twenty years before, it was not able now to play eleven, and did not attempt it again until 1852.

The year 1822 was an important one. It saw Mr John Willes at Lord's on the 15th and 16th July, playing for Kent *v.* MCC, make a big bid for the introduction of round-arm bowling. He was only allowed to bowl a few balls before he was 'no-balled,' and he left the ground, declining to go on with the match. A substitute was found, and Kent won easily by an innings.

Mr Willes has the credit of introducing roundarm bowling, and there can be little doubt his attempt in this match created the agitation which led to its adoption a short time afterwards. This is the story told of how he learned it. He had been very ill, and to recover strength fell back upon the game he loved so dearly. He was not quite strong enough to bowl, so he enlisted the aid of his sister to bowl to him. The straight ones troubled him more than the old style of bowling; rising more quickly off the pitch, and traveling differently. A little reflection revealed that his sister in delivering the ball turned her hand over it, hence the change. As soon as he got well he practised it, and found he could do more with the ball. Unfortunately, his temper was stronger than his respect for the laws; for not only did he leave the match, but made up his mind to give up playing altogether a decision which he adhered to. It will not do to condemn his action too severely. He is not the first who has had a pet theory pooh-poohed, and given it up in a moment of petulance. Five years later, if he had retained his proficiency, he would have been a perfect godsend to the Gentlemen, and have helped to speed the good cause with F. W. Lillywhite, J. Broadbridge, and Mr G. T. Knight. It should be remembered that Tom Walker, of the Hambledon Club, practiced it also.

The year 1827 saw the new bowling having a fair trial. Lillywhite and Broadbridge were the most proficient at it, and placed Sussex in the position of being able to play All-England. The first match came off on the 4th June, at Darnall, Sheffield, and was looked upon as a comparative test of the two styles of bowling England being represented by underhand bowlers. Alas! for the underhand representatives! they were out of it altogether, Sussex winning by seven wickets. Why the match was played in Yorkshire I do not know, unless it be that the cricketing authorities in the South were desirous, in the interests of the game, to give cricketers in the North an opportunity of witnessing first-class play. Cricket had made tremendous strides in Nottingham, Sheffield, Liverpool and Manchester in the last half-dozen years, and the policy of the MCC in playing a representative match there was in keeping with the forward spirit it has ever shown since the welfare of the game was placed in its hands.

The second match was played at Lord's a fortnight later, Sussex again winning, but only by 2 wickets. The defeat upset some of the players who represented England, and a number of them, with more temper than judgment, met and signed the following document:

> We, the undersigned, do agree that we will not play the third match between All-England and Sussex, unless the Sussex bowlers bowl fair that is, abstain from throwing.

Fuller Pilch's name was among the signatories, but reflection brought wisdom, and the third match was played at Brighton, the 23rd, 24th, 25th July, England winning by 23 runs. Ten years later Pilch, playing for Town Mailing *v.* Reigate, scored 160 against Lillywhite's bowling.

Round-arm bowling had now taken a hold, and here will be the place to say a word on behalf of one of the earliest and finest exponents it has ever had.

Frederick William Lillywhite was born at West Hampnett, near Goodwood, Sussex, 13th June, 1792. There is no record of his doings until he was thirty years of age, and his first appearance at Lord's was on 18th June, 1827, in his thirty-sixth year, playing for Sussex *v.* England. His height was only 5 ft 4 ins; but he was substantially made (weighing 11st. 8lbs.), and possessed exceptional stamina. He played right up to the day of his death, 24th August, 1854. The introduction of round-arm bowling was his opportunity, and no one then had a greater command over the ball. His pace would be considered slow today, but his accuracy of pitch was something marvellous, and a ball off the wicket was a rare thing. A wide ball rom him was not expected and rarely given; he only bowled some half a dozen in his whole career. He was what is now called a 'head bowler', always on the look-out for a weak spot in the defence of the batsman, and trusting more to catches than to wickets bowled down. He knew that the batsmen of that time had not been used to over after over of straight, good-length balls, and that sooner or later he would tempt them to hit. For years Broadbridge and he carried everything before them. Broadbridge was medium-pace also, and had been before the public as a good man some ten years before. The batting for some years had had the upper hand of the bowling; but Lillywhite and Broadbridge restored the balance, and showed the importance of being able to defend one's wicket as well as hit.

In 1832, Mr Alfred Mynn appeared at Lord's. In his way, he was quite as celebrated as Lillywhite, and was certainly a more striking figure. He was born January 19th, 1809; height, 6ft 1in.; weight, 18st. He was of the most lovable temper, and no player was cheered more heartily by the cricket-loving public; and he was a rare good batsman, hitting severely, and scoring faster than any player of his time. The hitting of his time compares unfavourably with the rapidity of the scoring today, 30 runs an hour being considered fast. His bowling was round-arm, very fast, but in the early part of his career very erratic aiming at beating the batsman by sheer pace. His delivery was peculiar, described by one writer as noble and majestic. He walked up to the crease, head erect like a soldier on parade, and the ball shot from his hand at a pace worthy of so strong a man.

Mynn and Lillywhite were the two bowlers who were now looked up to as possessing the styles to be copied – Mynn, very fast, relying on his pace; Lillywhite, a good length, relying on his accuracy. Mynn had the greater number of followers for a time followers who bowled at a pace much beyond their strength and went quickly to pieces. Lillywhite's accurate length appealed to the thoughtful player, and raised both bowling and batting to a more scientific position.

Sir Freserick Hutchinson Harvey Broadhurst was born 30th June 1807. Height, 6 ft; weight, 13 st. He was a first-rate round-armed bowler, and, like one or two fast bowlers I have mentioned, had rather a low delivery. Very few amateurs have continued playing at so advanced an age, and with such great success; for when he was 53 years old he represented the Gentlemen of Hampshire on several occasions, bowling in most of their matches, and rarely failing to come off: one match in particular, against the United England eleven, he showed that he had lost little of his wonderful command of the ball.

He represented the Gentlemen *v.* Players in 1837, the 'Barn Door' match, and continued to do so until 1854, when he was in his 48th year. Most years he bowled for them with more or less success; but in 1853, at Lord's, he carried everything before him, bowling unchanged in both innings a feat which had never been performed before by either Gentleman or Player in those matches. In the first innings he bowled 132 balls, 24 maidens, 19 runs and captured five wickets; in the second, 140 balls, 20 maidens, 31 runs, six wickets; and there can be little doubt the Gentlemen were indebted to him and Mr Kempson for winning the match on that occasion.

He was not a scientific bat, going in for hitting, and taking little trouble about defence, like many of the great bowlers of that time, and I do not remember any very large scores to his name. But he was a very fine fieldsman, and one of the greatest supporters of the game we have had. He was President of the MCC in 1857, and a constant attendant for many years at the great matches played at Lord's.

Mr C. G. Taylor (height, 5 ft 9 ins; weight, 10 st.), two years later, made his first appearance at Lord's, playing for Eton *v.* Harrow, and for the next twelve years shared the amateur batting honours with Mynn. He belonged to Middlesex, and was born 21st November, 1815.

July 11th, 1836, at Lord's, was the beginning of North *v.* South matches; the North winning by six wickets. Lillywhite was ill, and did not play, or the result might have been different. In the return at Leicester, six weeks later, the South won by 218 runs. Mynn was in his best batting form, scoring 21 not out, first innings; 125 not out, second. In his last four innings he had scored 283 runs, twice not out a feat which was considered a record for four consecutive innings in great matches. Lillywhite was just as effective with the ball in this match, capturing five wickets first innings, six second. Fuller Pilch played on the side of the North; but 1837 saw him batting for the South, which he continued to do for the remainder of his career.

Messrs W. Marcon and H. W. Fellows, as exceptionally fast bowlers, attracted attention in 1841. Both played for Eton *v.* Winchester at Lord's, 29th, 30th July of that year, and in the fulness of strength were contrasts physically. Mr Marcon was 6 ft in height; weight, 11 st. He was born at Swaffham, 28th March, 1824. Mr Fellows was 5 ft 9¾ins. in height; weight, 15 st. He was born at Rickmansworth, Hertfordshire, 11th April, 1826. Mr Marcon played a great deal, and, like George Brown of Stoughton, required two longstops, and tested the nerve of every wicketkeeper who tried to take his bowling. It is said of him that, with a very fast ball, he broke a batsman's leg at Oxford. As a player, I should like to have seen this particular fast ball and the unfortunate batsman who tried to play it. My medical experience has shown me that some legs are easily broken; but I have been always of the opinion that the legs, like the heads, of Varsity men have been exceptionally hard nuts to crack. I have had many an interesting chat with Mr Fellows; but, as far as I know, he has no such extraordinary testimony to his powers, although his bowling was considered dangerous to bat against, and the ball as it travelled hummed like a top. On one occasion he hit a stump so terrifically hard that it fell into the longstop's hands 11 yards distant! Both gentlemen had rather a low delivery, something between under-hand and round-arm.

The year 1845 was another of the eventful years. George Parr played for the North *v.* MCC at Lord's. He was then in his twentieth year, and, though he did not score largely, eventually became the best batsman in England a position which he held for many years. He had splendid defence, and hit particularly well all round, but excelled in hitting to leg. He had also a good knowledge of the game, and made an excellent captain; and his name was on the lips of every player for twenty years. He was born 22nd May, 1826, at Radcliffe-on-Trent: height, 5 ft 9 ins; weight, 12 st. 12 lbs

The 17th July of that year is the date of the first match played at Kennington Oval. Originally a market garden, the Montpelier Club secured the ground in 1844, and formed themselves into the Surrey Club the year after. After a number of ups and downs in the next ten years, Surrey suddenly blossomed into a most powerful club, and became second only to its next-door neighbour, the MCC, in power and influence. The members in 1855 numbered 230, income £500; in 1861 they had increased to 1,000, income £2,000, and every year since then may be said to have increased.

The 25th August, 1845, is another landmark. On that date the now famous club, the I Zingari, began its wanderings over the face of the earth, seeking for rising clubs; but more particularly for gentlemen bowlers who should wrest the supremacy from the professionals, and make the Gentlemen *v.* Players match a closer contest.

The club became a most popular one, and did good work for the game whenever it played. Crowds naturally flocked to see an eleven which comprised most of the best amateur bats of the day. Originally small in number, its strength today is something to be proud of, and to be enrolled among its members is considered a very high honour. I have in my possession a copy of its first Rules and Regulations, and give a selection:

RULE III.
A candidate for election shall be placed at a wicket, with or without a bat as the club may decide, and be bowled at. One straight ball to exclude. The number of balls given not to exceed the number of members of the I Z.

RULE V.
That the entrance be nothing, and the annual subscription do not exceed the entrance; but that the expenses of a match (i.e. of the I Z. umpire, &c.) be defrayed by the members engaged therein.

RULE VII.
That all directions connected with the game may be conveyed in the French or Italian languages.

SUPPLICATION.

Members playing in I Z. matches are more than most earnestly requested to abstain from wearing any coloured shirt, jacket or trousers. A Zingari belt or cap or ribbon should be the only distinguishing badge.

IRRITATION.

I Z. batsmen and fieldsmen being hit are not entitled to scratch or rub.

PROHIBITION.

Health drinking and dry toasts.

REITERATION.

Keep your promise, keep your temper, keep your wicket up.

The club flourished at a great rate, and in 1862 was made up of Active Members, Agents, Half-play Members liable to be called out, Members unattached to Cricket but attached to the I Z., and Candidates for the Asylum for Aged and Decayed Zingari.

2

The All-England & Other Elevens

The All-England eleven was formed in 1846. Before that time cricket in England was confined to certain districts. It had always flourished in such counties as Kent, Hants, Surrey, Notts, and Sussex; but outside of them it had been limited to a few country clubs, which were more or less attached to some nobleman or gentleman's residence, and were in fact supported by them. Such for instance was the Kingscote club, in Gloucestershire, under the auspices of the good old cricketing family of that name. Lord Ducie had a club atTortworth, and the Marquis of Lansdown at Bowood. True, there were important clubs in such large towns as Liverpool, Manchester, and one or two others; but the members were mostly in good positions, and were usually elected by ballot. At the weekly meetings of those clubs, the younger members came to play, the older ones to criticise, and sides were picked. A few matches were played during the season with clubs of the same strength who were within driving distance.

The dinners played no insignificant part at those gatherings, and many a good bottle of port was cracked before the evening was over. It is related that the Kingscote club nearly ruined itself by its hospitality to the Epsom club after a friendly match. Three haunches of venison were consumed, besides other delicacies, and the cellar ran dry. The chairman is said to have closed the innings of the claret with the remark: 'Gentlemen, I am sorry to say there is only one bottle left, and as it would be ridiculous to divide that among so many, with your permission I'll drink it myself.' That sort of social cricket existed, and very enjoyable cricket it was; but cricket among the people was scarcely known until the All-England eleven appeared.

Guy, Park, A. Mynn Esq., W. Denison Esq., Dean, Clarke, N. Felix Esq., Hillyer, Dorrinton, Pilch, Sewell, Martingell, O. C. Pell Esq., Lillywhite

Amateur efforts do not, as a rule, meet with success, for the reason that too often no one is responsible and the element of self-interest wanting. The I Zingari club has been a brilliant exception; but since it was formed a hundred clubs could be named which, conducted on somewhat similar lines, have died after a few years of struggling existence. The All-England eleven was started by one man, and conducted on business principles; and while it lived it was exceedingly active, and helped to spread a knowledge of the game. William Clarke was the founder; the majority of the players who composed it were the best professionals in England in every branch of the game, and under his leadership were open for engagements anywhere, as long as they obtained their price. As the eleven grew in strength and popularity, the desire to be considered, worthy of a place in it became the aim of every young and rising cricketer, and on more, than one occasion some of the celebrated amateurs were to be found playing in its ranks for the honour alone. Of course the difficulty was to find clubs of any strength to compete against. Usually the number of their opponents was twenty-two; but very often that was found inadequate to make a fight against so strong a combination of talent, and recourse was had to players outside of the club. In many cases two or more professional bowlers were allowed, and by that means interesting contests were played, and the eleven compelled to put its best foot forward.

William Clarke.

Every player of the twenty-two was naturally anxious to do his best against such celebrated players, for well he knew that his success would be talked about over the length and breadth of the land. To keep up one's wicket for half an hour, even without scoring, against the best bowling in England, was to create a reputation locally; to score a double figure and be praised by one of those great men, was something to boast of for a lifetime. A good many of us can date our first experience of first-class play from witnessing the famous All-England eleven, and hundreds will tell with glistening eyes of the good old times when they were considered worthy of a place against it.

The first match played was against twenty of Sheffield, on 31st August, 1st and 2nd September, 1846, Sheffield winning by five wickets. The All-England eleven players were:

Mr A. Mynn, W. Martingell, W. Clarke, T. Sewell, J. Dean, G. Butler, W. Dorrinton, V. C. Smith, F. Pilch, W. Hillyer, J. Guy.

That was a team that could hold its own against any eleven in England; but not to be compared with the team of 1847, or a year or two later, which had such good men in it as G. Parr, F. W. Lillywhite, and J. Wisden.

Clarke was the central figure, and for years met with phenomenal success as a slow underhand bowler. As a leader he knew the value of a change of bowling, believing the greater the difference of style the greater the chance of success. Mynn, Lillywhite, Hillyer, Wisden and he, ranging from fast round to slow underhand, were variety enough for all purposes, and there can be little doubt that their opponents were in many cases paralysed by it. It was an amusing sight in those days to watch the procession of local players to and from the wicket, dismissed by fast roundhand at one end and insinuating slow underhand at the other. I cannot think of a time when the All-England eleven, during the first twenty years of its existence, did not possess slow and fast bowling, and in that lay half its strength against weak twenty-twos who had only been accustomed to one extreme or the other. Clarke's personal success was the astonishing part to his opponents. They could understand being bowled by a fast ball of indifferent length, which they but dimly saw after it pitched; but to be clean-bowled by slow underhand was a mystery to them. They forgot the head that was behind Clarke's bowling. Just as F. W. Lillywhite was the first to prove the power of a good-length medium pace, round-arm ball, so was Clarke the pioneer of good-length slow underhand. Both had thoughtful heads on their shoulders, could tell very quickly what a batsman could play and what he could not, and when they found a weak point bowled at it until they got their man out. I question very much if we have had a slow underhand bowler of the quality of Clarke since. His pitch was so accurate that when he made up his mind to bowl at a particular spot, he could bowl within two inches of it as long as he desired.

Clarke's eleven visited something like forty different districts the first three years of its existence, and many other fresh places were visited in later years. It is difficult to get at a trustworthy statement of the bowling averages, but in 1850 Clarke bowled in thirty matches and captured 303 wickets.

William Clarke was born at Nottingham, 24th December, 1798, so that he was in his 48th year when he started the All-England eleven. His height was 5 ft 9 in.; weight, about 14 st. He appeared, for North *v.* South, at Lord's in 1836, when he was 37 years old; but he made little impression then. Twenty years previously his name appears in the Nottingham eleven, showing that he must have played at a very early age; but the advent of the All-England eleven was his opportunity, and he bowled with great success until the year of his death in 1856. Like Lillywhite, he was well advanced in years before he made his mark, and it was the occasion that created the man. The success which had attended such fast bowlers as Sir F. Bathurst and A. Mynn, fast roundarm, and Messrs Fellows and Marcon, fast underhand, had created a rage for fast roundarm bowling, and slow underhand had been completely neglected. Clarke saw that, and his accurate length, precision of pitch, and curl from the leg to the off, completely baffled the batsmen. Most of them were in two minds about playing back or running out, and he generally managed to bowl them before they got out of their indecision. But like most bowlers who are also captains, he had the weakness of keeping himself on too long. Against Pilch, and one or two others who collared him at times, he would try just another over, which invariably did more harm than good. Success brought him the usual number of followers, who jumped to the conclusion that the secret of his bowling success lay in his pace, not in his length. Slow underhand bowling became the rage for a year or two, and clubs were just as diligent in practising slows without length, as they had been in cultivating pace without length.

The appearance of the All-England eleven at Bristol against twenty-two of West Gloucestershire, in June, 1854, was my first experience of first-class play. I was nearly six years old, and had paid more than one visit in the spring of that year to the field at the back of the 'Full Moon' Hotel, Bristol, while it was being relaid for this special match, and the names of Clarke, Parr, Caffyn, Julius Caesar, Anderson, and Willsher, were discussed constantly at home. My father, uncle Pocock, and brother Henry, were playing, and with boyish eagerness and delight I sat in the pony-carriage by the side of my mother and watched the play. Bickley and Clarke were in great bowling form, particularly the former. He bowled:

Innings	Overs	Maidens	Runs	Wickets
1st	38	30	10	8
2nd	13	12	2	5

Clarke captured 11 wickets first innings, 7 second. And how Parr and Caffyn hit our bowling all over the field! Clarke's figure stands out in my memory yet.

The year after they came again to the same field, and met the same club, but Clarke was not in the eleven. He wrote to my father some time before the match, saying that, owing to ill-health and failing sight, he would be unable to play. He was present as an onlooker during the three days, and was so delighted with E. M.'s performance as longstop that he presented him with a bat. E. M. had owned many a bat before; but this one had a spliced handle with a strip of whalebone down the centre of it, and was very much prized. My father, uncle, brothers Henry, Alfred, and E. M., all played in this match, and the twenty-two got dreadfully beaten. Bickley was again the most successful bowler, and at one part of the match was unplayable. His analysis was:

Innings	Overs	Maidens	Runs	Wickets
1st	38	24	24	6
2nd	41	23	30	10

His first 14 overs in the first innings made almost a record: 14 overs, 0 runs, 4 wickets. The next five showed: 19 overs, 17 maidens, 2 runs, 6 wickets.

Three of the All-England eleven played in top-hats.

At the conclusion of the match Clarke presented my mother with a copy of *Cricket Notes by W. Holland, with a letter containing Practical Hints by William Clarke*. He had remembered my mother's enthusiasm the year before, and the group of boys who gathered round when he talked to her, and he knew the book would give her and them pleasure. I have the book in my possession now; it is before me as I write, and his handwriting stands out distinctly:

PRESENTED TO MRS GRACE BY WILLIAM CLARKE, SECRETARY, ALL-ENGLAND ELEVEN.

You can imagine how that book was treasured and read by the younger members of the family.

Between the years 1850 and 1860 a large number ot first-class players appeared. The All-England eleven created great interest everywhere, and it brought to light names which otherwise might never have been heard of. I have only to mention Lockyer, Julius Caesar, Caffyn, John Lillywhite, Wisden, Anderson, Willsher, Tinley, H. H. Stephenson, Jackson, Carpenter, Daft, T. Hayward, and Tarrant. All of them I have met at some time of my career, and I can say without hesitation they could have held their own against any combination of the present time.

Four other players might be mentioned who appeared in the decade I have been referring to – James Grundy, James Lillywhite, W. Slinn, and Isaac Hodgson. Grundy was much the best of the four, and a good all-round man. The other three did not play so prominent a part as those I have already named. They were frequently engaged by twenty-twos in their contests against the All-England eleven, and did some good performances in bowling.

With such an array of talent as I have enumerated, and a large number of young promising players, it will be readily conceived that there was little difficulty in finding players enough to fill up the All-England eleven. Indeed there were more than enough to fill up two elevens; and very soon a second was formed, under the title of the United England eleven. There had been a good deal of grumbling in the early part of 1852 about Clarke's management of the All-England eleven. One or two of the players were dissatisfied with his treatment of them, and did not hesitate to say so. Clarke had formed the eleven, conducted it in his own way, and successfully; and, like most successful men, he was a little bit arbitrary, and disinclined to changes which did not agree with his mode of thinking, and which would affect his future management. A little consideration to the opinions of the grumblers might have kept the original team longer together, although the increasing number of good players every year would very likely have led to the same result in a year or two. Clarke did not see his way to making the changes desired, and so the United England eleven was formed that year.

The United England eleven played its first match against Twenty Gentlemen of Hampshire at Portsmouth, 26th, 27th, 28th August

1852. The eleven representing it on that occasion was certainly not of the strength of the All-England eleven; but there were three players in it who had done good work for Clarke's team, and whose places it would be difficult to fill. Wisden, Grundy, and John Lilly white were the three, and Wisden and Dean were appointed joint secretaries of the new eleven. Quite evidently the two teams were not on the best of terms, or rather I should say the members of the United were on terms of proclaimed hostility to Clarke; for at a meeting of the members of the United eleven at Sheffield, 7th September, the following agreement was drawn up and signed:

> That neither of the members of the United Eleven shall at any time play in any match of cricket, for or against, wherein William Clarke may have the management or control (county matches excepted), in consequence of the treatment they have received from him at Newmarket and elsewhere.

The manifesto did not have any effect upon Clarke, or weaken the interest attached to the All-England eleven matches, for both he and the club continued their successful career. Of course the two elevens were eager to stand well with the public, and the managers of both tried to enrol in their list of members the best players of the day. The All-England eleven seems to have been the more attractive; for Willsher, after playing for the United in 1853, went over to the All-England in 1854. There was plenty of room for both, and the cricketing public had now greater opportunities of witnessing first-class play. Caffyn left the All-England for the United in 1854; but it was not until 1858, when Carpenter appeared, that the United was seen at its best.

After Clarke's death, Parr became manager of the All-England eleven, and a better feeling prevailing, a match was arranged between the two elevens, at Lord's, on the 1st, 2nd, 3rd June, 1857, for the benefit of the Cricketers' Fund, which the All-England eleven won by 5 wickets. The teams were made up entirely of professionals on that occasion. Messrs F. P. Miller and F. Burbidge were down on the list of the United; but the All-England objected on the ground of their being amateurs.

The Cricketers' Fund was originated in 1857, and matches on its behalf were played annually at Lord's, between the All-England and United elevens, down to 1867. In 1864 it was re-established on a sounder basis, and it has made satisfactory progress since; especially after 1884, when Lord Harris became president. I have taken the following from a print in my possession:

THE CRICKETERS' FUND FRIENDLY SOCIETY.
President: LORD HARRIS.

PROVIDES FOR THE RELIEF OF CRICKETERS,
being Members of the Society, who, from
OLD AGE, ILLNESS, ACCIDENT, OR OTHER INFIRMITY
are incapable of following their profession; and the temporary
assistance of
WIDOWS AND CHILDREN
of such Members, who have been left destitute.
Qualification for Membership:
Any person earning a livelihood from the game of Cricket can be
admitted on filling up the necessary forms
The Society numbered nearly 120 Members on January 1st, 1891.
CLAIMS PAID TO THE SAME DATE: £3,000.
Donations will be thankfully received by the President and the
undermentioned, who are Trustees of the Society:
V. E. WALKER, Esq., Arnos Grove, Southgate, C. E. GREEN,
Esq., 13 Fenchurch Avenue, E. G. A. J. W. BIDDULPH, Esq., The
Chalet, Burton Park, Petworth, Sussex. J. MCLAREN, Esq., Old
Trafford Cricket Ground, Manchester. THOS. HEARNE, Sec.,
MCC House, Ealing Dean, W.

I cannot find words strong enough to express my appreciation of the good work the Society is doing, or the interest that is taken in it by all classes of cricketers; but it is to be hoped that still more professional cricketers than is now the case will become members. A deservedly high compliment was paid to it by the MCC and Australian elevens in 1890, when they played a match for its benefit at Lord's, from which the Society received close on £600.

The United eleven had to go through a similar experience to the All-England before it disbanded in 1869, seventeen years after it was formed. Some of its prominent members seceded, and formed themselves into the United South of England eleven.

Pooley, John Lillywhite, Griffith, T. Humphrey, Silcock, J. Lillywhite, Charlwood, G. F. Grace Esq., W. G. Grace Esq., Southerton, Jupp, R. Humphrey.

The United South of England eleven played its first match on the 11th, 12th, and 13th May, 1865, against twenty-two of Ireland, and gave evidence that it was likely to prove a formidable rival to the other two elevens. I give the original team, from which it will be seen that it was made up entirely of Southern Players and comprised some of the best bowling and batting talent of the time:

T. Humphrey, T. Lockyer, H. Jupp, T. Hearne, G. Griffith, T. Sewell jnr, W. Mortlock, John Lillywhite, Julius Caesar, E. Willsher. James Lillywhite, Willsher was made secretary; John Lillywhite, treasurer.

The split affected the All-England as well; in fact, it might almost be considered a split between the Players of the North and the Players of the South. In the year 1862, Northern and Southern Players were continually bickering, and county matches suffered accordingly. The formation of the United South of England eleven was the final wrench, and the All-England eleven was composed entirely of Northern players afterwards.

The All-England, the United, and the United South were the three principal elevens which travelled over the United Kingdom between 1846 and 1876. They had many imitators, the most important being:

The 'United All-Ireland Eleven,' which started in 1856, and broke up in a few years.

The 'New All-England Eleven' in 1858, which lived two or three years only.

Another 'New All-England Eleven' in 1862, which died the same year.

A 'North of England Eleven' in 1863, which played one match only.

The 'United North and South of England Eleven' in 1867, which played two matches.

The 'New United South of England Eleven' in 1875.

Others sprang up from time to time; but they were of mushroom growth and existence, and need not be given.

It is impossible to state the number of wandering amateur elevens which existed at that period. They were nearly all conducted on similar principles to those of the I Zingari, without grounds of their own, and playing anywhere. Of course they were not of the strength of that famous club. As there is always a rage for extraordinary titles among young clubs, I have no doubt the few I give will be of interest. I would just remind hon. secs. that some of them are still in existence, and that the names may have been registered. I should be sorry if any rising and enterprising club were to be accused of appropriating the property of older and established ones:

The Knickerbockers, Accidentals, Inexpressibles, Dingle Wanderers, Anomalies, Gnats, Perfect Cures, Active Fleas, Perambulators, Et Ceteras, Limits, X.Y.Z., Owls, Rouge et Noir, Jolly Dogs, Odds and Ends, Caterpillars, I.O.U., Waifs and Strays, Butterflies, Desperadoes, Eccentrics, Hic et Ubique, Gryphons, Nonentities, Grasshoppers, Casuals, Harum Scarum, I Vagabondi, Idle Boys, Variegated Annuals, Rose of Denmark, Unmitigated Duffers, Fossils, Cock-a-doodle-doo, Pelicans, Don Quixotes, Cochin Chinas, Bohemians, The Fly by Nights, The Calves, Will-o'-the-Wisps, Lavender Kids, Spiders,

Anythingarians, The Witches, The Wretches, Omnium Gatherums,
Incapables, Rovers, and The Other Johnnies.

There can be very little doubt that for some years the All-England and
United elevens spread a knowledge of cricket, and in that way did
good to the game; but by-and-by, when county and other important
matches began to suffer, opinions rapidly changed, and travelling
professional elevens, in the minds of the cricketing authorities, came
in for a certain amount of condemnation. The jealousies of the two
elevens had little sympathy at headquarters or anywhere else when
important matches were spoiled by them. Occasionally when a player
was asked to play for his county he demurred, on the ground that he
would be playing for one or other of the elevens on that day. It was
not a very pleasant state of affairs, and rather a difficult one to solve.
County cricket between 1846 and 1860 was not of sufficient interest
to draw large crowds. A professional had to consider the gate: it was
his means of living; and when that is remembered, it can be easily
understood he would go where the greatest remuneration was to be
had. It certainly was to be had in connection with the All-England
eleven, for its engagements lasted from May to September. Nor was
the remuneration a question of weather, or in any way affected by the
result of the match. A sum was guaranteed by the club played, and
each player had his share, and could rely on a steady engagement as
long as he kept up his form. It was not likely a player would throw
up an engagement of that kind to play a county match, even though
he were offered the same remuneration, unless he obtained permission
from the manager of his eleven. Unfortunately, as I have already said,
the managers of the two elevens were not too complaisant, and so
county cricket suffered.

The cricketing authorities were alive to the difficulty; but could not
see their way out of it, as there were not sufficient counties at that
period for committees to work together and promise players even half
the number of engagements a travelling eleven fulfilled.

The counties which played between the years I have mentioned
were few in number. The Gentlemen *v.* Players was an annual match,
and the MCC was doing excellent work all over the country. Then, as
now, the premier club sent its eleven all over England, and even across
the Channel, keeping in view the sacred trust of fostering the game

which had been placed in its hands. Oxford *v.* Cambridge had their yearly contests, and were now considered the most likely nurseries of recruits to strengthen the amateurs.

But, undoubtedly, the contests of the year were the All-England eleven *v.* The United eleven, and the North *v.* South, at Lord's, especially the former. When the two famous elevens met reputation was at stake, and both strove to put their best teams in the field. There was no half-hearted play then. Thought was put into every ball bowled, and neither batsman nor fieldsman spared himself. It was the match of the year from a player's point of view, and crowds testified to it by turning out in thousands. It was not always so in the North *v.* South matches. More than once an eminent player cried off at the last moment, and occasionally the sides were poorly represented.

And now it began to be realised that the game had taken a hold outside of England. September, 1859, saw Parr's team batting against twenty-two of Lower Canada: and two years afterwards, on the 20th October, 1861, the first English team, under the captaincy of H. H. Stephenson, sailed for Australia. Little thought we then that 17 years later Australia should have progressed sufficiently to be able to send a team to us which should hold its own against the strongest of our clubs!

On the 18th and 19th July, 1861, my brothers, Henry and E. M., made their first appearance at Lord's, playing for the South Wales Club *v.* MCC Both gave a fine display of cricket, Henry scoring 63 not out, first innings; E. M., run out 14 first, and 41 not out, second. E. M. was still more successful with the ball, capturing 8 wickets first innings (6 of them clean bowled), and 7 second. He was in his twentieth year, and bowled both roundarm and underhand. South Wales won by seven wickets.

Between 1846 and 1862 few changes were made in the laws. The MCC, while it has always been watchful in the interests of the game, has never been hasty in altering or amending laws which had worked smoothly, wisely preserving a position of neutrality to outside appeals, and only acting when it became absolutely necessary. There were grumblings about this or the other bowler infringing the law in raising his hand above the shoulder in delivering the ball; and some of the umpires were accused of favouritism, or want of firmness, in not speaking out. It was well enough known that most of the bowlers offended occasionally; but as long as they did not make a practice of it, the umpire was silent. Possibly he had been a bowler himself, and knew how difficult it was for a roundarm bowler to bowl over after over with a horizontal arm and keep a good length; and what a relief it was to raise the arm now and then a little bit above the prescribed position, and how much quicker it made the ball come off the pitch.

Grumbling was pretty general in the beginning of 1862, and no one was surprised that an explosion occurred before the end of it. England was playing Surrey at the Oval on the 25th, 26th, 27th August of that year; and a memorable match it turned out to be in more ways than one. England commenced batting on the Monday, and kept possession of the wicket until 5.30 the next day, compiling the exceptionally large total of 503. Hayward headed the list with 117; Grundy came next, with 95; Carpenter third, with 94; and Willsher fourth, with 54. There was only one 'duck' in the score; and that, strangely, was to Daft's name, caught at the wicket. Right glad were Surrey when that innings was over. With them it was not now a question of winning the match, but a question of saving it. It was one of those charming evenings we are occasionally favoured with in the month of August not a breath of wind, the sun fast setting, and the shadows stealing over the ground; and one of the largest crowds ever present at the Oval. Mortlock and T. Humphrey appeared at the wickets about six o'clock. Mr V. E. Walker and Willsher were the bowlers; and John Lillywhite and T. Sewell, the umpires. Only a few balls were bowled when Humphrey hit out at a curly one of Walker's, and the ball travelled at a great rate to Grundy, who was standing at deep short-leg. Grundy sprang into the air, and with his right arm fully extended brought off a magnificent catch. The cheering was immense. Willsher was bowling steadily, as usual, at the other end; and Mr F. Burbidge, who had taken Humphrey's place at the wicket, and Mortlock had to play carefully. Willsher commenced his third over, and immediately the ball left his hand Lillywhite cried, 'No ball!' Willsher continued to bowl; but after being 'no-balled' six times in succession, he threw down the ball, and walked away. With the exception of Messrs V. E. Walker and C. G. Lyttelton, the remainder of the eleven representing England followed suit.

To say that the excitement was intense is to convey but a faint idea of the sensation among players and spectators. Nobody knew why Willsher had been 'no-balled; 'his delivery looked as fair the third

Edgar Willsher.

over as it did the first, or at any time in his bowling career. Lillywhite thought otherwise: in his opinion his hand was above the shoulder when the ball left it, and it was his duty to call 'No ball.' Play was stopped for the day. There was no demonstration, but it was generally believed that a very big nail had been knocked in the coffin of the law bearing on the point, and that the law would have to be either stretched or altered. A night's reflection found Lillywhite in the same belief; and to enable the match to proceed, Street was put in his place. There is no need to say if the action was a wise one. Lillywhite was made the scapegoat; but he could console himself with the thought, a year or two afterwards, that by his firmness on that occasion he had caused the law-makers to act.

A fortnight before that match my brother E. M. had caused a sensation of another kind at Canterbury. His score of 118 against Wootton and Grundy at Lord's, for the South Wales Club, had set the critics talking, and his doings the previous two years were recalled.

In 1860 he played 44 innings, average 41; his principal scores being:

150 for West Gloucestershire *v.* Clifton.
114 for Lansdown *v.* Trowbridge.
183 for Lansdown *v.* Plummer's XI.
118 for Ashton School *v.* Ashton.

In 1861 he played 60 innings, average 34; his principal scores being:

102 for for Lansdown *v.* Batheaston.
112 for Lansdown *v.* Frenchay.
100 for Berkeley *v.* Knole Park.
119 for Lansdown *v.* Clifton.

They were not first-class matches, but good enough to show that he possessed batting powers of a very high quality.

For years, during the cricket week, my father and mother had visited Canterbury, where they had many friends, and were cordially welcomed in cricket circles. The match, the first part of the week in 1862, was England *v.* Fourteen of Kent; the second part, MCC *v.* Gentlemen of Kent. The Hon. Spencer Ponsonby Fane, who was managing the matches for the MCC, had experienced great difficulty in getting together a good team for England; and at the last moment Hayward was taken ill and could not come.

In the evening my father suggested E. M. to the Hon. Spencer Ponsonby, who promptly said: 'Communicate with him at once, please; and I shall try to arrange with Mr Baker, the Secretary of the Kent County Club, that he shall be allowed to play as an emergency for the MCC in the second match.' Mr Baker acceded to the request very heartily, and E. M. turned up at Canterbury on Tuesday, and for England scored a 'duck' first innings, 56 second. Willsher, Sewell, and Mr Lipscomb were the bowlers, and his 56 included 9 fours and 6 twos.

There was a little friction over the second match. The Captain of the Gentlemen of Kent objected to E. M. playing for MCC, not being a member; but Mr Baker very firmly said: 'I have given my promise to the Hon. Spencer Ponsonby that Mr Grace shall be allowed to play; and if you insist upon your objection being enforced, then I have no alternative but to resign the Secretaryship of the County Club.' That put an end to the discussion, and E. M. carried everything before him.

Kent scored 141 first innings. E. M. went in first for the MCC at one o'clock on Friday, and after seeing 4 wickets go down for 65 runs, he began to hit. He hit all that day, and was 105 not out at the end of it. A good deal of rain fell during the afternoon, and the wicket became heavy, but he made the ball travel at a great rate. Next morning he was in the same vein, and finished up with 192 not out; total, 344. His score was made up of 26 fours, 7 threes, 9 twos, and singles. He broke one bat in compiling it; but Lord Sefton, on behalf of the MCC, presented him with another.

The story of his being out first ball, and Fuller Pilch giving him 'not out' on the ground that he 'wanted to see the young gentleman bat,' is a myth. In the early part of the innings the bowler appealed for a catch at the wicket, but Pilch unhesitatingly said, 'Not out.' He was chaffed for his decision afterwards, but said he had no doubt about it. Then laughingly added, 'Perhaps I should not have given him out if I had. I wanted to see Mr Grace do a bit of hitting.'

The second innings of the Kent Gentlemen lasted a little over three hours, E. M. capturing all 10 wickets.

He bowled both roundarm and lobs, but was most successful with the latter.

The Hon. Spencer Ponsonby had the ball mounted with silver, and presented it to E. M. on behalf of the MCC

I can remember E. M. in his twenty-first year. He is now in his fiftieth, with more than the average share of energy and activity left; at twenty-one he was as agile as a cat, and could field at point better than any player I have met. A very good judge said of him once: 'The only thing that man cannot do in the cricket field is keep wicket to his own bowling!'

The fame of E. M.'s doings spread everywhere, and his style of batting was freely criticised. The critics found fault with his cross hitting, and said he was not above hitting a straight, good-length ball; but all agreed that his hitting was something wonderful. It has always been a mystery to me how he timed the ball so accurately. Good-lengths, half-volleys, and long-hops were all the same to him. He got them on the right part of the bat, and neither bowler nor fieldsman could tell to which part of the field the ball was going. One hit they might expect. Give him a ball a little bit up, about a foot to the off, and they could depend upon it travelling to long-on. Many a fieldsman was placed there for a catch, but very rarely was the ground large enough for that particular hit, and a rough wicket made little difference to him. Do not imagine he could not play with a straight bat, or a defensive innings if he wanted. I have seen him defend his wicket as correctly and patiently as any one. From his twentieth to his thirtieth year his eyesight and quickness were exceptional, partly owing to his temperate and active habits.

In 1862, and for a good many years afterwards, his scores and averages were certainly remarkable; and when we compare them with the doings of the great players of the past and of his own time, we can understand the sensation he created between 1862 and 1865.

Mynn and Pilch were two of the best batsmen between 1830 and 1850. I give their doings in 1843 and 1844:

Mynn in 1843 played 28 innings, scored 471 runs, average 16.23; most in an innings, 73.

In 1844 he played 36 innings, scored 439 runs, average 12.7; most in an innings, 48.

Pilch in 1843 played 22 innings, scored 525 runs, average 23.19; most in an innings, 89.

In 1844, 41 innings, 592 runs, average 14.18; most in an innings, 50.

In 1862 and 1863, Anderson, Hayward, Daft, Parr, and Carpenter were the crack batsmen:

1862	Average	Innings
R. Carpenter	31.20	38
R. Daft	22.6	22
T. Hayward	21.12	62
G. Anderson	19.5	53
G. Parr	13.39	43

E. M. Grace: 40 innings, 2,190 runs; average, 40.30.

The year 1862 is hardly a fair comparison, for the majority of the matches in which E. M. played were not first-class. The year after, when he played for the All-England eleven, South *v.* North, and Gentlemen *v.* Players, is a fairer test:

1863. *First-class Matches only.*

	Innings	Runs	Average
R. Daft	9	313	34.7
G. Anderson	10	287	28.7
P. Hayward	16	392	24.8
R. Carpenter	22	447	20.7
G. Parr	16	204	12.12

E. M. Grace: 27 innings, 964 runs; average 35.19.

The result was sufficient to stamp E. M. as the most successful batsman of that year. An average of 20 was considered remarkable in 1850. In 1860 it did not create so much astonishment; in 1863 E. M. raised it to 35. In the matches in which he took part that year, he played 78 innings, scored 3,074 runs, and averaged 39.32.

3

My Family, Home, & Early Cricket Days

My father, Henry Mills Grace, was born at Long Ashton, Somersetshire. He was a fair cricketer, though not possessing the skill of either of my brothers. When a boy he played a great deal, and if he had had the opportunities afforded to his children, he would have attained a good position as an all-round player. Clubs were few in number in his boyhood, and grounds were fewer still. For one that possessed a ground of its own, a dozen had to be content with the open common. Nor were schools so considerate about playing cricket in his time, and players had many difficulties in the way of practising and learning. The greatest difficulty he had to contend against was the distance to the ground. Clubs in the neighbourhood of Bristol were singularly fortunate in one respect: they had plenty of open ground then, as they have now. Durdham Downs were available, and, though not looked after as they should have been, a very fair pitch could be obtained.

When my father became a medical student, it was impossible for him to get away during the afternoon or evening, as most students do in the present day, and if he had not resorted to extraordinary hours he would have been compelled to give up playing. Two to three days a week throughout the cricketing season, he and a number of companions were in the habit of going to the Downs and practising between the hours of five and eight in the morning. In that way only could he continue the game he loved so well; and I remember we tried to follow in his footsteps in after years, at not quite so early an hour. He had the great qualities of perseverance and concentration, and he diligently impressed upon us the need for cultivating them.

I can remember his words now:

> Have patience, my boy; where there's a will there's a way; and there
> is nothing you cannot attain, if you only try hard enough.

My father and mother were married in the year 1831, and settled
down in Downend, Gloucestershire, where they lived the rest of their
lives. Downend is about four miles from Bristol, and was not a more
important village sixty years ago than it is now. At the time my father
made it the place of his labours, it was a small scattered village, and
tourists when they travelled that way rarely paid it the compliment
of staying long in it.

My father had to make his way in life, and was at the beck and
call of every sick person within a radius of twelve miles. He had not
an hour he could call his own. The early morning saw him riding six
miles eastward; at midnight he was often six miles to the west.

There was not much time for cricket. The village had not a club
of its own; so my father had to be satisfied with running into Bristol
now and again, to look at the matches of the Clifton and Bristol clubs
about the only two at that time within available reach.

My brother Henry, the eldest of the family, was born on the 31st
January, 1833. At eight years of age he was sent to school, and every
time he came home would talk of nothing but cricket. My father
realised that he would be compelled sooner or later to create time to
help him, if he desired to keep in touch with him physically as well
as mentally. He was strong in the belief that if you want to educate
and influence a boy thoroughly it is as important to play with him as
to work with him; so he took time by the forelock, and had a cricket
pitch laid in front of the house. It was not much of a pitch, nor was it
full size; but it was sufficient to teach the rudiments of the game.

The villagers and surrounding neighbours began to take an interest
in cricket, and nothing would satisfy them but that my father must
take the initiative in forming a club. Why should not Downend have
a club of its own? It was not strong enough to form one; so the
neighbouring villages were invited to help, and a club was established,
and named 'The Mangotsfield'. Rodway Hill was the most convenient
spot for the majority of the players, and, indeed, about the only place
where ground could be had. It was common ground; but the members

set to work with a will, and levelled and railed in about 40 yards square at considerable expense. The West Gloucestershire club was formed about a year later by Mr Henry Hewitt and the students living with the Revd Mr Woodford, the clergyman at Coalpit Heath.

And now my father became more enthusiastic than ever, and prevailed upon some of his old Bristol friends to come over and help the good cause. My uncle Alfred Pocock responded heartily, and walked twice a week between the two places, a distance of 12 miles. He was a first-class racquet player; and, though he had not played cricket until he was twenty-three years of age, was not without hope that he might become a first-class cricketer also. He, too, possessed my father's enthusiasm and perseverance; so it can be readily understood the Mangotsfield Club began to improve rapidly.

My father was 5 ft 10 ins. in height; weight, about 13 st. He batted right-handed; but bowled and threw in with his left No man was more alive to the importance of choosing an eleven carefully for match play. A week or two before a match, he would take out his notebook and write down his team:

'First,' said he, 'I must have two good bowlers.

'Also two good change-bowlers.

'A wicketkeeper and long-stop.

'The rest, as long as they can bat and field, will make up a fair team.'

Good fielding was his strong point, and he used to insist upon his team practising throwing and catching all round the field. Another important order was that, one night a week at least, sides should be chosen, and every one play as if it were a match.

My uncle Alfred Pocock was 5 ft 9 ins. in height; weight, 12 st. 7 lbs When he first played for the Mangotsfield Club, he did not possess the skill which made him so valuable to E. M., Fred, and myself; but, infected by my father's earnestness, he practised diligently and acquired great power with both bat and ball. He made many good scores for the club, and his bowling won many a match. Nothing pleased him so much as watching a correct style of play; and he would bowl willingly for hours to a promising youngster, and was delighted to see him punish an indifferent ball. He bowled roundarm, medium pace, could break both ways, and was very straight. I have known him hit a single stump six times in twenty balls, and he was not satisfied unless he did it.

There is no need to say that, with two such enthusiasts as my father and uncle, the Mangotsfield Club increased in numbers and began to hold its own in contests. The West Gloucestershire Club held a distinct lead for a year or so, pretty much owing to the skill and influence of Mr Hewitt, who was ably supported by the pupils of the Revd Mr Woodford, at Coalpit Heath. Mr Woodford about this time had half a dozen college boys reading with him, who had learned their cricket under able teachers, and who were much more proficient with bat and ball than the majority of local talent. About the year 1845 the Mangotsfield was much strengthened by the appearance of two nephews of my mother, Mr William Rees and Mr George Gilbert, who came to stay with us during the holidays. The holidays lasted nearly two months, and my cousins showed both clubs that they had a great deal to learn in every branch of the game. Both were almost in the first class as batsmen, much above the average as bowlers, and fielded with dash and certainty.

The 'Mangotsfield' became too much for its sister club and the majority of the clubs which played against it. The year 1846 saw it still improving, and the West Gloucestershire had to admit its superiority. Amalgamation was agreed upon the year after, and the West Gloucestershire Club chosen as the more dignified and most suitable name. Rodway Hill was the more convenient ground, and there they played for the next twenty years.

The principal clubs in the neighbourhood of Bristol about that period were Clifton, Kingscote, Lansdown, Westbury-on-Trym, and Bedminster. Lansdown had been in existence since 1825, and was the strongest opponent of the West Gloucestershire; the others had very little chance against it. In later years Cheltenham College was included in the list, and became the most exciting match of all. Forty years ago there was not the same limit as to age at Cheltenham, and the XI. were often nearer twenty years than sixteen. The College XI. became a thorn in the side of the West Gloucestershire, in proving that it was not omnipotent. Mr M. Kempson was in residence at that time, and by his fine all-round play gave the West Gloucestershire many a hard day's work. He gave them a taste of the bowling skill which was to be of somuch service to his side in the Gentlemen *v.* Players match in 1853. Mr, now Sir Henry, James was there also, and helped with both bat and ball, and altogether the match was the most exciting and enjoyable of the year. I ought to say matches; for most years two were played. The annual fixture was in the month of June; but hardly a year passed in which a second was not played in September or October when the boys returned from the holidays.

The year 1846 was the club's first experience of very fast bowling. Mr Marcon was in the neighbourhood that year, and played against them. Their wickets went down like ninepins, and half of the batsmen never saw the ball when he bowled. Every fieldsman was behind the wicket, and there were two longstops: the first stood 15 yards behind, and was supposed to be the wicketkeeper; and the second about 30 yards farther away. Mr Marcon did not trouble about the length of the ball. He aimed at the wicket, and the ball flew straight from his hand to it without touching the ground; and nearly every time it hit the bottom of the stump, the stump was smashed. Runs were scored now and then from a snick to leg or slip, but not one of them could hit him in front of the wicket. A member of the team said it could be done ought to be done, and *he* would do it!

'It is no use grounding your bat and waiting until he bowls,' said he. 'No! have your bat in the air in hitting position, and let fly at him.' He was certainly big enough and strong enough to do as he said; so in he went, and stood waiting with the bat in the air, ready to hit.

Mr Marcon came with a rush, and our enterprising member hit. The ball hit the bat high up about the shoulder, and bat and ball went right through the wicket.

My brother Henry was fifteen years of age when he played his first match for the club in 1848. He did not make much of a show that year; but two or three years later he could show an average of 17 for seven innings, and was very successful with the ball also. My cousins were at their best then, and the West Gloucestershire had now become a very strong club.

The year 1852 saw the departure of my cousins. They had begun the work of life, and holidays of two months' duration had become a thing of the past. The brunt of the fight had again to be undertaken by my father and uncle; but they faced it pluckily, for the sake of the boys who were springing up. Henry was still improving in his play, and my uncle and he were considered the two best all-round players in the district. They could both bowl very straight: my uncle was the steadier, with plenty of patience, but my brother was the faster, and on a rough kicking wicket met with great success. They would go any distance to play, whether the match were good, bad, or indifferent, and some of their experiences of country cricket were rather amusing.

Mr Williams, a player of University reputation, who was living at Thornbury, got together an eleven; but he could not lick them into match form, and almost gave up in despair. He did not like to cry 'Beaten,' and thought he might as well have a try against some of the clubs, about the end of the season, when one or two of their best men were away holidaykeeping. Bristol was the club chosen; but, unfortunately for Mr Williams, Henry and my uncle had been asked to play, and they were on the ground waiting when the Thornbury team appeared. The chances were about 100 to 1 against Thornbury, and the certainty came off on that occasion; for Mr Williams and his hopeful lot were ignominiously defeated. With more pluck than judgment, and doubtless to encourage his disheartened eleven, Mr Williams said at the conclusion of the match: 'The result was a piece of luck. My lot could play the same team any day, and I should not mind putting twenty-five pounds on the result.'

'Do you mean it?' said the captain of the Bristol.

'I do!' said Mr Williams, and the match was fixed for a fortnight later, the first week in October.

My father was told of the match, and blamed both Henry and uncle for allowing it to be made, and considered it was nothing short of robbery. They said they had nothing to do with the making of it, and had not a sixpence on the result. My father, however, did not like the look of matters, and said he would play for Thornbury and pay part of the money.

'Understand now and for good, you boys,' said he, 'I shall not allow you in future to take part in any match which is played for money, as it is introducing a form of gambling into the game, which is wrong and must do harm to it.'

Mr Williams turned up on the appointed date. The Bristol team was even stronger than on the first occasion, and could not keep from laughing at the team opposed to them. Mr Williams and my father chatted together, without the slightest sign of dismay on their faces. The remainder of the Thornbury eleven were nearly all strangers, and hardly one of them had been seen in a good match before.

Some of the Bristol eleven suggested to their captain that the money should be posted before the match commenced. He had no intention of proceeding to that extremity; but the spirit of mischief prevailing was too much for him, and he was compelled to approach Mr Williams and make the request. Mr Williams put his hand in his pocket and produced notes to the amount, much to the surprise of the Bristol captain, who had to make the humiliating confession that he had omitted to bring his part.

Such a scene as followed has not often been witnessed at the beginning of a match. Mr Williams and my father waxed indignant; and did not hesitate to tell the Bristol captain that his conduct was far from gentlemanly, and unworthy of so manly a game; and they declined to go on with the match until the amount was produced. The whole team could not raise the sum among them; but a few watches and what money they had in their pockets were accepted as an equivalent, and deposited in safe hands.

Thornbury won the toss.

'What shall we do, doctor?' Mr Williams asked.

'We may as well bat,' said my father. 'It is a one-innings match, and we shall have the best of the wicket.'

Mr Williams and my father went in first, and my uncle and Henry bowled. There was no tempting my father to hit; for he had made up his mind to keep up his wicket. At the end of an hour and a half, when Mr Williams was bowled, the score was 60, of which he had made 45 in brilliant fashion. My father was not out 12, and they had run three byes. Half an hour later the innings was at an end: the total 75, my father not out 17.

The match began rather late in the day, and it was 3.30 when Bristol began to bat. With the exception of my father, there was not one of the Thornbury lot who had ever been known to bowl, and it was thought the match would be over by 5 o'clock. It was over earlier than that.

My father bowled the first over, and a good one it was; not a run scored off it. Laughing was general when Mr Williams commenced at the other end. He fell back on the old, old resource when everything else has failed underhand grubs! There was not quite so much laughing at the end of the over, when he had clean-bowled one man, and the scoring sheet was still blank.

Snow had fallen during the day, and the wicket cut up badly. My father bowled as steadily and patiently as he had batted; and Mr Williams slung in his grubs, and got a wicket nearly every other over. The match was all over by 4.45, and Bristol had scored something less than 50 runs. To say that the Bristol XI were laughed at, is to express very faintly what took place.

My uncle and Henry, when they got back to Downend, were chaffed unmercifully; and it was many a long day before they heard the last of that match.

During the rise and progress of the Mangotsfield and West Gloucestershire Clubs, great changes had been taking place in our home.

There was, as I have already mentioned, Henry, born 31st January, 1833. Then followed Alfred, born 17th May, 1840; Edward Mills, born 28th November, 1841; myself, born 18th July, 1848; George Frederick, born 13th December, 1850; and four girls between Henry and myself.

Downend House, where my father and mother had been living since Henry's birth, had now become rather straitened in accommodation, and a move was made to 'The Chesnuts' across the road sometime in 1850, where my father and mother lived for the rest of their lives.

The change was an improvement in many ways. For one thing there was an orchard attached to it, which meant for my brothers and myself a more convenient pitch on which to practise. My father, Henry, and uncle set to work early in 1851, and had a good wicket ready by the beginning of the cricket season. The orchard was about 80 yards in length, and thickly studded with apple trees, a few of which had to be sacrificed. On the left of it was a high wall; on the right, Mr Cave's wood and a deep quarry full of water.

The first year or two the pitch was small; but E. M. enlarged and improved it as he grew up, and I cannot remember when it was not in a condition worthy of a first-rate club. There was no restriction in our hitting, but undoubtedly the situation was its greatest attraction: we had only to step out of the house and begin play, and that to a medical family whose duties took them so far from home was a priceless boon. Many a time my father and brother Henry returned from their work too pressed for time to be able to go to Rodway Hill, and so had to give up the desire of half an hour's practice. That was obviated now. They could partake of a hasty lunch, and join in the practice that was carried on most days during the season. I should say during most months in the year, for we commenced as early as March and did not leave off until October. To my father and mother there was a great charm in the new arrangement, for it kept the entire family together. Rarely did we practise without my mother being present as an onlooker. My sisters did not play the game, as has been so often stated; but my mother and they fielded the ball if it travelled their way, and bowled a ball or two occasionally to Fred and myself when we were boys. That was the extent of their efforts.

My memory carries me back to my sixth year. Most boys at that age have more to do with the nursery than a cricket ground; but it must be remembered that my family was a cricketing one in every sense of the word, and a cricket ground in front of one's home at that time rare and exceptional. It was as natural for me and every one at home to walk out to the ground, as it is for every boy in England to go into his nursery; and what boy with a choice at his command would prefer the latter? Alfred and E. M. were showing great promise, though not quite good enough to play for the club, and spent every moment of their spare time practising.

My uncle made a point of coming to Downend frequently to coach us, and an excellent coach he made. His bowling was not fast enough to frighten us, but straight and accurate enough to enable us to learn the first principles of batting; viz., good defence. Very fortunately, at that period of my life I was given a bat to suit my strength. I say fortunately, for my uncle and Henry tell me a mistake had been made with regard to E. M. in that respect. Who was to blame, I know not; but E. M., long before he reached manhood's years, was in the habit of using a full-sized bat, and to that they attribute in some measure his cross-hitting. A little thought will show that there is a deal of reason in their argument. It is possible for a boy to handle a bat a little bit over his weight, and even play straight with it; but it is impossible for him to do so when it is inches too long. That is a point that cannot be considered too carefully in coaching a boy, if a correct style and freedom be aimed at. Good players can be reckoned by the score, who will tell you that a mistake of that kind was made with them in their early days, and that they never got thoroughly over it.

To my uncle great credit is due for teaching me, and I sincerely wish that every boy who reads this may possess a teacher as patient and as capable. His first piece of advice was:

> Use a bat suited to your height and strength, and if you stand properly and play straight, you ought to be able to keep the ball from hitting your wicket.

Then he would show me how to hold the bat so as to use it freely; give me guard according to the side of the wicket he bowled; place my feet in the proper position, and impress on me the need to stand upright. For months, for years I might say, I had to be content with simply stopping the ball, happy if I could keep it away from the wicket.

'Keep your left shoulder well forward, and get over the ball,' he kept drumming into our heads, 'until you do that, you will never do any good. And keep your eye fixed on the bowler, and never lose sight of the ball from the time it leaves his hands. There must be no playing or hitting wildly.'

I did all that in my own mind as conscientiously and persistently as any boy works at anything he loves; but somehow I could not make the progress I longed for. Too soon would come a ball on the blind spot, and I was beaten. I should like to be able to say that I had no difficulty in learning, and that proficiency came to me much easier than it comes to other boys. The reverse is the truth. I had to work as hard at learning cricket as I ever worked at my profession, or anything else. Very quickly I learned that there was no royal road there, and that if I wanted to be a good cricketer I must persevere. I was fortunate in having a good tutor, and a strong gift of perseverance; that is as much as I can say to students of the game.

For the next two or three years I had to be satisfied with short innings in family practice games. The rule was, fifteen minutes each to the senior members, five minutes to the juniors or more if time allowed; however, I had plenty of fielding, and worked hard at it. E. M. kept us busy in that way; and as Mr Cave's wood and the quarry were in the direction of long-on, it suited his pull from the off beautifully, and he took a special delight in hitting the ball there.

From first to last we had three dogs, whose services were invaluable: Don, Ponto, and Noble. Noble was a most intelligent retriever, and would go into the water for the ball without hesitation. Ponto took his position at the side of the bowler, and watched the flight of the ball with as much care as the batsman; and when it was hit over the trees, would listen carefully until he heard it crash among the branches and then make straight to the spot where it fell. His instinct was remarkable, and with a little training we got him to do wonders. A ball bowled to the off he expected to be hit on that side, and he did not take kindly to E. M.'s pulling. They had plenty of pluck, too; for they would present their chest to the ball, no matter how hard it was hit, and time after time I have seen them catch it on the bound with their mouth.

By the time I was nine years old I had got over the elementary stage of stopping the ball, and was slowly acquiring power in meeting it firmly and playing it away. Playing with a straight bat had become easy to me; and my uncle told me I was on the right track, and patiently I continued in it. In my tenth year I could play a ball from my wicket with a fair amount of confidence. 'Do not allow the bowler to stick you up, or it is all over with you,' he said. I could now play forward as well as back; but, of course, had to be content with less firmness in that stroke, quite satisfied if I could meet the ball with a straight bat.

The next year saw me still improving, and I was considered good enough to play for the club. My cousin, W. Rees, was staying with us for a week or two. His appearance was of great interest to me, and I watched his play most carefully. It was six years since he played last for the West Gloucestershire, and his old skill had not deserted him; for he played three innings, and scored 102 runs. He was one of my godfathers; and, after seeing my defence, thought me such a promising young player that he presented me with a bat before he left My godfather was of the same opinion as my father and uncle about the bat being suited to the height and strength of the player, for the one he gave me was not full size. But it had what I had long wished for, a cane handle.

What was I doing in the way of bowling? will be asked. A great deal; though perhaps not giving it the thoughtful attention I bestowed on batting. I was not blind to the fact that, if I wished to become a good cricketer, I must cultivate every branch of the game. A year or two ago there was some talk of training boys to begin bowling at a shorter distance than 22 yards. With that suggestion I heartily agree;

for I am perfectly certain that very few boys between the years of ten and fifteen have strength enough to bowl the regulation distance any length of time without becoming tired and bowling short. 18 yards was the distance we were taught to begin at, and a good length was the principal point drilled into our heads. I pegged away very perseveringly, and I believe in my twelfth year was paid the compliment of being considered the forlorn hope when the regular bowlers of the club had failed. A very dubious compliment, I admit, but I considered it a very high one. It was very encouraging to me, and I did my little best to justify it.

The year 1860 saw E. M. in great batting form for the West Gloucestershire Club, and I too helped to swell the total of the scoring sheet. Against Clifton the Club did a good performance, scoring an aggregate of 381, and winning easily. E. M. and my uncle went in first, and made 126 before they were parted. Altogether E. M. scored 150, without the semblance of a chance, and his hitting was clean and hard. I was down on the sheet as eighth man, and at the end of the first day scored 35 not out very patiently and correctly, they say; and next day added 15 more. I was not quite twelve years of age, and played with the bat my godfather gave me. A little later the same year we played Gloucester and Cheltenham combined, and won by an innings and 27 runs.

The year 1861 was not an encouraging one to me or my teachers; for in ten innings played I only scored 46 runs. The matches were principally for West Gloucestershire, against Clifton, Lansdown, Knole Park, and Bedminster then, as now, the best clubs in the neighbourhood of Bristol. I was now very tall for my age, and could get well over the ball. The club had one or two peculiar experiences that year, which were strongly illustrative of country cricket.

In the Lansdown match scoring was very one-sided. Partly owing to the weather, only seven men put in an appearance for Lansdown when the match began, and my uncle and E. M. disposed of them for 33 runs. There was little in that to discourage them; but at the end of the day, when the same pair had scored 147 without being parted E. M. 75, uncle 69, one or two of the Lansdown players did not hesitate to say that there was neither reason nor fun in the match, and hoped that the West Gloucestershire eleven would not mind if they abandoned it. The West Gloucestershire only laughed; for they could remember a similar experience against the same club in 1847, when Lansdown had the laugh on their side. Then Lansdown scored 74 first innings; West Gloucestershire, 6 only. Only nine overs were bowled, and it was a most inglorious procession. At the end of the day Lansdown had scored 128 for 5 wickets in their second innings; and West Gloucestershire, considering the task too much for them, said they would give them the match. At that time, when a match got very one-sided, giving it up was a common occurrence, and neither side thought it unsportsmanlike.

But the match of matches for a startling and unexpected finish was West Gloucestershire *v.* Redland, at Rodway Hill, on 28th July, 1858. With the exception of Fred, all the members of the family, uncle included, were playing, and a good match was expected. We were on the ground practising before the Redland turned up, and had a fair number of spectators even at that early hour. One onlooker, who had been drinking rather freely, lay full-length unpleasantly close to where we were playing, and all our persuasions to get him to move further away were unavailing. When the Redland eleven arrived, an attempt was made to clear the ground, but our noisy critic resented, and my father, much against his will, had to resort to force of arms Calling up my brother Alfred, who had a fair reputation as a boxer, he ordered him to remove the obstinate individual; he did not seem to object, and the unusual sight of a fight before a cricket match was witnessed. Two minutes proved that Alfred had a very easy undertaking, and he dealt very lightly with his opponent who had the sense, or feeling, to cry 'Enough,' and left the field altogether. The little preliminary excitement added to the interest of the match, and a keen and enjoyable one it became.

Redland scored 51 first innings, 116 second. West Gloucestershire scored 67 first, and were 84 in the second for 5 wickets, with about an hour remaining to play, when our friend of the morning turned up again. This time he brought his friends with him, who asserted that he had been unfairly treated. It seemed absurd that a cricket match should be delayed a second time for so small a matter; but there was no alternative. Alfred had a tougher task this time; but, rising to the occasion, he polished off his opponent in an artistic and satisfactory manner.

That did not satisfy him or his friends; for they betook themselves to a convenient heap of stones, and a free-fight ensued. For a little while the West Gloucestershire and Redland, fighting side by side, had rather the worst of the contest; but, charging shoulder to shoulder with stumps and bats, they drove the crowd from the heap of stones, and assumed the offensive. A lively state of affairs prevailed the next half hour. In the meantime my father had ridden off hurriedly to the nearest magistrate, who returned with him, and threatened to read the Riot Act if they did not disperse. Fortunately for the reputation of the two clubs and the villagers, so extreme a measure was unnecessary, and the opposition collapsed; but the match had to be abandoned.

The year 1862 found my father aiming at the formation of a County Club; and his suggestion being well received, what was undoubtedly the first match of Gloucestershire County was played at Clifton that year, under the title of The Gentlemen of Gloucestershire *v.* Devonshire. That was a step in the right direction, and on the high-road to first-class play.

The West Gloucestershire Club, while it owed much of its early success to my cousins, W. Rees and George Gilbert, was at its best between 1860 and 1867. In those years E. M. was a host in himself; Henry, Alfred, and my uncle as good as they had ever been; and Fred and I improving every year. We all played in the eleven in 1863, and I could show at the end of that season an average of 26.12 for nineteen innings.

That year the club was strong enough to play twenty-two of Corsham, and win; and in 1866, Ross, Hereford, and Monmouth were also included. The last three were played in succession, commencing at Ross on the 10th and 11th September, and finishing at Hereford on the 14th and 15th. It was a most enjoyable week. The twenty-two of Ross and District scored 35 and 40 to West Gloucestershire's single innings of 129. E. M. and myself bowled right through: E. M. had ten wickets for 14 runs first innings, and twelve for 21 runs second; I had ten for 18 first, and e8 for 14 second.

The twenty-two of Monmouth did rather better, scoring 47 and 57 to our 85 and 84. E. M. and I again bowled unchanged throughout. E. M. had 13 wickets for 24 runs first, and 12 for 29 second; I had 7 for 23 first, and 8 for 25 second. Rather an amusing incident occurred in that match: E. M. and myself had taken our positions at the wicket to commence batting, when the captain of the Monmouth twenty-two asked if we had any objection to playing with a ball which was slightly soiled and had been in use for a few overs. I did not see any particular objection to it, and was willing to go on; but E. M. insisted upon the rules of the game being observed, and would have none of it. There was no alternative but to send down to the town for another, and we had to wait patiently for over a quarter of an hour until the messenger returned. I was bowled first ball, much to the delight of my opponents.

The twenty-two of Hereford was much the strongest combination, and defeated us by 43 runs.

The year 1867 was the last of the West Gloucestershire club. It had lived for more than twenty years, and held its own against all the clubs in the neighbourhood. Its last match was against twenty-two of Holt, and proved a very one-sided affair. The twenty-two scored 56 and 109; West Gloucestershire scored 413 in a single innings, of which E. M. scored 200, Henry 17, and my share was 93.

First innings	Overs	Maidens	Runs	Wickets
E. M. bowled	25	7	28	12
W. G.	25	13	26	7

The second innings we stepped aside, and allowed Fred to bowl:

	Overs	Maidens	Runs	Wickets
Fred bowled	40	18	44	15

At that period Henry was in his 35th year, E. M. in his 27th, Fred in his 17th, and I in my 20th.

I have dwelt at some length on the doings of the West Gloucestershire Club, as it had almost become a family club for some years before it stopped playing; and it was in connection with it that E. M., Fred, and I gained much of our skill. It ceased to exist owing to the many first-class engagements which we had offered to us, and which my father and mother thought we ought to accept in the interests of the game. It had fulfilled what my father had in view when he formed the Mangotsfield Club to spread a knowledge of the game in the district, and teach his boys to play. That its success as a club gave him pleasure I do not require to say. My uncle and he little thought their efforts would bear such fruit, or that the orchard at Downend would be cherished so dearly. They had watched their boys grow into men, able to hold their own in the cricket-field, and accepting defeat and victory in the right spirit. It was a stern school to learn in, but it was thorough. We pursued it earnestly, never grumbling at the work to be undertaken.

The matches played by the West Gloucestershire Club against the following clubs, from 1846 to 1867 resulted as follow:

	Total Matches	Won	Lost	Drawn
Lansdown	14	8	4	2
Knole Park	12	9	2	1
Clifton	15	10	4	1
Cheltenham College	12	3	3	6
Bedminster	13	12	1	0
Westbury	11	10	0	1
Kingscote	3	2	0	1

The Gentlemen of Gloucestershire *v.* Gentlemen of Devonshire, at Clifton on the 8th and 9th July, 1862, was our first county match, and the result was very gratifying, and encouraged us to proceed. We did not lay claim to first-class form; but after defeating Devonshire by an innings and 77 runs, we naturally considered that we were not far from it. E. M. was undoubtedly the hero of that match; for he scored 57 out of a total of 219 runs, and captured 6 wickets for 47 runs first innings, and 7 for 21 second. Mr J. J. Sewell, of Marlborough College fame, played a splendid innings of 65 runs, and with E. M. put on 115 runs for the first wicket. Rarely had any county club made so favourable a start, and my father was delighted with the result. My uncle, Henry and Alfred played; but I was not considered good enough, although I watched every ball bowled.

The return, at Teignbridge on the 25th and 26th August, was rather disappointing to us, for we lost it by 33 runs. It was the first important match I played in, and I scored 18 runs, but did not bowl. Henry made 19, and our total first innings was 92. In the second, with the exception of E. M., 21, and my brother-in-law, Dr. Bernard, 21, everyone came to grief, and our total was 68.

In the year 1863 I made great progress in batting, scoring freely against our crack local clubs Clifton, Lansdown, and Knole Park, and was looked upon as one of the principal bowlers of the West Gloucestershire

Club. Our first match against the Gentlemen of Devonshire illustrated the changing fortune characteristic of cricket. It was played at Tiverton on the 24th and 25th July. Devonshire winning the toss, batted first, and scored 227; two players, Messrs J. H. Coplestone and A. D. Gill, scoring 141 runs between them. We scored 135 of which I made 15, not out, and had, of course, to follow our innings. E. M., Henry, Alfred, and my uncle grumbled terribly at the condition of the wicket, and spying a big roller at the extreme corner of the field, all hands were enlisted to bring it up, and we spent the time allowed between the innings in rolling. A change came over the look of affairs; for E. M. was in one of his uphill fighting moods, and played magnificently. He hit very hard, and scored 132 out of a total of 294. Mr J. J. Sewell scored 42, my brother Alfred 32, and Henry and uncle 23 each. Devonshire was left with 203 to win, certainly not an impossible undertaking; but they were not equal to it. My uncle did one of his finest bowling performances, capturing 7 wickets for 36 runs, and getting rid of our opponents for the small total of 78.

The return match, played at Clifton 20th and 21st August, proved even more disastrous to us than the return match the previous year; for we were defeated by an innings and 61 runs.

Three days later we played Somersetshire at the Sydenham Fields, Bath, and won by 87 runs. I was top scorer with 52 not out, and obtained 4 wickets for 17 runs first innings; 2 for 26, second.

On the 31st August, 1st and 2nd September, of the same year, I played my first match against first-class professional bowling. The All-England eleven played twenty-two of Bristol, at Durdham Down, on those days, and I was eager to measure my strength against players who ranked so high. Nine years had elapsed since the All-England eleven played its second match at the back of the Full Moon Hotel, and great changes had taken place in the team. Clarke, the founder, was dead, and Bickley, owing to ill-health, was unable to play. Willsher, H. H. Stephenson, Anderson, Julius Caesar, and A. Clarke had played in 1855; but Tarrant, Hay ward, Jackson, Tinley, and the others we had not seen. It was well known that cricket in Bristol had made great strides in the last half-dozen years; how much, we could not say. The team representing the All-England eleven was considered as strong as the two previous ones, and the result would indicate the extent of our improvement.

E. M. was our captain, and had now played for and against the All-England eleven; Messrs Sewell, Daubeny, and Bramhall had good local reputations, and altogether the twenty-two was representative of cricket in the neighbourhood. Personally, I was anxious to do well, and practised diligently with bat and ball for weeks before. I knew right well that the contests in which I had played the last year or two were not to be compared with the contest on this occasion.

E. M. showed that the All-England bowling had no terrors for him; for he began hitting the first over, and made 37 altogether. One hit rather amused us. It went almost straight up and mountains high to Jackson, the bowler. 'I have got it!' said Jackson, running up the pitch; but thinking he had misjudged it, he ran a yard or two back again, then ran forward again, and allowed the ball to fall a yard or two behind him. Messrs Sewell and Daubeny played splendidly for 38 and 44. I batted tenth man.

'Have you ever felt nervous at the beginning of an innings?' has been repeatedly asked of me; but I believe I have always parried the question. Well, I did feel very nervous, or anxious call it which you like; and if it is any encouragement to young players, I may say that I experienced the same feeling for many years afterwards. When any player of note tells you that he plays the first over or two without a slight feeling of that kind, and that he is as cool and confident then as he is the last over, do not be discouraged if it be different with you, or say, 'That accounts for his scoring more freely than I do.' Perfect command of nerve at the beginning of an innings is much to be desired, if it do not lead to over-confidence; but the very few I have met who said they possessed it have always given me the impression of being too eager to score the first over or two, and hit rather wildly to accomplish their end. That, in my opinion, is not so likely to lead to long scores as a slightly nervous feeling, as long as it does not have the mastery of you.

Before I began batting in this match I practised for a little during the luncheon hour, and Tarrant was kind enough to bowl to me for five or ten minutes, a kindness which turned out very useful. When I began my innings Jackson and he were the bowlers; and being nearly of the same pace, in an over or two I felt quite at home, played confidently, and hit out. Tarrant was shunted, and Tinley took his place and bowled lobs. A change from fast round-arm to lob-bowling has never affected the rate of my scoring. E. M. bowled lobs at home as long as I can remember, and I used to hail the change with delight.

Tinley's first over I played carefully; in the second I decided to hit, and hit him into the scoring-tent. The hit was loudly cheered; I was pleased, felt elated, got overconfident, and paid the penalty. In my haste to repeat the stroke, I ran out too far in the third over, missed the ball altogether, and was clean bowled. I had scored 32, at 15 years of age, against the All-England eleven, the heroes of the cricket world, and there is no need to say that I was delighted.

But my delight did not cause me to slacken my desire to progress. On the contrary, I realised that I had given promise of excellence, and must strive harder not only to justify it, but to improve on it.

The All-England eleven made a poor show in its first innings, Jackson and H. H. Stephenson scoring 33 between them, the others 53; total, 86. A small total we thought, and due to the effective bowling of E. M. and E. T. Daubeny, who divided the wickets.

E. M. justified his selection as captain. When E. Stephenson and Willsher got set in the second innings, I was put on to bowl, and E. M. went out to the longfield. 'Throw up one or two for Stephenson to hit,' said he, which I promptly did, and E. M. brought off a magnificent catch the first over.

The All-England eleven was defeated by an innings and 20 runs.

To be asked to play for the All-England eleven may be considered a distinct step forward. That was my position in the early part of 1864, when I was in my sixteenth year. E. M. had not returned from Australia with the other members of Parr's team, and I received an invitation to play against Eighteen of Lansdown on the 30th of June. For some reason or other, Lansdown had not then asked me to play, and I accepted the All-England eleven invitation with much pleasure. Henry was equally pleased, though playing for the Eighteen, and was anxious that I should acquit myself creditably. Lansdown batted first, but did not do well against Tarrant and Hayward, only scoring 75. Mr J. W. Haygarth scored 27, and Henry was not out 11. In the second innings they did better, making 162, E. T. Daubeny, 78. John Lillywhite, for the eleven, did what he liked with the Lansdown bowling, scoring 105 out of a total of 260. I batted sixth man, which I considered rather a high compliment in so strong a team, and was in for over half an hour while I made 15. Just when I got set an unfortunate mistake of Lillywhite's caused me to be run out. But I did not mind that: I had played for the All-England eleven, and had helped to defeat a strong local Eighteen by an innings and 22 runs.

Ten days later I made my first appearance in London, playing at the Oval for the South Wales Club. Henry and E. M. had played repeatedly for the same club; but E. M. was still on his homeward journey from Australia, and they had to do without him this match. My uncle and brothers were well known in Wales, having played at Newport, Cardiff, and elsewhere against the All-England eleven, and that led to their connection with the South Wales team, with whom they made an annual trip to town for years. Henry suggested that I should take E. M.'s place; and I was booked to play against Surrey Club and the Gentlemen of Sussex. My engagement nearly fell through. I was on the ground, with Henry, ready to play in the Surrey match on the 11th July. The captain of the South Wales team approached Henry, and asked him if he objected to my standing out against the Gentlemen of Sussex at Brighton, as he had the offer of a very good player, and he believed their opponents were exceptionally strong. Henry objected very much. 'To begin with,' he said, 'the boy was asked to play in both matches, and he shall play in both matches or none; and I only hope every member of the team will do as well as I expect him to do.' Henry scored 11 and 49 against the Surrey Club: I scored 5 and 38, and nothing further was said about my standing out.

The Brighton match was played on the old Hove Ground, on the 14th, 15th, and 16th of July, and it was my first appearance at that famous watering place. The wicket was in excellent condition, as it was always there; and after the discussion between Henry and the South Wales captain, I was eager to do well. Henry was not playing, and I felt that the entire responsibility of the family credit was resting on my shoulders. Up to the last moment we hoped E. M. would turn up; and I desired it eagerly, if only to give me heart. His ringing voice and cheery tones would have been invaluable to me; but I had to be content with a paragraph in the newspapers to the effect that the Revd Mr Grace, who had done such wonders in Australia, was expected to play. We have had E. M. described times and forms innumerable; but that was the only occasion we ever had him given as the 'Revd,' and we never could make out whether he considered it in the light of a compliment or as a bit of sarcasm. The match has been reported and criticised more than once, so I need not enter into minute details. South Wales won the toss, and I batted first wicket down. Before the second wicket fell, Mr Lloyd, the South Wales captain, and myself raised the score to close upon 200 runs; and at the end of the first day the total was 356 for 9 wickets, of which I had scored 170 made up of 19 fours, 9 threes, 17 twos, and singles without giving a chance. I was out in attempting to cut a wide ball getting over it too much, and cutting it into my wicket. We had news the same afternoon that E. M. had stepped on English soil, and he was wired to turn up next morning. He did not; possibly satisfied that there was no need for him after our long score.

The Gentlemen of Sussex scored 148 first innings, and had to follow on. They gave us a fine bit of leather hunting in their second innings, scoring 341, and leaving us 134 to win. Time did not permit us to finish; but at the end of the third day we had scored 118 for 5 wickets, of which I had made 56 not out.

They gave me a bat, which I have today and am very proud of. The handle and the blade are of one piece of wood: it was the only one to be had on the ground at the end of the innings; however, I value it for the reason that it marks the date of the beginning of my long scores. I was not quite 16 years of age, and had gained my first experience in playing steadily and consistently through a long innings.

A week later I played for the same club at Lord's against the MCC; and before the end of the month against the I Zingari. In the first match I scored 50; in the second, 34 and 47; and for South Wales Club that year I had an average of 48 for nine innings. In first-class matches I scored 402 runs for seven innings, average 57; and at the end of the season I had an aggregate of 1079. I had played well enough to merit an opinion from John Lillywhite's *Companion*, in its summary for the season: 'Mr W. G. Grace promises to be a good bat: bowls very fairly.'

That was my progress and position at the end of 1864, when I had completed my sixteenth year. The lesson I have desired to convey to young players is, that my doings in the cricket world at that period of my life, if they are of any value, were owing to my father and uncle's stimulating examples, and perseverance on my own part. When the associations and surroundings are favourable, there can be little doubt that perseverance will work wonders, if love and enthusiasm go with it. Love and enthusiasm we all possessed from the oldest to the youngest, and we possess it today.

And we have always been a temperate family. Intemperate smoking, in my opinion, has more to do with nervousness and small scores than moderate drinking. E. M. and I have never smoked. Another point to be considered is constant exercise of some kind throughout the year. We were known to be fond of hunting, shooting, and fishing, as well as cricketing. Immediately we laid down the bat, we took up the gun or rod; and my father, brother Alfred, and E. M. hunted as long as professional duties permitted. I find a day's shooting or fishing, or a run with the harriers or beagles, of great use during the winter months, and I take care to have plenty of walking. In the months of February and March I begin to prepare for the season, increasing the amount of exercise, and by the beginning of May I feel fit enough to face the cricketing season.

The spring and dash of life have somewhat abated in me, and perhaps I am less careful today in the matter of sleep than I was ten or fifteen years ago; but I cannot remember when I did not at the beginning or middle of the season take care to have a fair amount of rest. Every player must judge for himself whether he require six, eight, or ten hours. It has happened on many occasions that I have been up half the night, and scored heavily next day; but that proves nothing, unless, perhaps, that I possess exceptional physical powers.

A good story comes to my mind, which, while it goes against my theory, is too good to be lost. It occurred during the Scarborough week, where good cricket and good cheer go hand in hand. Three or four of us were on the way to our rooms in the early morning, after an enjoyable dance; and being more in the mood for chatting than sleep, we, with one exception, decided to spend an hour or two longer comparing reminiscences. The 'exception' had commenced his innings that day, and was not out when play stopped.

'You can do what you like,' said he; 'but I'm off to bed, as I mean to make a hundred tomorrow.'

I forget how long we sat up certainly later than we should have done in the beginning of the season, but next day every one of us scored largely; while our friend was out first over, without adding to his overnight's score! I sincerely hope young players will not follow our example, though it was not attended with disastrous results.

I have assumed that what I have been saying about my family and home, and early training, my readers would equally apply to the training of my youngest brother, Fred. He was just as enthusiastic as any of us, and practised as diligently at home as E. M. or I did, though he lacked some of our opportunities. My brothers Henry and Alfred had married, and were living some miles away from Downend, when he was old enough to begin; and E. M. was very much away. Fred had to fall back upon the services of the bootboy and nursemaid, and he kept them busy bowling to him all day long. My mother looked after his progress, and saw that he had every encouragement to improve, and he showed promise of excellence at quite as early an age as I did. I remember we had some difficulty in getting him out of the habit of practising left-handed. He was strong for his age, and played with a determination worthy of a much older boy. School training brought him forward rapidly, and before he had completed his tenth year he had played his first match and distinguished himself as a bowler locally, clean bowling ten of his opponents' wickets, and having two caught off him. Steadily he grew in skill and strength, and at the end of 1864, when E. M. and I had done sufficient to attract attention outside of Gloucestershire, he, in his fourteenth year, was a well-known figure to every cricket club in the district. He did not play with so straight a bat as I did, but, for his age, he was much more resolute in his hitting, and in the field showed something of the dash and certainty which characterised him in that branch of the game in after years.

There was a marked difference in the batting styles of E. M., Fred, and myself. I do not require to particularise E. M.'s again. He went in for hitting in his peculiar way as long as I can remember him, and he invariably brought it off. There was one special feature in it which helped him in his long scores; the flight of the ball after he hit it. When he got the ball clean on the bat it travelled low and fast, and the fieldsman had to be on the spot to have any chance of catching it. His strong nerve was invaluable to him and the side he played on, and the quality of the bowling made little difference to him. I have seen more than one bowler, who had been performing splendidly, go all to pieces as soon as E. M. had hit him once or twice; and one match I shall not readily forget. Gloucestershire was playing Notts, in 1877, when Morley and Barnes were at their best. The first dozen overs or so Morley was simply unplayable, and four of the Gloucestershire wickets were down for less than 30 runs Fred's, Townsend's, and my own among them when E. M. went in to bat. 'Keep your eye on Morley, and play carefully, Ted,' I said. 'All very well to talk,' said he. 'I should like to know what good the steadiness of you fellows has done for the innings? It looks to me like a clear case of funk, and I am going to stop it!' And stop it he did. In his very first over, Morley gave him one slightly to the off, which he promptly cracked to the boundary at long-on. In the next he pulled a good-length straight one to the same spot; and Morley lost his head and did not know where to bowl to him. Afterwards, Moberly and E. M. put on runs at a great pace, and eventually we beat them by an innings.

Gloucestershire *v.* Lancashire, in 1889, at Liverpool, was another illustration of it. Lancashire scored 73 and 102; Gloucestershire 80 first, and had lost 5 wickets for 42 second, the wicket unplayable. E. M. was our last resource, and he justified it. Very early in his innings Briggs favoured him with a ball about a foot to the off, which was sent to leg. Two or three extra fieldsmen were placed on that side for him, and Briggs tried him again. He gave him a good-length ball, a little outside the off stump, which E. M. hit between cover-point and mid-off and scored four by it; and then, to show it was no fluke, repeated it an over or two later. Briggs was all at sea, and E. M. had the measure of him afterwards, and, with the help of A. C. M. Croome, won for us a splendid and unexpected victory by three wickets.

It was hitting and nerve of that kind which made E. M. the terror of local clubs when he played for West Gloucestershire, between 1860 and 1867; and it was more than once seriously proposed that he should not be allowed to play. And he was just as successful with the ball. I give some of his exceptional performances, to show the quality of his play at that time:

Aug., 1861. – For Berkeley *v.* Knole Park, he scored 100 not out in a total of 119, and took every wicket 2nd innings.

Aug., 1861. – For Lansdown *v.* Clifton, 119 not out, and took every wicket 2nd innings.

Aug., 1862 .– For MCC *v.* Gentlemen of Kent, 192 not out, and took every wicket 2nd innings.

Aug., 1863. – For Lansdown *v.* Clifton, 61 not out, and took every wicket 2nd innings.

May, 1865. – For an Eleven *v.* an Eleven, at Clifton, 69 not
out, and took every wicket 2nd innings.

Aug., 1867. – For Marshfield *v.* Corsham School Club, 98 not
out, and took every wicket 2nd innings.

April, 1864. – Single-wicket Match, E. M. Grace *v.* Six of
Maryborough, Australia. E. M., 106 not out; the Six not
being able to get him out.

Fred's hitting was quite as clean, but more orthodox, and he had better
defence. He stood very upright, but had the habit of placing part of
his left foot in front of the wicket. He, too, scored heavily against
local clubs, and met with great success as a bowler; but somehow
he did not frighten his opponents so much as E. M. I do not think I
frightened them so much either; for local clubs have always welcomed
me, when I could find time to play with them. If I might be allowed to
compare my own style with E. M.'s and Fred's, I should say I had the
advantage in height, and played straighter; and I think I have always
had greater patience.

A word or two more, and I have done with the Family Sketch
and our early training. When we took to first-class cricket, play and
practice suffered to some extent in the orchard at Downend; but we
kept the wicket in good condition until the home was broken up and
always used it a month or two before the season began. We kept in
constant touch with the home-circle right through the season; either
wiring the result of every first-class match, or posting the scoring card
at the end of every day's play. That much they expected, and I think
we rarely disappointed them.

My father died in the year 1871. He had lived to see his sons grown
to manhood's years, taking part in the duties of life, and occupying
a high position in the game he loved so dearly. His last effort was to
establish the Gloucestershire County Club on a sound basis, which
he was successful in doing in the year 1870. My mother remained
among us thirteen years longer, and was present at every county
match at Clifton College. She took great interest in cricket all round
the neighbourhood, and treasured every telegram and report of our
doings. Local papers did not give much space to cricket twenty years
ago, and rarely reported matches played outside of the county; and as
London papers did not reach Downend till late in the day, we made

a point of telegraphing or writing to her the result of every match played from home. E. M. and I were playing for Gloucestershire *v.* Lancashire, at Manchester, on 25th July, 1884, when we received the telegram announcing her death. It came with painful surprise to us, and for the moment we knew not what to do; but my friend and comrade of many years, A. N. Hornby, the captain of the Lancashire eleven, grasped the situation, and, with a promptness and consideration which E. M. and I can never forget, immediately stopped the match, and we hurried home to have the last look at her who had loved us so wisely and well.

4

Cricket Schisms & County Cricket 1863-69

County Cricket made satisfactory progress in the year 1863. A number of county clubs were then formed, which took root, and have flourished with more or less success since. They had to contend against the popularity of the All-England and United elevens, who still received liberal encouragement wherever they appeared; but lovers of the game could see, even at that date, that a county club was more likely to establish the game on a firm footing than a travelling eleven which owed its existence entirely to gate money. The success of the two elevens was no doubt owing to the quality of the players representing them; but their jealousies and constant bickerings began to tire their supporters, and when the North and South took sides, matters for the moment looked serious. I suppose we shall never get to the bottom of the various schisms which created so much ill-feeling about that time, and which spoiled so many important matches; and I question if it be worth the trouble to try. A short recapitulation of them will be sufficient.

First, we had Clarke's management of the All-England eleven called into question, which led to the formation of the United eleven; second, there was jealousy on the part of the northern men about the selection of H. H. Stephenson for the captaincy of the first English eleven which went to Australia; then we had the Nottinghamshire dispute with Surrey for first place in county honours, which caused them to steer clear of meeting each other for years; and, finally, we had the divisions of the different elevens into North and South.

It was not an uncommon thing for two or three members of an eleven to combine and object to another member playing. For some reason or other, G. Atkinson absented himself from the Yorkshire team against Nottinghamshire on the 9th, 10th, and 11th July, 1863. Seven days afterwards, eight of the most prominent Yorkshire players wrote to the Honorary Secretary: 'We, the undersigned, have made up our minds that we will not play in the forthcoming Yorkshire *v.* Surrey match if George Atkinson plays.'

It was a most unhappy position for a Secretary to be placed in; but the eight gained their point, for Atkinson did not play in the Surrey match.

The North *v.* Surrey match at the Oval, 3rd, 4th, and 5th August the same year, was also spoiled, owing to Parr's 'combination' objecting to play. Parr, Anderson, Daft, Hayward, Carpenter, Tarrant, and Jackson were all absent, and it was not a case of their being unable to play, but that they would not play against Surrey. When England played Surrey a fortnight later, they were in the same mood, and remained in it in the North *v.* Surrey match, at Manchester on 20th, 21st, and 22nd August. In the latter match the North, though playing a weak team, was strong enough to win, and a certain amount of satisfaction was felt that the team should have been able to do it without the dissentient players. A lively newspaper correspondence ensued, and it must have been unpleasant to the players who stood out to read:

> The Northern Managers have experienced great difficulty in getting together their strength, and while endeavouring to smooth down the feeling which exists between certain players and the Surrey authorities, they have shown that they are not wholly reliant upon a particular division to supply an eleven to represent the North.

In the early part of 1864 an agitation was set going in one of the leading sporting papers which had for its aim the formation of a 'cricket parliament' to depose the Marylebone Club from its position as the authority on the game; but it met with little countenance, and the old club, which had now played on its present ground for fifty years, was allowed to carry on the work which it, and it alone, seemed to be able to do with firmness and impartiality. If evidence were wanting of the MCC's interest and consideration for the game at that period, we have only to look at the number and quality of matches played by it. During the year 1864 it played as many as 34 matches, including such clubs as Cambridge and Oxford Universities; Eton, Harrow and

Rugby Schools, the Army Club, Royal Artillery, and some of the minor counties. Show us how we can do good to the game and we shall endeavour to do it, has always been the aim of the Committee of the MCC, and it would have been a thousand pities if the Club had been deprived of its powers at that critical period of cricket history.

June the 10th of the same year saw an important alteration in the laws. The Willsher episode of 1862 was still fresh in the memories of players, and after vainly trying to get umpires to 'no-ball' a bowler when he raised his arm above the shoulder, it was finally decided that Law X. should read thus: 'The ball must be bowled; if thrown or jerked, the umpire shall call "no-ball."'

That settled for good the vexed question of the height of arm in delivering the ball, and bowlers and umpires breathed more freely afterwards. Surrey and Nottinghamshire met in July, and it was thought their differences were at an end; but when England met Surrey a month later, the crack Northern players would not come; and they also absented themselves from the North *v.* South match, in September. In the last match the North was poorly represented, and the South won very easily. So indignant were the Southern players that at the end of the first day's play they met and drew up the following protest:

> We, the South of England, decline playing at Newmarket on the 6th, 7th, and 8th October, as they, the North of England, refused to play in London. (*Signed*) T. Lockyer, W. Mortlock, E. Pooley, James Lillywhite, jun., G. Bennett, T. Humphrey, H. Jupp, C. H. Ellis, T. Hearne, T. Sewell, jun., G. Griffith, John Lillywhite, and Julius Caesar.

That did not improve matters; in reality it widened the breach, and created a schism between North and South, which led to the formation of the United South eleven, and the North of Thames *v.* South of Thames matches; and in after years the All-England and United elevens were seen very little in the south.

It was a most unhappy state of affairs and, but for the firmness of the MCC and the leading amateurs of the various counties and clubs, might have had serious consequences. Fortunately, a love for the game was springing up all over the United Kingdom, and good players were increasing in number rapidly. Very soon equally good players could be seen outside of the famous elevens, and the demands of the different players in some cases reasonable, in others unreasonable could either be granted or firmly refused. The MCC was now playing the Colts of England, for the purpose of discovering rising talent; and county clubs were doing the same thing. Public schools, colleges, and other clubs were also adding to the number. The Na Shuler Club, holding pretty much the same position in Ireland as the I Zingari in England, was formed in 1863; and there was another and more powerful combination, named the Free Foresters, which had been in existence since 1856, and which for seven years could show a record of 102 matches played, 62 of them won. Then there was the Southgate Club, which, owing to the famous Walker family, had a great reputation in the neighbourhood of London and out of it. It was very busy about that time, playing almost a first-class eleven, and sixteen of it were strong enough to defeat the United England eleven by an innings and 65 runs.

A very pleasing and encouraging feature at that time was the growth and interest taken in the game outside of England. Scotland and Ireland were developing rapidly, and began international matches with each other; and an English eleven, under the leadership of Parr, was causing great interest in Australia. England *v.* twenty-two of Victoria, on the 1st, 2nd, 4th and 5th January, 1864, at Melbourne, brought out a great crowd, as many as 40,000 attending during the four days. For a parallel to it in England we have to go to the Eton and Harrow match at Lord's, in the height of the London season, when something approaching 20,000 were present in two days.

The All-England *v.* United England, and Gentlemen *v.* Players matches, though far ahead of the Eton and Harrow match in a cricketing sense, were not to be compared with it in attendance. The Players were still far ahead of the Gentlemen, and that year's defeat made the eighteenth in succession.

But, undoubtedly, the most encouraging feature of that season was the progress made by the counties. Surrey county had a very fine record: 14 matches played 8 won, 1 lost, 5 drawn.

	Played	Won	Lost	Drawn
Middlesex	8	5	2	1
Sussex	8	5	2	1
Cambridgeshire	3	3 (Yorkshire 2, Notts 1)		

Notts	7	3	4	–
Yorkshire	7	2	4	1
Kent	9	–	–	9

A very sad show for Kent, considering that 13 of that club played an eleven of England twice that year.

Lancashire played 9: 3 won, 3 lost, 3 drawn; most of them against minor counties and local clubs. Hampshire played in matches of one kind and another, and Buckinghamshire played two against Middlesex. Amateur elevens were quite as busy; the I Zingari playing 23 matches, the Incogniti 23, and the Free Foresters 14.

I began to take an active part in first-class cricket in 1865. I was only 16 years of age, but I was over 6 feet in height and 11 stone in weight. Before the end of the season I had played for the Gentlemen of the South, the Gentlemen of England., England *v.* Surrey, and for the Gentlemen *v.* Players twice, with what success will be seen later on. Before touching upon the doings in 1865, it will be useful to revert for a little to the past.

The All-England and United All-England elevens were still in full swing, playing as many as thirty matches during the season. Scotland and Ireland were now included in the list of their engagements; but rarely was either eleven seen in the South. They still possessed the cream of the professional talent; and when they played against each other, the display was still the finest of the season. Down to the year 1864 the two elevens had met fourteen times, and results showed six wins each, two drawn. And, so far, not a single member of either eleven had scored 100 runs in an innings. Carpenter scored 97 in the 1859 match; but that was the nearest approach to it. The reason, no doubt, was owing principally to the quality of their bowling and the rough wickets which were played on then. It is told of Clarke's eleven that on one occasion when it visited Cornwall a man fielding at long-on flushed a covey of partridges, and that a patch 40 yards by 10 was the only part of the ground that was ever cut or rolled. But it might, in a degree, be attributed to the fact that professional players did not cultivate batting as much as bowling, knowing that, however good they might be at the former, they must excel in the latter to secure an engagement with a club of any importance. The aim of every club was to engage a good bowler as soon as its finances permitted. The player who averaged a double figure at the end of the season was considered to have batted exceptionally well; and when a good bowler did it he was looked upon as an all-round first-class cricketer indeed, and could command a very high price for his services.

The averages of a number of the prominent batsmen of both elevens in the annual matches played against each other from their inauguration in 1857 will show the quality of the batting at that period. At the end of 1864:

	Innings played	Average
R. Carpenter	19	25.6
G. Parr	21	24.18
T. Hayward	18	16.13
R. Daft	18	16.11
T. Hearne	17	16.13
H. H. Stephenson	24	16.2
G. Anderson	14	13.9
J. Jackson	18	13.11
W. Caffyn	24	12.5
J. Grundy	24	11.11
R. C. Tinley	21	10.5
E. Willsher	24	10.3
J. Wisden	17	8.6
G. Tarrant	9	7.6

Those were the most celebrated players of both elevens.

When we turn to the doings of the Gentlemen and Players there is a different story to tell. These matches were commenced in 1806. At the end of 1864 results showed that the Players had won 39, the Gentlemen 14, and 3 were drawn; and that the century had been exceeded 8 times; seven of them to the credit of the Players, one to the credit of the Gentlemen.

If we remember that in the majority of the matches won by the Gentlemen, they were either playing extra men, or had one or two players given them, it will be easily seen that the best of our amateur talent was very far behind the best of our professional. From 1854 to 1864 the Gentlemen were completely out of the running. Out of the 19 matches played between those years, the Players won 18, and 1 was drawn.

That was the state of affairs at the end of 1864; and when it was announced that 60 young players had applied and been recommended to play in the Nottinghamshire Colts' Match on Easter Monday, 1865, and that other counties were full of promising talent also, the prospects of professional players looked very rosy. University and public school cricket were in full swing also, and the number of first-class amateur batsmen was rapidly increasing.

At the end of 1865 County Cricket showed that Nottinghamshire and Surrey were at the head of the poll.

In purely county matches Surrey won 7, lost 3, and 2 were drawn; Nottinghamshire won 6, lost 1; Middlesex won 3, lost 1, and 1 was drawn; Kent won 2, lost 3, and 2 were drawn; Sussex won 1, lost 4, and 2 were drawn; Cambridgeshire won 1, lost 1, and 1 was drawn; Yorkshire won 0, lost 6, and 2 were drawn. Buckinghamshire, Hampshire, and Warwickshire played against each other with varying results.

Nottinghamshire's performance was a very fine one; four wins being ridiculously easy, especially that against Sussex at Trent Bridge, 1st, 2nd, and 3rd June, which was won by an innings and 86 runs. Parr and Daft batted consistently for their county all that season; the former doing specially good work with the bat, considering that he was now in his fortieth year, and had represented Nottinghamshire for 21 years. Then they had such good bowlers as Grundy, Wootton, Jackson, Alfred Shaw, and Tinley. Grundy was very successful on that occasion, the Sussex batsmen being perfectly helpless against him. In the second innings he bowled 100 balls, took five wickets, and only 6 runs were scored off him. The one match lost was the return against Surrey at the Oval on the 13th, 14th, and 15th July, and there was a tremendous amount of excitement and feeling over it. Parr declined to play, which did not make matters pleasant to begin with; and rarely have two counties fought so keenly as those two did on that occasion. Surrey in the second innings had 14 runs to make to win when the ninth wicket went down. They obtained them; but the Nottinghamshire players and some spectators alleged that Sewell, the last batsman, had been run out, and spoke bitterly of the umpire's decision. Quite a crowd gathered in front of the pavilion at the finish, and neither of the elevens measured their language, nor forgot to rake up old sores. The relationship between the two counties had become so strained, that the committees of both clubs decided to abandon the match in 1866, and contests between them were not resumed for three years.

Yorkshire's performances were sadly disappointing to its supporters; but the committee had to contend against internal dissensions, and on more than one occasion were without their full strength. Five of the regular eleven refused to play against Surrey at Sheffield on the 19th, 20th, and 21st June; and afterwards the committee tried all in their power to do without them, with the result that every match was lost. The county had commenced the season with satisfactory hopes, too; and among their fixtures was a match against the All-England eleven, which turned out to be the most humiliating defeat a good eleven had experienced for years, the county losing by an innings and 255 runs. Carpenter and Hayward scored over a hundred runs each for the All-England eleven, and every member of the team made a double figure; and in the second innings Wootton took all 10 wickets.

On the 22nd June I played my first representative match. The Gentlemen of the South met the Players of the South at the Oval on that day, and it was my good fortune to be on the winning side, the Players being defeated by an innings and 58 runs. Mr I. D. Walker was the successful batsman, scoring 91 out of a total of 233. I need not say I was anxious to do well, and was chagrined at being stumped without scoring.

The captain of the team sent me in first wicket down, a compliment which I keenly felt I had not justified; but I was on better terms with myself at the end of the match, after having bowled with success unchanged through both innings. In the first innings I took 5 wickets for 44 runs, in the second 8 wickets for 40.

Ten days later I made my first appearance for the Gentlemen v. Players at the Oval, in response to the invitation of the committee of the Surrey Club. On that occasion I was placed eighth on the batting list, and scored 23 first innings, 12 not out second. Mr R. D. Walker scored 92 the second innings; Mr R. A. H. Mitchell, 53 first and 33 second: but we lost the match by 118 runs; and I realised that while there were as good batsmen in the Gentlemen's eleven as in the Players', the former were still much behind in bowling. It was the ninth time that this match had been played at the Oval, and on each occasion the Players had won rather easily. It was easy to understand that against such an array of talent as the Players then possessed, the Gentlemen had a formidable task before them to win one of the two matches that were now played annually between them. Our defeat was all the more annoying that the Players' eleven was not at all representative on that occasion; for the northern cracks Daft, Parr, Jackson, Hayward, Carpenter, Tarrant, and Anderson had all declined to come.

The return match, at Lord's, on the 10th and 11th July, was more encouraging to us; the Gentlemen winning it by 8 wickets. It was their first win since the year 1854. Hayward, Carpenter, and Parr were among the Players, and this added considerably to our satisfaction in defeating so strong an eleven. I batted first, with my brother E. M., in both innings. Mr B. B. Cooper made 70 for the Gentlemen, and Mr R. A. H. Mitchell 44 not out; and G. Parr was highest for the Players, making 60 in their second innings.

I had another, and what I considered a very high, compliment paid to me on the 17th, 18th, and 19th July. The second of those dates was my eighteenth birthday, and I spent it playing for The Gentlemen of England *v.* The Gentlemen of Middlesex, on the Middlesex County Ground, at Islington. The result showed that both teams had plenty of batting strength, for 822 runs were scored for thirty-six wickets. My brother E. M. was most successful for England, scoring 12 and 111; and my share was 48 and 34. Mr A. J. Wilkinson scored 28 and not out 84 for Middlesex; and Mr C. F. Buller made 71 for the same side.

At the Oval, on the 21st and 22nd August, I played for England *v.* Surrey, and going in first with E. M., raised the score to 80 before we were parted.

I have dealt more fully with my own doings in those matches than I had intended; but, as it was the first year in which I contended against the best of the amateur and professional talent, I believed it might be of interest and encouraging to beginners to have the results. It will be seen that, at times, I was fairly successful with both bat and ball; but that now and then I shared the common experience of doing very little with either. First-class professional bowling I found to be a widely different thing from the amateur bowling which I had played chiefly against in the last year or two against local clubs. My slight experience against the All-England eleven had in a measure prepared me for it, and I took no liberties: but most of the bowlers were new to me, and their styles varied; and I learned that before I could do much against a man, I must know something about his bowling. It was trial enough to be compelled to play over after over of straight, good-length balls; but I had to watch tricky ones as well. Patience I found to be my greatest friend, and before the season was over I had gained something in confidence. But, of course, I was disappointed at not scoring a hundred runs at least once during the year, although I knew that was a feat rarely accomplished at that time against first-class bowling. My highest score was 85, for the South Wales Club *v.* I Zingari; but my most encouraging performance was in bowling for the Gentlemen of the South *v.* Players of the South, in the match I have already mentioned, and for which the Surrey Club presented me with a ball, with the following inscription on it:

> Presented to W. G. Grace, Esq., by the Surrey County Cricket Club, for his great performance in the match of Gentlemen of the South *v.* Players of the South at the Oval, June 22nd and 23rd, where he bowled five wickets first innings for 44 runs, and 8 second for 40.

I had plenty of cricket of one kind and another that year, playing in all 54 innings, and scoring 2169 runs; and one of the innings was for Suffolk County Club. It came about in this way. The MCC was playing that county at Lord's, and I was in London at the time. I strolled on to the ground the second day; and Suffolk being two men short, very kindly asked rne to play. I did not wait to be asked twice, and could have wished to have done better for them. We were sadly defeated, only scoring 58 and 62; while the MCC scored 269 in a single innings. E. M. scored 82 for them, and knocked the Suffolk bowling all over the ground.

There were two or three good individual performances during the year; one of them being Jupp's 216 for the Players of the South *v.* Fourteen Gentlemen of the South, at Southampton in September. The Gentlemen were a very weak lot; but Jupp's score was made without a chance. Pooley scored in by hard hitting in the same match. Another fine effort was my brother E. M.'s against the United England eleven, for Eighteen of the Lansdown Club, at Bath in the month of June. Out of a total of 299 he made 121; and he, my eldest brother Henry, and myself took all the wickets in both innings.

Over a hundred runs in an innings, in good matches, was scored by Messrs C. G. Lyttelton, R. D. Walker, A. Lubbock, Spencer

Leigh, S. A. Leigh; and among the Players, by W. Oscroft (twice), H. H. Stephenson, Bennett, T. Humphrey, Hayward, and Carpenter.

My brother E. M. came in for a hot reception at a match played at the Oval on the 28th, 29th, 30th September. Playing for Eighteen Gentlemen of the Surrey Club against the United South of England, he scored 64 and 56, and received his 75th presentation bat; it being the custom of the committee ot the Surrey Club at that time to give a bat for every score of 50 runs. Mr I. D. Walker and he bowled unchanged in both innings; Mr Walker's underhand lobs and E. M.'s fast round completely beating the United South batsmen. Jupp was most at home with them, and got set in the second innings. 'The problem is to get Jupp out,' said I. D. to E. M. 'All right!' said E. M.; 'I can do it with a lob.' Very shortly after he gave him a lofty one, which fell right on to the top of the wickets, and a scene followed. Cries of 'Shame!' and 'Unfair bowling!' were shouted all over the ground; and a large number of the spectators advised Jupp not to go out. The match was stopped for the greater part of an hour, finally resuling in a win for the Eighteen by 155 runs.

ALL-ENGLAND ELEVEN played 30 matches that year: won 19, lost 5, drawn 6.

Carpenter was at the head of the averages with 31 innings, average 24.23; G. Parr, 28 innings, average 17.16. In bowling: J. Jackson captured 206 wickets, average 5.21 per innings; G. Tarrant, 250 wickets, average 5.40 per innings; and Tinley, 301 wickets, average 7.28 per innings.

THE UNITED ALL-ENGLAND ELEVEN played 9 matches: won 3, lost 3, drawn 3.

Carpenter played 14 innings, and averaged 17.2; J. Thewlis played 14 innings, and averaged 16.5.

In bowling: G. Atkinson captured 61 wickets, average 5.1 per innings; J. Grundy, 48 wickets, average 5.3 per innings; G. Wootton, 35 wickets, average 4.3 per innings; Tarrant, 33 wickets, average 8.1 per innings.

THE UNITED ALL-ENGLAND ELEVEN played 14 matches: won 4, lost 4, drawn 6.

Jupp and Humphrey were the most successful batsmen; Willsher and Jas. Lillywhite the most successful bowlers.

A marked improvement was witnessed in batting in the year 1866. Hardly a week passed without an individual innings of a hundred runs in an innings being recorded in some match or another; and before the season was at an end, 200 runs was exceeded four times. The averages reached a figure undreamt of a few years before, and the once-coveted double figure had become quite common. An aggregate of 1000 runs, which was at one time considered a very exceptional feat, was accomplished by eighteen batsmen, ten of them amateurs; many of the batsmen, however, played few or no first-class matches.

The All-England eleven again showed excellent results: 30 matches played won, 15; lost, 6; tie, 1; drawn, 8. The United All-England played 22 won, 14; lost, 2; drawn, 6. The United South played 17; won, 4; lost, 7; drawn, 6.

In County Cricket, Surrey, Middlesex, Kent, Sussex, Cambridgeshire, and Lancashire were well represented: but Yorkshire was again a failure, only playing three matches, and losing two of them; the other was unfinished. Nottinghamshire only played six matches home and home with Cambridgeshire, Yorkshire, and Middlesex; winning 2, losing 1, while 3 were drawn.

The All-England eleven *v.* United All-England eleven match was played, as usual, at Lord's, for the benefit of the Cricketers' Fund, on 21st, 22nd, and 23rd May, and a large crowd witnessed the contest. The teams were composed entirely of northern players: both elevens were well represented, and a very good match took place, the United winning, and making the record of matches played between them 7 wins each, 2 drawn. But after that, representative matches North *v.* South, and Gentlemen *v.* Players were completely spoiled, owing to the northern players declining to play. No less than thirteen players in the North refused, and at last the committee of the Marylebone Club spoke out clearly and firmly. At a committee meeting of that club, held on May 21st, the following resolutions were passed:

1. That as the committee must decline to enter into the disputes among the professionals, or take the part either of northern and southern players, another eleven be selected to play in the North *v.* South match.

George Parr.
(*From an old print.*)

2. That the selection of players for the match Gentlemen *v.* Players
    having been considered in reference to the refusal of the northern
    players to meet the southern men, the players in all matches at
    Lord's be selected from those who are willing to play together
    in a friendly manner in the matches on that ground.

Of course, the resolutions were passed too late to have any effect that
season; but they bore fruit two or three years later.

The match between the Gentlemen and Players at Lord's, on the
25th June, was not representative of the players; although it was
strong enough to beat the Gentlemen by 38 runs, chiefly owing
to the magnificent batting of Tom Hearne, who scored 122 not out
in the second innings.

The return match at the Oval was no better, but the Gentlemen turned the tables, and won by 98 runs.

The South *v.* North, at Lord's, on the 2nd July, was a miserable failure. There were only a few players in the North team that could be called first-class, and the match was robbed of all interest. The North scored 95 and 65, to the South's single innings of 203, and the spectators who witnessed it did not hesitate to speak out about the conduct of the absent northern players.

I cannot say that I played a very important part with the bat in any of these three matches. In the first and second I scored 77 runs for four innings; in the third I made 19 in my single innings. But I met with fair success with the ball in both matches against the Players, obtaining 6 wickets in the first and 9 in the second.

I have often been asked if I had much faith in myself before I commenced my big innings of 224 not out for England *v.* Surrey, at the Oval, on the 30th July of that year. My memory is a blank in that respect. I was a little over eighteen years of age at the time, and the years that followed were busy ones; and that particular match, and one or two others, have become dim memories. I know I travelled up to town the same morning, and felt slightly nervous the first over or two; everything afterwards I have forgotten, except the shouting which followed at the end of the innings, late in the afternoon of the second day. And I remember Mr V. E. Walker, the captain of the England team, was kind enough to let me off the last day to compete in the 440 yards' hurdle-race of the National Olympian Association Meeting at the Crystal Palace, which I won in 1 minute 10 seconds over 20 hurdles.

My score of 173 not out, for the Gentlemen of the South *v.* Players of the South, at the Oval, 27th and 28th August, is also a hazy remembrance. I have a faint idea that there was more hitting in it than in the previous match, and that I played more confidently. I had been thinking hard, during the season, that the arrangement of the field in first-class matches was not quite what it ought to be. There was a prevailing opinion at the time that as long as a bowler was straight, a batsman could not score off him, and that no men in the long field were necessary. The opinion had, I believe, been handed down from old W. Lillywhite's time, who, when a straight ball was driven over his head, used to take off his hat, rub his pate, and say: 'That's a very pretty game, but it aint cricket.' My brother E. M. was the first to upset that theory, and I determined to copy him, and so every time I had a ball the least bit over-pitched, I hit it hard over the bowler's head, and did not trouble about where it was going. My height enabled me to get over those that were slightly short, and I played them hard: long-hops off the wicket I pulled to square-leg or long-on, without the slightest hesitation.

The year altogether was a busy one, and the game had now taken a greater hold than ever.

I have been repeatedly asked when I played first in the Midland and Northern counties, but was at a loss to answer. I stumbled across an old score the other day, which recalls the date and circumstances. It was on the 4th and 5th of June, 1866, at the old Hyde Park Ground, Sheffield, when I captained Eighteen Colts of Nottingham and Sheffield against the All-England eleven. I have represented many a team in my life, but this seems to my mind the most curious, and I shall not readily forget the impression the match made on me. The ground was on the top of a hill which took some climbing to reach, and everything in connection with it was of the most primitive description. I am more used to Yorkshire ways and arrangements now; but at the time I felt as if I had got to the world's end, and a very black and sooty end it seemed! I was only a boy of 17, and had never before had the honour of leadership on my shoulders against an eleven of worldwide fame. My brother E. M. had been asked to undertake the responsibility, but could not go, and recommended me to take his place. The All-England eleven beat us by an innings and 8 runs, and I was very much impressed with Parr's leg-hitting. The ground was not much to look at, but the wicket was a good one; and after scoring 9 and 36, I was complimented on having captained the team and with playing creditably.

Scorers of 1,000 Runs in all Matches in 1866.

	Runs	No. of Innings	Not Out	Highest Innings
Mr W. G. Grace	2,168	40	7	224*
Mr C. F. Buller	1,647	54	6	196
Mr M. A. Troughton	1,526	46	14	91
Mr J. J. Sewell	1,466	44	7	166

Mr R. A. Fitzgerald	1,420	60	6	147
Mr A. Lubbock	1,383	34	9	220
Mr E. B. Fane	1,265	37	3	151*
Captain Taylor	1,237	56	7	99
Mr Ashley Walker	1,213	47	1	126
Mr C. F. Lucas	1,081	36	3	135
H. Jupp	1,605	68	8	165
Sergt. W. McCanlis	1,580	45	8	172*
T. Hearne	1,335	52	2	146
J. Smith	1,163	62	2	80
H. Holmes	1,118	42	10	105
R. Carpenter	1,102	37	11	97*
J. W. Burnham	1,060	42	7	115
T. A. Mantle	1,010	44	9	93

*Not out.

The Marylebone Club opened the season of 1867 with a match on the continent. It sent twelve of its members across the Channel to play a friendly game against twelve of the Paris Club, on the new ground in the Bois de Boulogne, in the hope, no doubt, of spreading a knowledge of the game. It was the first time the MCC had played out of the United Kingdom, and judging by the names of the players who represented Paris, it might have been a contest between two English elevens. The MCC won very easily, defeating their opponents by an innings and 135 runs; Mr A. Lubbock scoring 102 in brilliant form. The match took place on the 22nd and 23rd April, and on the two succeeding days the I Zingari played on the same ground, against the same club, and won just as easily; Mr A. Lubbock again being the top scorer with 72 not out. History does not report that the French nation was stirred or excited over the visit of two such important clubs, nor does it say that cricket clubs were formed and flourished on account of it.

A month later, on the 23rd, 24th, and 25th May, the All-England and United All-England elevens met at Manchester for the benefit of the Cricketers' Fund. The match had been played on Whit-Monday at Lord's since 1857; but as both elevens were now composed entirely of Northern men, and the schism which had raged for years between North and South was still active, very little surprise was felt when the fixture was announced to take place on the old Trafford

Ground. The MCC realising that the two elevens meant to travel their own way respecting that march, as they had done in the North *v.* South matches, met in the early part of the season and passed the following resolution:

Taking into consideration the conduct of certain of the professionals of England during the season of 1866, it is no longer desirable to extend the patronage of the Marylebone Club to the Cricketers' Fund exclusively; but a fund has now been formed which shall be called 'The Marylebone Professional Fund', which shall have for its object the support of the professional players who, during their career, shall have conducted themselves to the entire satisfaction of the Committee of the MCC.

The first match on its behalf was played at Lord's on the 10th and 11th of June, between an eleven of England and Middlesex County, and was largely attended. I had the pleasure of playing for England, and helping to speed the good cause. It was the first time Middlesex had played against England, and the result was far from encouraging to the county; for it lost by an innings and 25 runs. Mr A. Lubbock was top scorer with 129, and I supported him with 75; and while we were together runs came at a great pace. So far Mr Lubbock had shown that he was likely to take a high place in batting honours at the end of the season, his hitting and defence in the matches he had already played being consistently good.

At Lord's on 17th and 18th of June, North of the Thames *v.* South of the Thames was substituted for the old North *v.* South Match, and the wrench between Northern and Southern players was, for a time, complete. The match was one of the curiosities of a remarkable scoring season. Batting generally had so much improved that a total score of 400 runs created as little surprise as a total of 200 had done a year or two previously. The season, so far, had been dry, and favourable for tall scoring, and before the match commenced the opinion prevailed that this match would prove no exception. But the weather has spoiled many a match, and it spoiled that one for three innings were completed on the first day for a total of 195 runs. The South batted first, and were all out in 1 and 17 for a paltry 32. Wootton and Grundy were the bowlers, the former capturing seven wickets for 18 runs. The North did very little better; the first four wickets fell for 7 runs, and six of them were down for 16 in 36 minutes. They were all out in an hour and a half; total 61: for this I was mainly responsible obtaining six wickets for 23 runs.

The second innings of the South realised 102 runs; Mortlock being the highest score with 22 not out. Alfred Shaw did the mischief this time bringing off three remarkably good catches, and capturing three wickets in 39 balls for 2 runs. The North began their second innings next morning with a balance of 73 against them, and were all out in an hour and three-quarters for 46. The highest score was 8, and there was not a 'duck' in the innings. Not a single extra was scored; and the fielding was magnificent. My brother E.M. brought off four very fine catches at point, Pooley was brilliant behind the wickets, and James Lilly white took four wickets for 18 runs, and myself 6 for 28. It was a most exciting and sensational match from start to finish, and the keenness and closeness of it will be remembered for many a long day.

The match between the Gentlemen and Players, played at Lord's on the 8th and 9th of July, was almost a repetition of the one I have just described. The Players batted first, and were all out in an hour and fifty minutes for 79; Mr Appleby taking six wickets for 33 runs. The Gentlemen scored 87 in the first innings. Wootton was the most successful bowler capturing six wickets for 41 runs.

The second innings of the Players was more disastrous than the first, for they only scored 61; and three innings had been completed a little before seven o'clock on the first day. I was the successful bowler this time capturing eight wickets for 25 runs. The Gentlemen were left with 54 to win. A little over an hour sufficed to finish the match next day, on a difficult wicket; the Gentlemen winning by eight wickets.

There was no need to complain of the weather on that occasion. From beginning to end it was perfect; but, as Lillywhite said in his summary of the year, 'the wickets were decidedly bad even for Lord's ground.'

The return match between the Gentlemen and Players was spoiled by the weather, and could not be completed; but it will be memorable for the finely-played innings of 107 not out – in the second innings – by Mr A. Lubbock, the hard-hit 71 of my brother E. M., and the wicketkeeping of Mr J. Round. But I took no part in it, or in any match for over six weeks.

On the 14th of July I was laid up with scarlet fever, and was unable to play until the end of August, and I did not feel very fit then. It was a bitter disappointment to me; for while my bowling efforts had been quite up to my expectations, I had not scored so heavily as I had desired, and I was hoping for better things before the season ended. That was my most successful bowling year. I bowled faster than I do at present now and then putting in a slower one, which often deceived the batsman.

The year was a great one of individual performances with both bat and ball; 200 runs in an innings was scored by Messrs E. B. Rowley, E. M. Grace, and H. Clement, though not in first-class matches; and 100 runs was scored 171 times, but only eleven of them against first-class professional bowling. Mr W. Townshend scored 100 runs twice in a match for Rossall School. But, undoubtedly, the great batting performance of the year was Mr Lubbock's, who scored over a hundred runs three times two of them in first-class matches and who had the very fine average at the end of the season of 72.4 for 5 innings.

Wootton and Southerton both captured over 100 wickets in first-class matches; but Grundy, Emmett, Freeman, and one or two others bowled with finer results. Emmett and Freeman proved invaluable to their county, and it was owing entirely to their allround efforts that Yorkshire, after being at the bottom of the poll in 1866, was raised to the top in 1867 not losing a single match in the six played.

Neither Surrey, Kent, Cambridgeshire, nor Middlesex kept up its 1866 form; but Sussex and Lancashire showed improvement, and Nottinghamshire was still well to the front. Nottinghamshire played one match against the North of England, which practically meant the combined strength of Lancashire, Yorkshire, and Cambridgeshire, but was beaten by 112 runs. Freeman and Tarrant bowled unchanged in both innings against them, dividing the wickets and clean-bowling nine of their opponents.

Batting generally advanced with rapid strides in the year 1868. Total scores and individual performances exceeded everything in the past, and the cry was that the batting had now become too strong for the bowling. Two innings of 689 and 630 runs were scored; Mr Tylecote scored his memorable 404 not out at Clifton, and Mr W. J. Batchelor scored 289 for the Long Vacation Club at Cambridge. Totals and individual scores were the highest yet recorded in the history of the game. Altogether over 200 runs in an innings were scored by six players, and the century was exceeded at least 200 times. It was very much owing to the lovely weather which prevailed the greater part of the season, making the wickets dry and fast.

An eleven of Aboriginal Players of Australia visited England, and played their first match at the Oval on 25th and 26th May. They played 47 matches during the season; winning 14, losing 14, and 19 were drawn. In strength they were about equal to third-class English teams; and the result of their visit was satisfactory and encouraging to them in every respect. I had not the pleasure of playing against them; but I believe it was generally admitted that two players, Mullagh and Cuzens, showed very good all-round form.

County Cricket still progressed; Yorkshire holding its own, but not shining so conspicuously over the others as it did the previous year. Nottinghamshire played Lancashire for the first time, and home-and-home matches were resumed with Surrey.

Gloucestershire made a start, playing the MCC at Lord's on the 25th and 26th June, and winning by 134 runs; but it was two years later before the club was formed on a sound basis, and engaged in contests with other counties.

My brother Fred played on this occasion; but he had made his first appearance at Lord's on the 1st and 2nd of the same month, playing for England *v.* MCC He was only 17 years of age at the time; but he had already earned a great reputation in local cricket, and had represented the South of the Thames *v.* North of the Thames in 1866. I was of the same age when I first played for England, and I believe we are the only two players who have represented England so young. Fred had played for the United South also, and was thought good enough to go in first with me; and we now continued to represent that eleven most years.

Before the season was over I accomplished two or three good batting performances. On June the 1st and 2nd, for England *v.* MCC, at Lord's, played for the benefit of the Marylebone Cricketers' Fund, I scored out of 96 first innings, and 66 out of 179 second; and we defeated the old club by 92 runs. The MCC had not played England since 1856, and did not again until 1877.

The North of the Thames *v.* South of the Thames was played, in place of the North *v.* South match, at Lord's, on the 8th of June, and was one of the curiosities of those contests. The North eleven was not a particularly strong one, and the match was finished in one day, the South winning by 9 wickets. A shower of rain in the early part of the day caused the ground to kick, and in 5 hours 31 wickets were disposed of for 260 runs. Mr A. N. Hornby appeared in the North team on that occasion.

At Lord's on the 29th and 30th June the Gentlemen defeated the Players by 8 wickets, and I scored 134 not out in a total of 201. It was my first hundred in those matches; and the wicket was very hard and fast, which suited me splendidly. I hit very hard, and rarely made a mistake; and I believe even today that it was one of the finest innings I have ever played. The wicket played queerly, and everything was run out at Lord's in those days, and not once in the innings did Willsher, Grundy, Lillywhite or Wootton cause me any trouble; and I very seldom allowed the ball to pass the bat. I captured 6 wickets for 50 runs first innings; 4 for 31 second.

The return match at the Oval on the 2nd and 3rd July saw Mr I. D. Walker in magnificent batting form. He scored 165 out of a total of 379, and never played a better innings in his life. Every bowler was hit all over the ground by him, and Lillywhite and Willsher were on four times. In his score there were 2 sixes, 3 fives, and 17 fours. The bowling of Mr David Buchanan in the second innings was another feature of the match. He captured 9 wickets for 82 runs a very fine performance, considering that he was now 38 years of age, and that it was his first appearance in those contests. The Gentlemen won by one innings and 87 runs, this being their second win at the Oval. Their first win on that ground was in 1866, and Mr Burrup, the Secretary, was so elated over it, that he presented every member of the eleven with a bat. There was less excitement on this occasion, and at last the happy time had come when the Gentlemen could hold their own in these contests.

The return match between the North of the Thames and the South of the Thames, on the St Lawrence Greund at Canterbury, August 3rd, 4th, and 5th, was a remarkable, and in one respect historical, match. For the North the Revd J. McCormick scored 137 in the first innings in two and a half hours, and hit our bowling all over the field; in the second innings, Mr R. A. H. Mitchell scored 90, and Mr H. N. Tennant 45 not out. For the South, I scored 130 first innings;

102 not out second. Altogether, 1,018 runs were scored in the three days; and it was the first time I scored two centuries in a match. It should be remembered that the St Lawrence Ground was always an easy scoring one; and on that occasion, being hard and dry, it was particularly so, and suited me exactly. Besides, there were boundary hits at that date there, and I did not have anything like the running I had for my 134 at Lord's.

The year 1869 showed no decline in high scoring; in reality it showed an increase in three-figure innings and averages. The century was made close upon 250 times: nine times by myself; five times each by my brother Fred and Jupp; four times by Mr I. D. Walker; and three times each by Messrs B. B. Cooper, E. L. Fellowes, A. N. Hornby, C. I. Thornton, F. W. Wright, B. Pauncefote, C. J. Ottaway, T. Wise, Lieut. Scott, Daft and Rowbotham. My brother Fred also scored 206, and Mr L. C. Howell 201.

I had the honour of being elected a member of the MCC, and played my first match on the 13th of May, against Oxford University, at Cowley Marsh, and scored 117 out of a total of 229; and by the end of the season my results for that club were:

In batting: 12 innings, 724 runs; average, 60.4.
In bowling: 426 overs: 209 maidens; 570 runs; 44 wickets; average, 12.42.

And I scored over a hundred runs in an innings four times for it.

County Cricket was in favour of Nottinghamshire and Yorkshire that year, they running a dead heat for first honours. Surrey played as many as twelve county matches; but was defeated by both Nottinghamshire and Yorkshire. Cambridgeshire had ceased to exist as a county; although a match under that title was played against Yorkshire at Leeds, on the 10th and 11th July, which resulted in a great defeat for Cambridgeshire. Tarrant was seized with illness in the early part of the season, and did not play again, and Cambridgeshire without him was far below the best county form. Lancashire, Sussex, and Kent did not improve on their 1868 form; and Middlesex having lost their ground at Islington, only played two matches against Surrey one at Lord's, the other at the Oval.

The North *v.* South matches were resumed; but again Parr, Carpenter, and Hayward declined to play. With Freeman and Emmett at their best, however, the North could hold its own without them, and the contests ranked next in importance to those between the Gentlemen and Players. They met three times during the season, and the South won two out of the three. I batted six times, and scored altogether 258 runs. My best innings was in the second match played at Sheffield, when I scored 122 out of a total of 173, against Freeman, Emmett and Wootton. And I was fairly successful with the ball in the same match, capturing 6 wickets for 57 runs first innings. But Southerton's 7 for 34 runs in the second innings put all other bowling performances in the shade; although in the whole match Freeman took thirteen wickets for 86 runs.

The most remarkable match of that year was The Gentlemen of the South *v.* Players of the South, at the Oval on the 15th, 16th, and 17th July. It had been a scoring match most years; but 1869 outshone its predecessors, and at the end of the three days only 21 wickets had fallen for a total of 1,136 runs. The Players won the toss, and on a perfect wicket, and in favourable weather, batted all the first day and until 1.50 the next, for the large total of 475. Pooley and Jupp commenced the innings, and scored 142 before they were parted. Charlwood batted seventh man, and hit our bowling everywhere in his score of 155. Eight of us had a try at him; but it fell to the lot of my brother Fred to clean bowl him. My bowling average did not come out particularly well in that match. 'At last,' said the Players, 'we have got the best of them!'

Mr B. B. Cooper and I batted first for the Gentlemen, and the Players had close upon four hours of it before they parted us for a total of 283. Six of their regular bowlers nearly broke their hearts in trying to part us; but Mantle, the unexpected and about the last resource, caught and bowled both of us in six balls, Mr Cooper having scored 101, while my share was 180. But that was not the end of it. Mr I. D. Walker came afterwards, and smote them to the tune of 90; and it was five o'clock on the Saturday before the innings was at an end, for a total of 553. The 283 was a record for first wicket in a first-class match, and it is so today. The Players had an hour and forty minutes left to play, and in that time scored 108: Pooley, 50; Jupp, not out 43.

The All-England eleven played 23 matches; 8 won, 6 lost, 9 drawn.

The United All-England eleven played its last match that year. It was founded in 1852, and held its own against the All-England eleven and odds; but somehow or other it had never been so popular as its formidable rival and predecessor.

The Gentlemen won both matches against the Players: the first at the Oval by 17 runs, the second at Lord's by 3 wickets. The brunt of the batting was borne by Messrs I. D. Walker, A. Lubbock, and myself; the bowling by Messrs Absolom, Buchanan, and Appleby.

5

Cricket in My Manhood
1870-77

Most men who have lived active mental or physical lives have had their memories taxed to remember the various incidents in them. It has been so in my case, for the doings of some years stand out more clearly than others.

The year 1870 I can remember as being one of my best; indeed, I may say it saw me almost in my best batting and bowling form. Nine times I scored over a hundred runs in an innings, the majority of them in first-class matches.

For the MCC I played 12 innings, and averaged 55.6; for Gloucestershire County, who played first-class county matches for the first time that year, I played 4 innings, and averaged 91.2; for the Gentlemen *v.* Players I played 4 innings, and averaged 85.1; and altogether during the season I batted in 33 innings in first-class matches, scored an aggregate of 1,808, and averaged 54–26.

It will be inferred from those scores that the season was everything that could be desired in the matter of weather. And so it was. Wickets were dry and fast the greater part of it, and I scored at a great pace. My defence had grown stronger, and my hitting powers had improved also.

On the 9th and 10th of May a match, Left-handed *v.* Right was played at Lord's; but the Left-handed were not in it. The match was noteworthy from the fact that Carpenter, Hayward, and J. Smith again appeared on that ground, and it looked for the moment as if the North and South had once more clasped hands and blotted out the past. The South *v.* North, at the same ground on the 6th and 7th June, confirmed the good feeling; for all the Northern cracks, with the exception of Freeman, were present, and he was only absent on account of the first match played by the North of England eleven, at Dewsbury, of which Iddison he and were joint secretaries. That was G. Parr's last appearance at Lord's; he was 44 years of age, and scored 41 in fine form.

An important change in the laws affecting bowlers was passed at a special meeting of the MCC on the 4th of May. Before that date a bowler could change ends once only in an innings. The alteration now enabled him to change twice; but he was not allowed to bowl more than two overs in succession. The new rule was first carried into effect in the MCC and Ground *v.* Yorkshire match at Lord's on the 30th and 31st May.

MCC and Ground *v.* Nottinghamshire, at Lord's on the 13th, 14th, and 15th June, will be memorable for the unfortunate injury to Summers, one of the most promising players that Nottinghamshire had produced for years. They batted first, and scored 267, of which Daft made 117. The MCC scored 183 first innings, of which I made 117 not out. We had to follow our innings, and I resumed after 10 minutes' interval, and was bowled first over for a duck by J. C. Shaw. Messrs I. D. Walker, J. W. Dale, and C. E. Green came to the rescue, however, and we totalled 240. Nottinghamshire won a close match by 2 wickets. The injury to Summers occurred early in the second innings. The first ball bowled to him by Platts was a little bit short, and it bumped and hit him on the head, and concussion of the brain followed. Platts was in no way to blame, for the ball did not bump higher than many I had to play in the same match; but unfortunately Summers treated the blow too lightly, appearing on the ground next day in a hot sun, and afterwards travelling by rail to Nottingham, which shook him terribly, and developed symptoms which subsequently proved fatal.

It used to be said that the Gentlemen were seldom fully represented in the Gentlemen *v.* Players' matches: but it was the opposite that year, for the Players' eleven was far from being representative; and the consequence was, that the first was drawn very much in the Gentlemen's favour, while the second was won. In the match at the Oval, I scored 215 out of a total of 513 in the second innings so far, the highest individual performance yet recorded in those matches and Mr W. J. B. Money played two brilliant innings of 70 and 109 not out. In the return match at Lord's, I scored 109 in the first innings. It was my brother Fred's first appearance for the Gentlemen, and he was fairly successful with the ball; but he failed with the bat, having two ducks to his name in the first match, and only scoring 8 and 3 runs in the second.

A very good match was played at Beeston, Nottingham, on the 18th, 19th, and 20th August, between the Gentlemen of the North and the Gentlemen of the South, which showed Messrs A. N. Hornby, I. D. Walker, and my brother Fred at their best. The North batted first, and scored 287; Mr Hornby's contribution being 103, in which there were 1 eight and 17 fours. As usual, I commenced the batting for the South. I played what I thought a brilliant 77, and nearly every one of the eleven said so too; but I. D. Walker afterwards scored 179, and Fred carried out his bat for 189, very little was, therefore, thought about my performance. My lot, however, was not quite so unhappy an one as Mr G. Strachan's. For six hours he sat patiently with the pads on, waiting for I. D. or Fred to come out, and when his turn came he had to be content with two balls: the first he hit for 2; the second he was c and b Hornby. I ought to have said that Fred hit 34 fours in his score; I. D. Walker, 1 five and 25 fours and that the other eight batsmen scored 19 runs among them.

Another good bit of scoring was 166 for first wicket by Fred and myself, for the United South *v.* twenty-two of Sleaford with R. Iddison, at Sleaford, 9th, 10th, and 11th June. It is curious how some innings leave a greater impression than others. That one is vivid to me on account of an accident which happened to one of the twenty-two. He was fielding at short-leg to Iddison's lob-bowling, and was standing a little in front, about 12 yards from the wicket. Iddison would have him closer in, and eventually he was placed 4 yards nearer. I did not say anything at the time, but could not help thinking the position would have to be abandoned before Fred and I had finished batting.

Iddison pitched the first or second ball of the over a little too far up, and I stepped out and hit it on the full pitch. It went straight to the unfortunate fieldsman, hit him on the ankle, and then travelled far enough to enable us to run 4. 'He must be hurt,' I thought; but he did not show it. He was a rare plucked one, and never winced; but, as Jas. Lillywhite said, 'It is not in cricket human nature to hide that stroke, and I'll keep my eye on him;' and, sure enough, when the fieldsman moved to the long-field at the end of the over, and thought no one was looking, he began to rub vigorously. We saw little of him next day, and I believe he was laid up for some time afterwards. I think it cured Iddison of placing a man so near when bowling lobs.

Yorkshire was the most successful county that year, entirely owing to the very fine bowling of Freeman and Emmett. Lancashire showed a slight improvement; but Nottinghamshire, Kent, and Sussex did not come out favourably; while Surrey had an unprecedented run of ill-luck. I threw all my energies into Gloucestershire matches, and felt specially gratified at the results of our first year's play. We played Glamorganshire once, Surrey twice, MCC and Ground once, winning them very easily. The first match we played was against Surrey, 2nd, 3rd, and 4th June, on Durdham Downs. Our eleven was made up entirely of amateurs, while Surrey played ten professionals and one amateur. It was the closest match we played, and created considerable interest in Gloucestershire. Quite a large crowd turned out, and we had some difficulty in getting them to stand far enough back. I remember that in the first innings Pooley, who was batting very well, would not go on until they were moved. Eventually they did go, and he said he could now hit out to leg to his heart's content; but the change worked in another way it enabled long-leg to go farther out, and the first or second ball bowled Pooley hit into his hands, to the delight of the spectators.

Reference to the batting averages will show that Messrs W. B. Money, A. N. Hornby, I. D. Walker, and W. Yardley were in great form. Nearly every innings played by them was full of dash, and they scored at a great pace against all kinds of bowling. Mr Hornby, in particular, hit very hard, and exceeded the hundred eight times during the season, two of them in first-class matches. That feat I performed, as I have said, nine times, five of them in first-class matches; the highest and best being 215 for the Gentlemen *v.* Players, at the Oval.

The year 1871 was my most successful year with the bat. I was twenty-two years of age, and had played against every first-class bowler in England. Nearly all nervous feeling at the commencement of an innings had left me; but I guarded against over-confidence, and invariably played the first over or two carefully until I got my eye in. Grounds had improved wonderfully everywhere, and I aimed at placing every ball, however straight and good the length of it; for that was about the only way to score at all rapidly against the crack bowlers of the day, who could bowl over after over every ball on the wicket.

In the middle of May, I scored 181 for MCC *v.* Surrey; and I kept up my form right to the end of the season, exceeding the century ten times, all of them in first-class matches. The weather was rather unfavourable, and occasionally the ground caused the ball to kick badly; but I never lost patience, and in one or two matches in particular I very much desired to score largely. Willsher, H. H. Stephenson and John Lillywhite had benefit matches that year, and I was anxious to do well for them; for they had done excellent work for the game for many years, and were highly respected by all classes of cricketers. Willsher was unfortunate in the matter of weather in the match Single *v.* Married, played at Lord's on the 10th, 11th and 12th July, on his behalf; but I scored 189 not out for him, and got up another match in September, which helped considerably to increase the fund. In the second match, W. G. Grace's XI. *v.* Kent, I scored 81 not out first, and 42 not out second; and W. Yardley played a magnificent innings of 126 not out in the second innings of Kent.

North *v.* South, at the Oval on 31st July, 1st and 2nd August, was the match played on behalf of Stephenson; and I shall not readily forget his disappointment when I was given out lbw to J. C. Shaw the first ball bowled in the match. I was rather disappointed by it also; for there was a tremendous crowd present, and the wicket and the weather were perfect. 'Keep up your heart, H. H.,' I said; 'I shall take care that it does not occur in the second innings.' Fortunately the weather kept favourable all through, and I started my second innings about 4.30 the second day. After the first over or two I began to hit at a rare pace, and I paid particular attention to J. C. Shaw. At the close of the day's play my score was 142 not out, and only 2 wickets had fallen for 195. Stephenson was happy that night; and he was happier next morning, when the sun shone brilliantly and another large crowd came to witness the finish. I was out for 268, in a total of 436, at four o'clock on the third day, and had hit 3 fives and 28 fours. Stephenson was immensely pleased, and presented me with a gold ring.

The Gentlemen *v.* Players was the match on behalf of John Lillywhite. It was played on the old Hove Ground at Brighton, 14th, 15th and 16th August, in splendid weather; and with the third ball of the match J. C. Shaw clean-bowled me. Lillywhite's heart was sad indeed, particularly as he it was who gave me out lbw to Shaw in the first innings of Stephenson's match.

'I am terribly sorry, Lillywhite,' I said; 'I did want to do well for you.'

'Better luck next time!' He replied.

I cannot explain it; but, personally, I was not hopeful, and said so. Lillywhite did not share my misgivings; for he took two sovereigns out of his pocket, put them into my hand, and said:

'You take these, and pay me a sixpence back for every run you make in the second innings. I call it a fair bet.'

It was the greatest compliment I have ever had paid to my batting skill; and my fears vanished as I realised the fulness of it. You may guess how I laid on after the first over or two to wipe out the 80 runs which were required to pay off the two pounds. I commenced my second innings at three o'clock on the second day. The first wicket fell for 35, then my brother Fred joined me, and we raised the total to 275 before we were parted; and scored 240 in two hours and a half. After the first hundred runs, I forgot all about the bet. At the end of the day's play, the total was 353 for 3 wickets; my score being 200 not out. I had a great reception when I reached the pavilion, Lillywhite being particularly warm.

'I'll trouble you for five pounds on account,' he said.

'All right, Lillywhite, here it is,' I replied; 'but if you do not let me off for the rest of the bet, I shall knock down my wicket first over tomorrow!'

He made a virtue of necessity and cried, 'Quits!' I added 17 runs to my score next day.

No part of my cricket experience has given me more pleasure than my batting success in benefit matches. I always hoped to do something extraordinary on those occasions; and it is particularly gratifying to me today to remember that I nearly always accomplished it.

George Parr played his last match that year. He had been before the cricketing public for 27 years; and he finished his brilliant career at Trent Bridge on the 29th, 30th, and 31st May, in a manner worthy of his best days, scoring 32 not out, and 53 for Nottinghamshire *v.* Fourteen Gentlemen of Nottinghamshire.

In the Gentlemen *v.* Players' matches, the former had the best of it, winning one, while the other two were drawn slightly in their favour.

Among the counties, Gloucestershire held its own. Sussex did exceptionally well, but Surrey was again at the bottom.

I made a first appearance on four grounds that year, and scored well on all of them. At West Brompton I scored 118 in my only innings, and I do not remember having played there since. At Fenner's Ground I played for Gentlemen of England *v.* Cambridge University, and scored 162 in my only innings. Mr W. N. Powys had a great reputation as a fast bowler then, and he was expected to slaughter us. He did not. Mr C. I. Thornton, for the University, hit 20 off one over of Mr D. Buchanan's. At Trent Bridge I scored 79 first innings and 116 second against Nottinghamshire: the latter score was the first century scored on that ground. At Maidstone I scored 81 not out first, and 42 not out second, and did not play on it again until 1890, when I scored 109 not out, and 37.

And I played my last match on the old Hove Ground, Brighton, and scored 0 first, 217 second. It was on the same ground that I scored 170 and 56 not out for the South Wales Club in 1864, and I said goodbye to it rather regretfully.

The early part of the season of 1872 was unsuitable for heavy scoring, and the bowlers had the best of it until the end of June. Snow, sleet, and frost in May did not help the grounds, and scores up to the middle of the season were smaller than they had been for years. Like other batsmen, I suffered by it, and did not do so well as the previous year. I scored the century twice in May once for the MCC, the other for the United South; but my best displays began on the 1st of July, for the Gentlemen *v.* Players, at Lord's, and during the succeeding eight days I scored at a rate that I have rarely equalled and but once exceeded in my career. In two matches for the Gentlemen *v.* Players. in one week, I scored in three innings 77, 112, and 117; and two days later I made 170 not out for England *v.*Nottinghamshire and Yorkshire.

I was again fortunate in benefit matches. For Gloucestershire *v.* Yorkshire, at Sheffield, 29th, 30th, and 31st July, for the benefit of Roger Iddison, I made 150, and with Mr T. G. Matthews put on 208 runs the first day, our wickets still standing at the end of it. For the South *v.* North, at the Oval the end of July, I played for Griffith's benefit, and scored 114.

Eight times I scored over a hundred runs in an innings, and at the end of the season my batting results were:

For MCC – 13 innings, 528 runs, average 40.8.

For Gloucestershire County – 6 innings, 284 runs, average 47.2.

For Gentlemen *v.* Players – 3 innings, 306 runs, average 102.

For South *v.* North – 6 innings, 285 runs, average 47.3

For Gentlemen of England (Canadian Tour) – 11 innings, 540 runs, average 49.1

In First-class Matches – 26 innings, 1,485 runs, average 57.

In all matches – 63 innings, 3,030 runs, average 48.

For the United South eleven, principally against twenty-twos, I scored 316 runs for 8 innings: average, 39.4. I also played for twenty-two of Melton Mowbray against the All-England eleven, and for Sixteen of Grantham *v.* The United North eleven. My brother Fred and Jas. Lillywhite played for Melton Mowbray in the same match, and we caught Carpenter napping when he was batting for the eleven. Lillywhite was bowling and I was wicketkeeping, and Fred, I believe, was fielding at long-leg; anyhow, Carpenter hit one to leg, for which he ran two. Immediately he turned for the third run I ran out about 10 yards to meet the ball, and caught it first bound; and while he was trotting quietly up the pitch in fancied security, with his back to me, I let fly at his wicket. I could throw in those days, and was not surprised when the middle stump went flying out of the ground. The surprise was on Carpenter's side, the laugh on ours.

'Well, well! there's no fool like an old fool,' said he. 'To think I should have played cricket all these years, and get out in that way!'

Surrey came out excellently in county contests that year, and headed the list: Kent dropped to the bottom.

Lancashire made good progress also, and was much indebted for its success to two bowlers W. McIntyre and Watson. So well did those two perform, that Mr A. Appleby, almost at his best, played a comparatively small part in bowling for his county. Mr Hornby, too, was a host in himself, batting with great dash and invariably scoring. Daft and Selby did great things in batting for Nottinghamshire; and Mr W. Yardley was very successful also. He had one exceptional experience at Lord's on the 20th and 21st May, playing for the South *v.* North: he was out first ball in both innings, earning his spectacles in a way that he will not readily forget!

An experiment was made at Lord's on 9 May, in the match MCC *v.* Next Twenty. The wickets were fixed an inch higher and slightly broader than the law prescribed. The experiment was not a success.

The year 1873 was my tenth of first-class cricket, and my best display of all-round form. I could show a higher batting average in 1872; but my bowling average was not so good, although! captured exactly the same number of wickets. The early part of the season was very wet, and batting generally was not up to the standard of previous years. Two amateurs Messrs Frank Townsend and J. M. Cotterill took a high position, and Messrs C. J. Ottaway, I. D. Walker, A. N. Hornby and C. I. Thornton were consistently good; but the number of batsmen who averaged 25 runs per innings was below that of 1871. The proportion of amateurs in the list was greater than ever. Daft and Jupp were now the only two professionals who could be classed with the best of the amateurs; for at last the years began to tell upon Carpenter, and his wonderful skill was beginning to desert him. Emmett proved that he could handle the bat as well as the ball, and Charlwood and Lockwood were doing excellent work also.

But a colt appeared that year who was to raise the standard of professional batting far above everything yet reached. Arthur Shrewsbury made his first appearance at Trent Bridge Ground on the 14th and 15th of April, playing for twenty-two Colts against Notts County. He was 17 years of age, and scored 35 by scientific cricket, against A. Shaw, J. C. Shaw, M. McIntyre and F. Morley, four of the very best bowlers of that or any time. His defence was perfect, and his patience, for so young a player, exceptionally good. A month later at Lord's he confirmed the good opinions formed of him, scoring 4, and not out 16 for Fifteen Colts of England *v.* MCC

The amateurs were to receive quite as valuable a recruit in their ranks before the season was over. Mr W. W. Read was but 17 years of age when he was considered good enough to represent his county. Before the season was over, he played for Surrey *v.* Yorkshire at the Oval on the 11th and 12th of August. Few cricketers have delighted the cricketing public more than Mr W. W. Read and Shrewsbury during the last ten years. For their counties and in representative matches they have won many a great victory, and averted many a defeat. By-and-by I shall have occasion to describe their styles, and touch upon their brilliant performances.

The Gentlemen *v.* Players' matches were great victories for the former that year. The first was played at Lord's, and was won by the Gentlemen by an innings and 55 runs; the second at the Oval, which was won by an innings and 19 runs; and the third at Prince's, which was won by an innings and 54 runs. The results were entirely owing to the superiority of the Gentlemen in batting. Mr Hornby played a grand innings of 104 in the match at Prince's, and in my three innings I scored 158, 163, and 70.

Four matches were played between the North and South; the South winning 2, losing 1, and 1 was drawn. Gloucestershire and Nottinghamshire divided the honours in county cricket. The Gloucestershire eleven was composed entirely of amateurs; Nottinghamshire, of professionals only. Individual scores of a hundred runs and over in an innings were made about 230 times; and the number to my credit was seven, all of them in first-class matches. At the end of the season I took a team out to Australia. It was the third which had gone there, and, while we found cricket generally much improved, there was little doubt that England was still considerably ahead of Australia in playing the game, though very little in enthusiasm over it. I had the pleasure of meeting three players then who afterwards created great reputations Messrs H. F. Boyle, F. R. Spofforth and C. Bannerman. Of course, neither showed the form then which he displayed in later years.

The season of 1874 opened favourably: the weather was delightful, and continued so the greater part of it; and the consequence was, that the bat had again the best of the ball, and that century-scoring exceeded everything yet recorded. In matches of all kinds, individual innings of a hundred runs was scored close upon three hundred times; and over 200 was scored twelve times. Very little was thought of the first figure now, unless in first-class cricket; and the increase in the number was owing more to the improvement in the grounds than to any decadence of bowling. By the end of the season I had scored over 200 runs once, and over 112 times: the greatest number of centuries I have ever scored in one year. Nine of them were in first-class matches. Jupp exceeded the hundred three times in first-class matches; and, in my estimation, played finer cricket that year than he ever played before or afterwards. Thirty-seven completed innings for an average of 36.15 was a wonderful improvement on the professional batting form of 1862, and showed how the game had advanced.

Shrewsbury was considered good enough to represent his county; but no one was surprised that he failed to do much the first year. It takes more than one year's experience to master, or even fight successfully against, first-class bowling, as I found to my cost when I began to play in the great matches; and a very successful colt may be a very indifferent county representative for some time. The same may be said with regard to Mr W. W. Read.

Another and fine all-round cricketer commenced his brilliant career that year, and made his mark very quickly in first-class matches. I refer to Mr A. G. Steel, whose performances with both bat and ball have been the admiration of the thousands who have had the pleasure of witnessing them. I shall have occasion to speak at some length about him farther on; but I cannot help saying here, that I never envied a county the possession of any cricketer so much as I envied Lancashire the possession of Mr A. G. Steel. He was 15 years of age when he played his first match at Lord's on the 29th and 30th July for Marlborough College *v.* Rugby School, and scored 41 not out first innings.

The Players made rather a better fight against the Gentlemen that year, winning one match out of the three played, and losing the other two by 48 and 61 runs. Only one individual innings of a hundred runs was scored in the six innings played by both sides, and that fell to my credit.

One of the closest and most exciting matches of that year was the North *v.* South, played at Prince's on the 4th and 5th June for the benefit of the Cricketers' Fund. The South in its second innings had 27 runs to make to win, with 5 wickets standing, and yet lost by 3 runs.

I was again successful in a benefit match, scoring 167 for Gloucestershire *v.* Yorkshire at Sheffield on behalf of Luke Greenwood.

University cricket was now a different thing from what it had been ten or twenty years before; and very rarely were the Gentlemen without one or two University players in their eleven when they met the Players. A match entitled 'Gentlemen of England who had not been educated at the Universities *v.* Gentlemen of the Universities, Past and Present' was played at the Oval on the 15th and 16th June. A University education has always been considered a distinct aid to success, mentally and physically; but this match did not show that

University men were better cricketers than non-University men, for their representative eleven got severely beaten by an innings and 76 runs. But then their opponents had among them such players as A. N. Hornby, I. D. Walker, V. E. Walker, A. Appleby, G. F. Grace, and myself.

What was described as an 'American Invasion' took place early in the month of August. Eighteen American Baseball Players (who visited us with the idea of introducing the game of baseball) played seven cricket matches, and showed that they knew something of that game as well as baseball. Unfortunately they had been much underrated, and the engagements made on their behalf were against very third-class teams They won four out of the seven played, and the other three were drawn. There was one individual score of 50, but 25 was nearer the form of the best of them; and only once did the total of their innings reach as high as 130. Their fielding was exceptionally smart; and though their efforts to create a love for baseball were not rewarded, their skill was undoubtedly appreciated.

The All-England, United South, and United North elevens were still travelling all over the country; but county cricket was taking a greater hold, and they did not excite so much interest as they used to. With the United South, I visited Ireland for the first time, and against twenty-two of Leinster my brother Fred and I did a good performance, scoring 272 runs. My 153 was, so far, the highest innings made against a twenty-two; and I had now scored the century in England, Scotland, Ireland, Canada, and Australia.

Cricketers all over the country had occasion to grumble at the weather in 1875. It was both wet and miserably cold the greater part of the year, and wickets everywhere were sticky and very often unplayable. Batting averages went down considerably, and bowlers got great break on the ball. Slow and medium round-arm bowlers had their opportunity, and improved to some extent, and batsmen who had only been used to straight fast were a little bit abroad in playing them. Alfred Shaw at times did what he liked with the ball; and I shall never forget his wonderful performance for Nottinghamshire *v.* MCC, at Lord's, on the 14th and 5th June – 166 balls for 7 runs and 7 wickets, 6 of them clean bowled, my own among them. It took me an hour to make 10 runs, and I thought and still think as much of that hour's play as I do of many an hour in which I scored close upon a hundred. Mr G. Strachan did a very fine performance with the ball also. For the Gentlemen *v.* Players, at the Oval, he with 21 balls got five wickets, and no runs were scored off him.

That year was my greatest success with the ball; the sticky wickets suiting my bowling as nicely as the fast suited my batting, and I captured 192 wickets during the season, for an average of 12.166 runs. I had never done so well before, nor have I since.

Batting, as I have said, suffered in consequence. One young player, Mr A. J. Webbe, however, came to the front with a rush, and played two or three very fine innings during the season. For the Gentlemen *v.* Players, at Lord's, in the second innings, he and I put on 203 runs for the first wicket, and his defence and patience were perfect. He was 20 years of age at the time.

Two great bowlers dropped out of first-class cricket that year J. C. Shaw and E. Willsher. Freeman had dropped out a year or two before; so that three of the very best bowlers we have ever had had now left the ranks. I question if we have had three such really good fast bowlers since. Just about that time medium-pace bowling began to be cultivated, and very fast was neglected by both amateur and professional.

The Players won one out of the three matches played against the Gentlemen and one was drawn. The North *v.* South matches were not quite so interesting as in former years. When only two matches were played, the interest and excitement were great; but this year as many as seven were played in different parts of the country, and the public and the players themselves got tired of them.

County cricket flourished, and Nottinghamshire came to the front again.

My batting average dropped down to 32 that year, the reason being the weather. Quite naturally, critics thought 'I had gone off;' but in my heart I did not think so, for I felt as fit as I ever felt in my life. Two or three times that remark has been made about Messrs A. N. Hornby, W. W. Read, Shrewsbury, and myself; and I have been rather amused when one or the other scored a hundred runs the next match.

Charming weather prevailed during the greater part of the season of 1876, and at the end of it batting averages were very much higher than they had been for years. The bowlers had a very trying time, and were unfeignedly glad when the last ball was bowled. It was a year of exceptional batting performances for me, though my average was not quite so high as in two or three years I have already given. About this time I began to find that, in batting in particular, it took me longer to get into form and condition than in previous years. Increase of years and increase of weight may possibly account for it. I was close upon 28 years of age, and in weight about 15 st.

During May I played 8 completed innings, scored 163 runs; average, 20.3. In June I completed 12 innings, scored 464 runs; average, 39.5. In July I played 11 completed innings, scored 637 runs; average, 57.10. In August I played 10 completed innings, scored 1278 runs; average, 127.8. The month of August of that year was, I believe, the highest run-getting month in my whole cricket career; and I sincerely hope I shall not be considered egotistical in touching at some length upon one or two of the matches played.

It is now well known how Kent County scored 473 runs in its first innings against the Gentlemen of the MCC at Canterbury on the 10th August Lord Harris being the top scorer with a grandly played 154 and then got the MCC out the day after for 144. The MCC had to follow its innings a few minutes before five the same evening, and Mr A. P. Lucas and myself started the batting. Every one believed that the match was now a hopeless thing for the old club I and I was exceedingly anxious to get off that night, so that I might reach Clifton next day, and have a quiet Sunday's rest before meeting Nottinghamshire on the Monday. It was no use trying to play carefully; so I made up my mind to hit. I risked a little more than usual, helped myself more freely than I would have done under different circumstances, and everything came off. The 100 was scored in 45 minutes, and when stumps were drawn at 6.45 the total was 217 for 4 wickets, made in an hour and fifty minutes. My share was 133 not out; extras, 17.

Saturday was one of the hottest days of a very hot month; and I thought I might as well put my best foot forward in the early morning. My partner was Mr P. C. Crutchley, and he being in the scoring mood also, we kept the ball travelling at a great pace. The ground was in rare order, and from noon to luncheon-time we put all we knew into our hitting, only stopping for a few minutes while I borrowed a bat, having broken the one which had served me so well. The new bat was a good one, but much too small in the handle for me, and the pace slackened slightly; however, during the luncheon-hour the

Hon. Spencer Ponsonby Fane very kindly got hold of some thick twine, which he wrapped round it and brought it up to the right size. Tired nature began to tell its tale during the afternoon: but relief came from the officers' tent in the form of champagne and seltzer; and at it we went again, and were not parted until we had put on 227 runs, and raised the total to 430 for 5 wickets. The opinion of the Kent Twelve, Mr Absolom's in particular, was, 'that it had been a very hot day!' The total was 546 before I was out, my score being 344, made in 6 hours and 20 minutes, without a chance.

I had to travel by train to Bristol on Sunday; but by Monday morning the effects of it had worn off, and when I started the Gloucestershire innings against Nottinghamshire I felt very fit. I scored 177 in 3 hours and 10 minutes; and in it there were 1 seven, 2 sixes, 1 five, and 23 fours. My wicket went to the credit of Selby, and showed the value of a change, however indifferent the bowler. Alfred Shaw and Morley had been trying all they knew, and failed; so Seiby was called upon. He said he did not want any long-leg to his bowling; so my brother Fred promptly hit his first ball in that direction, and we ran 7 for it. The same over I hit him in the same place for 6; but in attempting it a second time, I got under the ball and was caught at long-on rather square. I believe the fieldsman was Barnes. He was in his right position at long-on when Fred and myself hit the 7 and 6 to long-leg, and had to go after the ball; for there was no boundary on the sloping side of the College Ground in those days. He quietly took his position almost square with the wicket and brought off the catch, and remarked afterwards that 'he knew something about placing the field to a third-rate bowler, if Selby did not'. Our total score was 400. Daft and Oscroft batted in magnificent form the first innings, but could not save the follow on; and on the evening of the third day Gloucestershire were left with 31 to win, which E. M. and Fred hit off in 25 minutes.

The Nottinghamshire men on the home journey met the Yorkshire eleven travelling down, and told them to look out for squalls at Cheltenham. Tom Emmett laughed, and said the 'big 'un has exhausted himself, and cannot do the century trick thrice in succession. If he does, I mean to shoot him, in the interests of the game; and I know there will be general rejoicing, among the professionals at least!'

I do not think I ever played on a better wicket than the one which had been prepared at Cheltenham, and I was not surprised that runs

Mr A. J. Webbe.

came at a great pace. At the end of the first day the score was 353 for four wickets: Mr Moberly, 73 not out; myself, 216 not out; and when we were parted about two o'clock next day, the total was 429; Mr Moberly having batted in his very best form for 103. It was rather a curious coincidence that the long stand should have been made by the 6th-man and myself both in this and the Canterbury match. Our total was 528, and my score 318 not out. Yorkshire made 127 for seven wickets.

I can say little about my 400 not out, for United South *v.* twenty-two of Grimsby, that has not already been said. I can just remember that the twenty-two thought our team rather a weak one; that the wicket was perfect; and that the grass was closely cut for about 40 yards square, but the rest of it a little bit long. Holmes, one of the eleven, had occasion to grumble when he was given out lbw to a ball that was far from being straight; but consoled himself the third day when the same umpire served one of the twenty-two just as badly. 'A perfectly fair umpire,' he said, 'but decidedly incompetent.' I did not feel half so tired at the end of my Grimsby score as I did after the Canterbury or Cheltenham scores.

There is another match I must say a word about the North *v.* South, played at Nottingham for Daft's benefit. The South had a very good team, and so had the North, and everyone was anxious that the match should turn out a real success. The weather was on its best behaviour; and I was upset at only scoring 16 first innings; in fact, neither side did much the first day: the first innings closing thus North, 102; South, 155. The third day was the exciting one. Splendid batting on the part of Messrs A. N. Hornby, R. P. Smith, Lockwood, and Daft himself, made the North score 242 in the second innings, and left the South 190 to win, and 3½ hours to do it. 'Rather a heavy task,' was the general opinion. Mr A. J. Webbe and myself hit 100 runs in 66 minutes; then he left at 101, for 41 a real good bit of batting. Mr I. D. Walker 20, and my brother Fred 10 not out, enabled us to score the necessary runs. They were made in 2 hours and 25 minutes; and I had the satisfaction of scoring 114 not out for one of the most popular and scientific cricketers of his or any age.

The Gentlemen *v.* Players' matches were decidedly in favour of the Gentlemen that year. Two were won by them, the other drawn. The North *v.* South matches were played as usual; the South winning 1, and 2 were drawn; and the All-England, United South of England, and United North were busy all the season.

Individual innings of 300 runs and over in an innings were scored 3 times; of 200, 14 times; of 100 runs, more than 400 times.

I had the pleasure of seeing Gloucestershire at the head of the counties again. My batting and bowling performances during the season showed that I had played:

	Innings	Runs	Average
For MCC	7	494	70.4
For Gentlemen *v.* Players	5	309	61.4
For South *v.* North	7	474	67.5
For Gloucestershire County	11	890	80.10
In first-class matches	42	2622	62.18

Bowling in first-class matches:

Overs	Maidens	Runs	Wides	Wickets	Average
1550.1	638	2,388	0	124	19.32

In 1877 County cricket had taken a firm hold, and created greater interest than the All-England and United South elevens ever did. There were as many as nine first-class counties playing: their contests were very exciting, and their doings were followed carefully from the beginning to the end of the season. 'Who is going to take first place in county honours this year?' was a question that was repeatedly asked. But it was one that required special knowledge to answer. Gloucestershire did great things in 1876, and was conceded pride of place; and when it was announced that Midwinter, an Australian of high reputation in both bowling and batting, had returned to England, and would now play for that county, every one concluded that it would again be well to the front. Midwinter was the first professional who played for Gloucestershire, and his bowling considerably strengthened it.

For some years Gloucestershire and Middlesex had been called the counties of amateurs, and it was entirely owing to their great batting skill that they had held their own against what may be called the professional counties. We have only to refer to the batting averages to find that the professionals were still very far behind the amateurs in that branch of the game. The fact seems to have impressed itself rather strongly upon the Lancashire and Surrey Committees about this time; for we find their elevens with a good sprinkling of amateur talent in them, by which they were much benefited. Mr A. N. Hornby, at the head of the Lancashire eleven; Mr G. Strachan, at the head of Surrey; and Lord Harris, at the head of Kent, were infusing vigour into their teams, and producing good results. Nottinghamshire and Yorkshire, while possessing the very best professional bowling talent of the day, were lacking in amateur batting, and did not do so well as they would have done if they had possessed both.

The Gentlemen *v.* Players, North *v.* South, and University contests were quite as interesting and exciting as county contests; but at last the All-England eleven, United South, and United North began to lose their attractions; for no one thought of going out of his way to watch the skill of a first-class professional bowler pitted against indifferent country batsmen, when he could witness county matches fought out from start to finish by the very best professional and amateur talent. The All-England eleven played two or three matches in 1876, but very little afterwards, and died out for lack of gate support. The United South lived two or three years longer; but after 1877 my medical studies demanded more of my time, and I could only play for Gloucestershire, MCC, and in the great matches. I believe the United South played its last match at Stroud in 1880.

Messrs W. W. Read, A. P. Lucas, A. J. Webbe and F. Penn had now taken a very high position among the amateurs, and batted in very fine style. Mr W. W. Read and Jupp, for Surrey *v.* Yorkshire at the Oval, scored 206 for first wicket, the second highest yet recorded in a county match; and Mr J. M. Cotterill and myself put on 281 runs between the fall of the first and second wickets for the South *v.* North at Prince's. Individual performances of 200 runs in an innings were scored 10 times, and the century was scored more than 500 times. G. Hearne, Mycroft, Morley and myself were very successful with the ball. For MCC and Ground *v.* Oxford University, Morley bowled 33.1 overs for 14 runs and thirteen wickets a feat that has not often been surpassed.

For Gloucestershire *v.* Nottinghamshire at Cheltenham, at the end of the match, I bowled 25 balls for no runs and seven wickets.

6

Australian Elevens &
First-Class County Cricket

It seems a good many years ago since, in 1878, the first Australian eleven visited England, and it is rather difficult to remember the exact feeling which prevailed about it at the time. I can just recollect we were very glad to see them, but not very much alarmed about being defeated by them. We had their victory against Lillywhite's team the previous year in Australia fresh in our memories, and inferred from it that the game had advanced rapidly in that country; but we never for a moment thought of classing them with an English representative team; although we thought that they might do fairly well against the best of our counties. Their first match was against Nottinghamshire; and A. Shaw and Morley being in their best form, they were defeated by an innings and 14 runs. Their bowling, batting, and fielding did not impress us very favourably in that match; and good judges of the game very naturally shook their heads, and predicted a weary and trying time for them before the season was over.

Their match *v.* MCC and Ground, on the 27th May, was a great surprise. It was all over in one day; the Australians winning by 9 wickets, against one of the strongest batting and bowling teams in England, or anywhere else. MCC – first innings, 33; second, 19. Australians – 41 first innings; 12 for 1 wicket, second.

The wicket was as bad as it could be, and small scoring was expected; but no one dreamt for a moment that in the Australian eleven there were two bowlers possessing the powers which Messrs Spofforth and Boyle displayed. For the rest of the season the Australian matches rivalled county matches in interest; and though the wickets were more or less moist all the year, exceptionally good cricket was shown. Results at the end of the trip showed that they were a match for the best of our counties, but not yet up to the form of a representative English team: that in bowling and fielding they could hold their own with us; but in batting were a good distance behind. Their proficiency in bowling was, undoubtedly, the strength of their play, and impressed us greatly. An amateur capable of holding his own against the best of our professional bowling had been a rare thing among us for many years, and the proportion had been about four professionals to one amateur. The Australian bowling was entirely in the hands of amateurs, and it did not suffer by comparison with English professional bowling.

Their batting was their weak point. C. Bannerman averaged, in eleven-a-side matches, 24.1 for 30 completed innings; the rest were under 20.

County cricket in England did not suffer much by the Australian invasion, and some very interesting and exciting matches were played. Middlesex, with a very strong batting team, took first place, and Gloucestershire and Nottinghamshire were close up.

Mr A. G. Steel's performance with the ball was equal, if not superior, to anything ever shown either by professional or amateur; and two professionals, Selby and Ulyett, handled the bat in a way worthy of Daft in his best days.

The Gentlemen won both matches against the Players; and, altogether, the year was one of great interest. Over 200 runs in an innings was scored by ten amateurs, and the century was scored about 350 times.

Before the first Australian eleven had completed its tour in England it was decided that a fifth eleven of English players should go out to Australia. On this occasion it was an invitation from the Melbourne Cricket Club to the amateurs of England; but a team made up of amateurs entirely was found impracticable, and two most popular professionals, Emmett and Ulyett – both belonging to Yorkshire – had to be included. Ulyett was a good all-round player, but not a very successful bowler on good wickets; and it was not expected that the eleven would show such favourable results as those which had preceded it. And so it turned out; for, while the batting generally was quite up to the quality of anything the Colonials had yet seen, the weakness of the bowling caused the tour to turn out rather an uneventful one.

An English eleven, made up of professionals from Nottinghamshire and Yorkshire, which visited Canada and America at the end of the season, had a different tale to tell when it returned. Of twelve matches played, nine were won and three were drawn; and it was the bowling that did it!

The season of 1879 in England was a very wet one from beginning to end, and the bowling beat the batting; Alfred Shaw, Morley, and Peate, in particular, showing grand results.

County contests were more exciting than ever, and the struggle for supremacy was a close and keen one.

Among the amateur batsmen, Messrs A. N. Hornby, Hon. A. Lyttelton, A. G. Steel, and A. P. Lucas did particularly well; and among the professionals, Flowers, Bates, Barnes, and Scotton showed excellent promise of things to come. I was still busy with my medical studies, and could not play so much as formerly, but in batting and bowling I did better than in the previous year.

A very gratifying feature of the year to me was the presentation of a national testimonial at Lord's, on the 22nd of July, by Lord Fitzhardinge, who had been one of the chief movers in getting it up. Two years previously the Duke of Beaufort, then President of the MCC, suggested the presentation, and the Committee of the old club taking it up heartily, a very liberal response came from every part of the kingdom. I need not say I was pleased. I had played the game from the time I could handle bat and ball, because I liked it; but I did not know until this year that in doing so I had given pleasure to so many and made so many friends. Lord Chas. J. F. Russell uttered words at the presentation which I shall never forget. Comrades and players, both amateurs and professionals, showered their heartiest wishes upon me; and I felt, more than I could express and feel it still, that everyone had been very kind to me, and that helping to speed the interests of the game so dear to us all was something to be proud of.

Very little surprise was expressed when another Australian XI. appeared on English grounds in 1880. Their first tour had been very successful, and it was only natural they should seek to strengthen the favourable impression they had made. We had been told to expect a great improvement in their batting, and wonderful performances with the ball by a bowler new to English players. Expectations were realised: for at least two of them, W. L. Murdoch and P. S. McDonnell, showed a conspicuous inprovement in their batting

Mr Wm. Lloyd Murdoch.

skill; and the new bowler, Palmer, was a great acquisition, and at times bowled with great success.

Results showed that they were quite up to our best county form, but still unable to cope with a picked eleven. The memorable match against an eleven of England, at the Oval on the 6th, 7th, and 8th September, in which Murdoch batted so grandly for 153 not out in the second innings and Spofforth was unable to play, may be advanced as an argument to the contrary; but I thought then, and I think still, that if three matches had been played between the same elevens, England would have won all three. The composition of the English team will be most interesting to students of the game, and will show how broadly county cricket was represented. There were three players selected from Nottinghamshire; three from Gloucestershire; two from Kent; one from Lancashire; one from Middlesex; and one from Yorkshire.

Two things were clearly revealed: that the Australians had in Spofforth and Murdoch a bowler and batsman of the very first class. Spofforth could show in eleven-a-side matches a bowling average equal to Alfred Shaw, who was undoubtedly the most successful English bowler that year; and in all matches, his 391 wickets for an average of 5.63 per wicket will bear comparison with anything recorded in the history of the game. Murdoch's average of 25.8 for 19 completed innings, while not quite up to the standard of our first-class batsmen, was a great advance on his 1878 performances.

County cricket was in no way affected by the Australian visit; for, if anything, the interest displayed during the season was greater than in any previous year. Nottinghamshire deservedly came out first, for it was the only county that lowered the colours of the Australian eleven.

Gloucestershire had now played for eleven years, and had held its own against all comers. I had taken a particular pride in its success, as every lover of the game does in the county he represents, and was pleased to know that my individual efforts with bat and ball had helped to give it a high position. But then I had been supported by a team of amateurs that many a captain might envy. To name them, and give their doings, would take more space than can be well afforded: but I cannot allow this year to pass without saying something about my brother Fred's share in the good work, for it was his last among us. He died before the season was over, and before he had completed his 30th year.

The blow to my family and Gloucestershire county was more than I can find words to express; indeed, no words can express it. But I know that not only Gloucestershire, but the cricketing world, sustained a heavy loss by his death. I think I may be allowed to say of him, with pardonable pride, that he was a brilliant field, a splendid batsman, and a fairly successful bowler in first-class company; and that his memory is cherished by every player who knew him. I give his batting performances for his county, and will let them speak for themselves.

He played:

	Completed Innings	Runs	Most in an Innings	Average.
1870–74	34	1,199	165*	35.26
1875	12	430	180*	35.83
1876	12	297	78	24.75
1877	15	441	98	29.40
1878	14	418	73*	29.85
1879	15	211	57	14.06
1880	13	320	83	24.61

The Gentlemen *v*. Players' matches resulted in a win to each. The first, at the Oval, the Players won by 37 runs, in a great degree owing to the fine bowling of Alfred Shaw and Morley, who bowled in great form, as they did the greater part of that year. The return, at Lord's, the Gentlemen won by 5 wickets, owing to consistently good batting of the eleven and the successful bowling of Mr H. Rotherham.

Very few of the old names now remained in the batting averages, and another generation of bowlers was springing up. A reference to the bowling and batting averages at the end will show a remarkable improvement on previous years. The doings, in particular, of Alfred Shaw, Morley, and Peate will bear more than one perusal. For years the first two had stood head and shoulders above every other bowler in the quantity and quality of the work done; and Shaw, in particular, might be called the bowler of the century. Other bowlers have been as successful in one or two seasons; but for consistent brilliancy, for ten years at least, he has had no equal in England, or out of it.

Lord Harris, the Hon. Alfred Lyttelton, the Hon. Ivo Bligh, and Mr A. J. Webbe were now batting in grand form; and the amateur batting of that year was of a very high quality. Professional batting came out favourably also; Barnes, Charlwood, and Ulyett showing excellent results.

Mr Renny-Tailyour scored 331 in a single innings for the Royal Engineers. Over 200 was scored 18 times by other players, and a 100 close upon 500 times.

The year 1881 saw Lancashire at the top of the tree. That County played brilliantly in all its matches, and came out very far ahead of the others. To begin with, it possessed in its captain, Mr A. N. Hornby, one of the ablest and most popular cricketers in England, who never spared himself, whether he were playing a winning or a losing game, and whose enthusiasm infected every member of the team. As a batsman, he had no superior that year; for not only did he perform grandly for his county, but he came out first in the averages in first-class cricket.

It was difficult to find a weak spot in the eleven. In batting and bowling they could compare favourably with any county; but it was very much owing to their brilliant fielding that such good results rewarded their efforts. It may be advanced against their success that five of the professionals were playing under residential qualifications; but it must not be forgotten that other counties would have been only too glad to have had them on similar conditions, and that it was owing to the Committee of the County Club and the excellent judgment of Mr Hornby that they had been originally selected and their powers developed.

Surrey was trying hard to recover its old position, and the Committee invited colts from all parts of the county to practise at the Oval under the eyes of good and competent judges. The old arrangement of having a colts' match once or twice a year had not produced favourable results, many a promising colt failing to do himself justice through nervousness or some other cause. Constant practice for a week or two was a better test, and showed whether they had the making of county players in them.

Nottinghamshire was in the unfortunate position of having good players and not being able to use them. Seven of the eleven after playing one match refused to play again unless they were all engaged for the rest of the season. It was a blow to the Committee, but one that had to be faced; for, if the malcontents had succeeded in their demand, county cricket would have suffered in Nottinghamshire and elsewhere. It said a great deal for the rising talent of the county that they could make a fair show against the other counties without the aid of the seven. Before the season was over, however, five of them admitted they had made a mistake, and were reinstated in the eleven, and afterwards the county showed something of its true form.

Yorkshire had a very good season, although during a part of it they were without the services of Hill and Ulyett; but they possessed a very successful and good bowler in Peate, while Bates and the evergreen Emmett did their share of the work.

Gloucestershire had a promising bowler in Woof that year. Middlesex was considerably strengthened by the bowling of Burton; and Mr C. T. Studd's all-round form, the brilliant wicketkeeping of the Hon. A. Lyttelton and Mr Vernon's dashing batting all helped to give it a good place. Kent suffered by the absence of Lord Harris a part of the season; and Sussex showed little sign of improvement.

The Gentlemen won their matches against the Players at the Oval and Lord's; but the latter were without their best eleven, owing to the Nottinghamshire rupture. They were both won by small majorities, however, and few better contests were played during the year. A third match, played at Brighton for the benefit of James Lilly white, who had represented Sussex in every contest for twenty years, had a very exciting finish. The Gentlemen were left with 113 runs to make in the second innings, and after making 50 without the loss of a wicket every one naturally thought the match was a gift to them; but, on Alfred Shaw going on to bowl, a complete change occurred, and, amidst the greatest excitement, the Players pulled off an unexpected victory by one run. I was unable to play in this match, and was rather sorry for it; for I knew how serviceable Lillywhite had been to his county.

Jupp also had a benefit this year South *v.* North, at the Oval, but a county engagement kept me away, and I had to be content with sending all manner of good wishes for the success of one of the finest cricketers Surrey ever produced. Individual scoring was good during the months of May, June, and July while the weather was dry and the wickets hard; but heavy rains set in early in August, and continued for the remainder of the season, which caused the pace to slacken considerably. A record was established by Mr W. N. Roe, on the 12th July, playing for Emmanuel L. V. C. against Caius L. V. C. at Cambridge, when he scored 415 not out, exceeding Mr Tylecote's score at Clifton in 1868 by 11 runs. Medical work took up much of my time that year, and I played less than formerly.

In 1882, the visit of the third Australian team was of great interest. Only eleven-a-side matches were arranged, an indication that the visitors meant to test the full strength of English cricketers. Murdoch was again at the head of the eleven and said to be batting better than ever. His huge score of 321 for New South Wales *v.* Victoria, in the

The Australians, 1884: Mr P. S. McDonnell, Mr G. Alexander, Mr G. Giffin, Mr G. E. Palmer, Mr F. R. Spofforth, Mr W. L. Murdoch, Mr W. Midwinter, Mr H. F. Boyle, Mr J. McC Blackham, Mr J. Bonner, Mr A. C. Bannerman, Mr W. H. Cooper, Mr J. H. Scott.

England (*v.* Australians), 1884: Pullin (umpire), Peate, Mr A. P. Lucas, Hon. A. P. Lyttleton, Shrewsbury, Farrands (umpire), Mr A. G. Steel, Lord Harris, Mr W. G. Grace, Mr W. W. Read, Ulyett, Mr S. Christopherson, Barlow.

early part of the year, proved that, and led us to expect greater things of him than he had done in 1880. He brought with him the best of the first team, and the weak members had been replaced by such good names as G. Giffen, T. W. Garrett, H. H. Massie, and S. P. Jones.

Their first match against Oxford University was a revelation of their powers, and established the reputations of three of the new members – Massie, Giffen, and Garrett. Their second match, played against Sussex, just as clearly showed that the old members, Murdoch, Palmer, Spofforth, and Bannerman, had gone forward and not backward. How well they fought against the best of our county elevens is a matter of history; not meeting with a single defeat, and conclusively proving that they were worthy of being classed not far behind the best of our representative teams The Gentlemen of England succumbed to them; but they were defeated by the Players, North of England and Cambridge University. Their great match against the combined strength of England at the Oval, on the 28th and 29th of August, will always be a pleasant memory to them.

	First innings	Second innings
Australia	63	122
England	101	77

England only wanted 85 to win in its second innings, and actually scored 51 for 1 wicket, and yet lost by 7 runs. Spofforth has done many great performances with the ball; but the finish of that innings will always be a good one to recollect, for the wicket was in fair condition, and he was fighting an uphill game against half a dozen of the best batsmen in England. Never bowler fought more successfully or pluckily than he did that day; and, supported by Boyle, he landed a victory for his side that stirred the hearts of his opponents and every one present. The shouting and cheering that followed I shall remember to my dying day, as I shall remember the quick hearty recognition of English cricketers over the length and breadth of the land that the best of Australian cricket was worthy of the highest position in the game.

In all, 38 matches were played during the tour, of which the Australian team won 23, lost 4, and 11 were drawn.

That, to my mind, was the best eleven of the seven which have now visited us, having no equal for all-round form. Their fielding and bowling were quite up to the English standard; their batting, slightly under it; and Blackham's wicketkeeping perfection.

It will not do to say that county cricket was not affected by the excitement which prevailed over the engagements of the Australian eleven that year. Undoubtedly it was. Lancashire and Nottinghamshire were equal for first place, the latter playing in its old form, owing to the perfect harmony which now prevailed between the committee and all the members of the eleven. Alfred Shaw and Morley were as effectual as ever with the ball; but Shrewsbury was not in the best of health, and did not play up to the form expected of him. Peate, of Yorkshire, had now become the acknowledged best slow bowler of England, and Emmett was as good as ever. Crossland, for Lancashire, strongly illustrated the usefulness of a fast bowler on a side. So good had become the wickets everywhere, that slow bowling was losing its sting, and good judges were of the opinion that it was the pace of the Australians' bowling which produced such excellent results.

Gloucestershire, Middlesex, Surrey and Kent were much in want of bowling of all kinds, and Sussex and Derbyshire were still far behind the others.

The Players won the first match against the Gentlemen at the Oval by 87 runs; but magnificent batting on the part of Messrs A. P. Lucas and C. T. Studd turned the tables on them in the return match at Lords, the Gentlemen winning by eight wickets.

A record score was made by the Orleans Club *v.* Rickling Green Club, at Rickling Green on the 4th and 5th August, the total amounting to 920. The first wicket fell for 20 runs; then Mr A. H. Trevor joined Mr G. F. Vernon, and they raised the score before they were parted to 623.

Individual innings of over 300 were scored 4 times; of 200, 19 times; and of 100 close upon 700 times.

For some years previous to 1883 grumbling had been general against the Law which admitted of the wicket being rolled only between the innings. Very often winning the toss meant that one side had a good wicket to play on the greater part of the first day; while the other had, perhaps, but an hour left before the stumps were drawn. If rain fell during the night, the wicket became unplayable next morning, owing to the in-side not being allowed to roll the pitch before resuming its innings. That grievance was now redressed; for early in this year the MCC passed an addition to the Law, which allowed the wicket to be rolled on the second and third mornings of a match, and a valuable addition it turned out to be.

A change was also made in the appointment of umpires. No one was selected to umpire in a match in which his own county was engaged.

County cricket had a better chance in the absence of the Australian eleven, and it was very encouraging to notice the increase of spectators. Travelling elevens were rarely heard of now, and county matches were fulfilling the aim of their promoters. Yorkshire and Nottinghamshire were well ahead of the others, both being strongly represented in batting and bowling. Middlesex came next; and at last Surrey began to creep up again, owing to the magnificent batting of Mr W. W. Read and the bowling of Jones. It was noticed that those counties which were lacking in good professional bowling were invariably low down on the list; Sussex, Kent, and Gloucestershire being in that unfortunate position. Midwinter's return to Australia weakened the Gloucestershire eleven, and there was no one springing up to take his place.

Professional batting was improving rapidly, and Shrewsbury and two or three others were in excellent form. If anything, they were playing over-carefully. The desire to show well in the averages was creating a school of slow scorers whose aim was to keep up their wicket and let the runs come. 20 to 30 runs an hour was a good pace of scoring with them. It was sound enough cricket, but rather tedious to look at.

The power of fast bowling had another exponent in Harrison, of Yorkshire, who met with great success; and Crossland was quite as successful as in the previous year: but those were about the only two fast bowlers who had a first-class reputation, and curiously they both had doubtful actions.

The first match between the Gentlemen and Players, at the Oval, 28th, 29th, and 30th June, resulted in a tie – the only tie ever recorded in those matches. Owing to a professional engagement I was absent from the ranks of the former, for the first time since 1867. The return, at Lord's, was productive of heavy scoring, and the Gentlemen won it by 7 wickets.

The fourth Australian team, which visited England in 1884, was considered the equal of its predecessors by many judges; but, weighing everything carefully, I still hold to the opinion that the third was the best we have yet had. The new men – Alexander, Cooper, and

Scott – were not up to the form of those left behind – Garrett, Jones, Horan, and Massie; and results will bear me out. In all, 32 matches were played: 18 won, 7 lost, 7 drawn, which was not quite so good a show as the 1882 team made. Three matches were played against the full strength of England, two of which were drawn, and England won the third. It was an unsatisfactory ending; for everyone desired to have three matches fought out to the end.

Spofforth was as effective as ever with the ball; Murdoch, McDonnell, Gifien, and A. Bannerman had lost nothing of their skill with the bat; and Blackham gave the finest display of wicketkeeping the cricketing world had yet seen.

I must speak favourably of the Philadelphians, who visited England that year for the first time, considering that they defeated the Gentlemen of Gloucestershire under my leadership, and enabled Lord Harris to have the laugh at me. It was a little bit unfortunate that they came the same year as the Australians; for while they played quite up to the expectations formed of them, their doings were discounted by the brilliant performances of Murdoch's eleven. They were certainly a good lot, and gave an excellent account of themselves against the amateur teams played; but they were not up to English county form. The most successful batsmen were Messrs Scott, R. S. Newhall, Thayer, and Stoever; the bowlers; Messrs Lowry, MacNutt, and C. A. Newhall.

Nottinghamshire had a great year among the coimties, not losing a single match; but then it had in its team Shrewsbury, Barnes, Gunn, Flowers, Selby, Scotton, A. Shaw, Attewell, Wright, and Sherwin, players who have made great reputations in all departments of the game. Middlesex and Yorkshire were in good form also; and Surrey took a step upward. G. Lohmann played for the last named coimty, and gave evidence of good all-round form; his bowling impressing the critics very favourably. Sussex was not quite so low as formerly, due in some degree to the fine batting of Mr W. Newham; and Lord Harris was the mainstay of Kent. Gloucestershire had to take a very humble position for want of bowlers; but could still hold its own in batting, being strengthened in that department by Messrs Brain and Pullen, two promising young players.

The Gentlemen *v.* Players' matches resulted in a win to each. Ulyett batted brilliantly in both, scoring 292 runs for three completed innings. Mr A. G. Steel was in great form with the bat and took first place in the averages. His best displays were against the Australians. He twice exceeded the century against them.

The wickets were hard the greater part of the season, and century-scoring was far in advance of anything yet recorded. Spofforth's bowling performances was the best of the year, and Emmett's results were very good, considering the number of years he had played.

The year 1885 was one of Mr W. W. Read's best; his batting being consistently good throughout the season. His hitting was brilliant against all kinds of bowling when he got his eye in and was well set. Shrewsbury and Gunn showed great improvement also, and were at the head of professional batting that year, as indeed they are at the present time.

A glance at the averages will show the marked change that was creeping over professional batting. For the first time since Carpenter, Hayward, Daft, and one or two others were the most prominent batsmen, the professionals could show a larger number than the gentlemen in the list of the averages. For more than ten years the gentlemen could show a proportion of two to one; in 1885 it was the other way. Shrewsbury had much the best average of the year, though it will be seen that he did not play half the number of innings which Mr W. W. Read played. His defence had become stronger than ever, and his wicket was about the most difficult one in England to capture. He did not go in for rapid scoring, but his hitting all round was clean and safe. Gunn's style was also admirable, but rather freer than Shrewsbury's.

Another professional who did great things that year was Briggs, of Lancashire. For years he had batted with success, and his fielding at cover-point had been most brilliant; but now he came out as a bowler, and by the end of the season proved that he had no superior as an all-round player. Lohmann, of Surrey, confirmed the good opinion formed of his bowling the previous year: and though his name did not appear high up in the batting list, he performed well enough to stamp him as a player of all round excellence. There were half a dozen other professional players, belonging chiefly to Surrey, Lancashire, Nottinghamshire, and Yorkshire, who all displayed good form; so it will be gathered that the Gentlemen had now a hard nut to crack when they met the Players.

Three matches were played between them that year. The first, at the Oval, was drawn in favour of the Players: Gunn, Briggs, and Shrewsbury being very successful with the bat; while Mr W. W. Read played a brilliant 159 for the Gentlemen. The second, at Lord's, was won by the Players by 4 wickets: Gunn, Shrewsbury, and Briggs being again the highest scorers; while Messrs F. M. Lucas and A. G. Steel did well for the Gentlemen. The Players had not won a match at Lord's since 1874. The third was played at Scarborough late in the season, and resulted in a crushing defeat of the Players by an innings and 25 runs. Neither side was fully represented; but I happened to be in my best batting form, and scored 174 out of a total of 273, while Messrs Christopherson and Evans were very successful with the ball. The Players scored 59 and 179 – Gunn, 88 in the second innings.

Three matches were played between North and South, and all were benefit matches. The first was played at Lord's, on the 25th and 26th May, for the benefit of the widow and children of F. Morley, and was won by the South by 9 wickets; the second was played at the Oval on the 25th, 26th, and 27th June, for the benefit of R. Humphrey, and was won by the North by 8 wickets; the third was played at Manchester for the benefit of Watson, and was drawn very much in favour of the North, Shrewsbury scoring largely in both innings.

There was no abatement in the interest taken in county cricket. Nottinghamshire did not show up so well as in the previous year, but was again at the head of the poll.

Mr J. S. Carrick created a new record by scoring 419 not out for the West of Scotland Club, at Priory Park, Chichester, on the 13th and 14th July, the total being 745 for 4 wickets; and Messrs L. Wilson and G. Wyld, for Beckenham *v.* Bexley Park, at Beckenham on the 1st August, scored 470 runs for no wicket. Barnes and Gunn distinguished themselves also, scoring 330 runs between the fall of the third and fourth wicket, for the MCC and Ground *v.* Yorkshire, which was record in a first-class match. It was a great year of individual performances, 200 and over being scored 33 times, and the century about 800 times.

Very little need be said about the fifth Australian eleven which came to us in 1886. A great deal was expected; but very little of importance was accomplished. The summary of the tour showed that 38 matches had been played: 9 won, 7 lost, 22 drawn. That was far below the standard of the previous teams, and the Australians were all more or less disappointed. Spofforth was not up to his old form, owing to an accident which caused him to play the part of a spectator for one month of the trip.

Giffen was the mainstay of the eleven, and without him the team would have fared very badly. Three representative matches were played, with the result that England asserted its undoubted superiority. Two of them were won by an innings, the other by 4 wickets. The opinion at the end of the tour was that they were up to County form, certainly not beyond it. The number of drawn matches was neither encouraging nor interesting. Giffen, Jones, and Scott had an average of 26, 24, and 21 respectively for the whole of the tour; but eight English players had an average of from 30 to 40 against them. Four of their team exceeded the century, while that figure was scored against them eight times by English players. I did it thrice, Maurice Read twice, and six other players did it once.

Giffen was also very successful with the ball, considering the amount of work he did; but his average was below both Emmett's and Lohmann's. Spofforth, Garrett, and Boyle did not show up so favourably as in former years, but Blackham at the wicket was finer than ever, and was, without doubt, far ahead of English wicketkeepers. The work he did was astonishing; and how his hands stood it was a mystery to everyone. He was as brilliant and safe in the last match as he was in the first.

An eleven of Parsees also visited England that year; and though they only won one match, yet they gave evidence of becoming good players, and they were as heartily received as either of the Australian or Philadelphian teams There was no desire to be critical, for every Englishman took it as a compliment that the noble game should have taken root in India. I played once against them at Lord's, and shall never forget their unbounded demonstrations of joy when they got me out. Any criticism of their play at that time would be out of place; they have made considerable progress since, and I may have occasion to speak more freely about them later on.

The season was a favourable one for scoring; but it could not be said that the batting was too good for the bowling. The professionals still held their own with the gentlemen in batting, and had almost a monopoly of the bowling in first-class matches. Brilliant things were done with the bat by nearly all the old players; and Mr A. E. Stoddart caused more than common interest. His 485 for Hampstead *v.* Stoics, at Hampstead, on the 4th of August, exceeded every individual performance yet recorded; and though it was made against very second-rate bowling, it will stand out in the history of the game as a remarkable display of welltimed vigorous hitting. He hit 63 fours; and when he left the total was 813 for seven wickets, made in the very quick time of six hours and a quarter.

Individual scoring was higher that year than any year since the game began: over 200 being exceeded no less than thirty-six times, and 100 more than a thousand times.

Nottinghamshire and Surrey had a very close race for first place in county honours, and finished about equal. Both now possessed very strong teams, the Surrey committee in particular straining every nerve to obtain promising recruits.

The Players won their match against the Gentlemen at Lord's by five wickets; while that at the Oval was drawn, very much in their favour. The opinion was gaining ground about this time that unless the Gentlemen cultivated bowling more, the Players would shortly have much the best of the contests.

In 1887, the old saying that 'It is a long lane that has no turning' was strikingly verified by Surrey. After a period of twenty-three years, the Committee of that County Club could breathe more freely, and realise that their efforts had been attended with success, for Surrey was again at the head of the Counties, and very fine results it showed. The eleven was a strong one, including such players as Messrs J. Shuter, W. W. Read, Roller and Key, with Lohmann, M. Read, Abel, Beaumont, Bowley, Jones and Wood. The batting and bowling could compare favourably with that of any other county. Lohmann was worth playing for his batting and fielding alone; but his bowling undoubtedly was then, as it is now, the backbone of the team. I cannot remember any county which has been so fortunate with its wicketkeepers during the last twenty-five years as Surrey. Lockyer created a great reputation; Pooley was a worthy successor, and Wood has proved that he might be classed in the same company.

Lancashire was second on the list, and owed its position to its bowling. Watson, Briggs and Barlow had few equals as all-round players; and Mr A. N. Hornby had lost none of his skill as a batsman, or enthusiasm and judgment as a leader.

Nottinghamshire was compelled to take third place a position lower than it had occupied for many years. Shrewsbury in batting had a fine average for it, having played 18 completed innings for 1,388 runs; average, 77.2: and he was well supported by Gunn and Barnes. His average, with the exception of my own in 1874 and 1876, when I played 7 and 11 completed innings for averages of 84 and 80, is, I believe, far in advance of any other player's average for his county since county cricket was played. Against Middlesex at Nottingham on the 15th and 16th August, he scored 267 in an innings, made without a chance, which occupied him ten hours and a quarter. Before the season was over, he scored over the century on six other occasions for his county; and that year, although he did not play in so many matches as he did in some years, was the most successful in which he had yet played. His display in first-class matches was a fine one indeed, and put in the shade all professional performances:

21 completed innings, 1,653 runs; average, 78.15. Individual batting performances were as brilliant as in any previous year, and we have to go far to find as good results as the following:

Over 200 in an innings, in *first-class matches*, was exceeded 6 times: twice by Mr W. W. Read, and once each by Messrs K. J. Key, A. J. Webbe, Shrewsbury, and Gunn. Over 100 in an innings, in *first-class matches*, was scored 123 times: six times by Shrewsbury, six times by myself (twice in one match), and more than once by two or three others. My two centuries in one match were made against Kent, at Clifton, on the 25th, 26th, 27th August, and it was the second time I had done it in first-class cricket.

The Players won both matches very easily against the Gentlemen: the first, at Lord's, by an innings and 123 runs; the return, at the Oval, by an innings and 16 runs. Shrewsbury, in the first match, batted excellently for in; but it was owing to the fine all-round play of the team that they did so well, and asserted their undoubted superiority. The successful bowlers were also successful with the bat, and their fielding was quite as brilliant as that of the Gentlemen. It was the strongest all-round team that had ever represented them. The bowling of the Gentlemen was their weak spot, and their eleven was over-matched in both contests.

Perhaps this would be the proper place in which to trace the steps which led to the formation of the County Cricket Council.

As long ago as 1868, when it was no unusual thing for a player to represent two or even three counties in the same season, Nottinghamshire, at a General Meeting, passed a resolution as an instruction to its Committee to this effect:

Under the impression that County Cricket, to be thoroughly appreciated by the public, a return ought to be made as near as may be to the manner in which those contests were formerly conducted, when no title but birth enabled any player, whether gentleman or professional, to take part therein; and that, consequently, it be an instruction to the Committee, in the selection of our future matches, to give preference to those counties who adopt that rule.

Secondly, that so long as the title to play in county matches is by residence as well as birth, the same may be acquiesced in by the Committee, on the understanding that no such player shall play in any respect of each such qualification during the season.

Lastly, that it be a further instruction to the Committee that they endeavour to prevail upon all the counties who do not at present do so, to adopt the principle of the last resolution. It is believed that Kent, Sussex, Yorkshire, Cambridgeshire and Nottinghamshire, at the present time, play only those who are county-born; and it is thought other counties would follow in their wake if the subject were properly introduced to their notice, as tending to promote a real and appreciable contest between county and county.

Four years later the Surrey Committee raised the question also; and at a meeting of the representatives of the leading counties in December, 1872, a resolution was passed:

That no player, either amateur or professional, play for more than one county during the season; but that he shall be free to choose at the beginning of the season whether he shall play under the birth or residential qualification.

A copy of the resolution was sent to the MCC, who weighed it carefully, and eventually the following rules were passed at a meeting of County representatives held in the Surrey County Pavilion at the

Oval, on the 9th June, 1873, and confirmed at a meeting of the MCC held in the Pavilion at Lord's on the 1st of July.

1. That no cricketer, whether amateur or professional shall play for more than one county during the same season.
2. Every cricketer born in one county and residing in another shall be free to choose at the beginning of each season for which of those counties he will play, and shall, during that season, play for that county only.
3. A cricketer shall be qualified to play for any county in which he is residing and has resided for the previous two years, or a cricketer may elect to play for the county in which his family home is, so long as it remains open to him as an occasional residence.
4. That should any question arise as to the residential qualification, the same shall be left to the decision of the Marylebone Club.

A further discussion of those rules arose at a meeting of County Secretaries held at Lord's in December, 1881, when Lord Harris moved, 'That the Committee of the MCC be requested to consider whether the two years' residential qualification might not be safely reduced to one year'; but the motion was rejected by 14 votes to 3.

At a largely attended meeting of County Delegates, held at Lord's on 12 July, 1887, Lord Harris in the Chair, it was moved and carried:

1. That a County Cricket Council be formed.
2. That the Council consist of one representative from each of the counties of Nottinghamshire, Yorkshire, Surrey, Kent, Lancashire, Gloucestershire, Middlesex, Derbyshire, Essex, Warwickshire, Norfolk, Sussex, Leicestershire, Staffordshire, Somersetshire, Northamptonshire, Hampshire, Durham, Hertfordshire, and Cheshire.
3. That it shall be competent for the Council to alter or amend the rules of County Cricket Qualification.
4. That upon all questions raised under the rules of County Cricket Qualification the Committee of the MCC shall adjudicate.

That was undoubtedly a step in the right direction; for the birth and residential qualifications had agitated the minds of County Club Committees for many years.

The air was full of rumours about the sixth Australian team which landed in England in 1888.

I have noticed that a really good bowler appears in the ranks of the professionals about once in half a dozen years, and among the amateurs about once in twelve. Australian cricketers have shown that the remark does not apply to them; for in the six teams which have visited us from 1878 down to 1888, at least half a dozen amateurs may be classed as great bowlers. There may be some difference of opinion respecting the positions which Allan, Palmer, Garrett, Giffen, Boyle, and Evans will occupy in cricket history; but there can be none about Spofforth, Turner, and Ferris. They will be emphatically classed among the great bowlers of the century.

Giffen, acknowledged to be the best all-round player who had yet represented Australia, was not with them on this occasion, and the number of players new to English soil was unusually large. By some the team was considered up to the standard of its predecessors, by others much below it; but nearly all were agreed that Turner and Ferris would uphold the reputation of Australian bowling. I question if any team started so favourably as that one did. Mr Thornton's eleven, Warwickshire, Surrey, Oxford University and Yorkshire went down before it in startling succession, the last four being defeated in a single innings, and quite a panic set in among certain cricketers. Turner and Ferris came off in bowling, and showed that they could bat also; and nearly all the other members of the team played up to their best form. Lancashire stayed the rot; then the Gentlemen of England scored heavily against them, and the Players defeated them by ten wickets, and the believers in English supremacy began to breathe more freely.

The play of the team was very much in-and-out afterwards, and before the season was over their form could be safely classed. Forty matches were played – of which they won 19, lost 14 and 7 were drawn. There is little need to analyse the matches; and the team may be put down, with one or two others, as being up to county form, but below English representative form. It is true that they met with a very sad stroke of bad luck when Jones, their best bat, was stricken with illness; but they were, undoubtedly, taken as a whole, below the quality of either of Murdoch's teams, and by a good many thought weaker than Scott's.

The bowling of Turner and Ferris will be remembered, but everything else will be forgotten. How those two slaved and toiled from the beginning to the end of the tour, and with what remarkable effect, is still fresh in the memories of most of us. Rarely have two bowlers been called upon to do so much work in one season, or acquitted themselves so admirably; Turner bowled over 10,000 balls; Ferris close upon 9,000; and Turner's average will compare favourably with Spofforth's, or any bowler that ever lived. Without them the team would have been a failure. McDonnell, the captain, was blamed for working them too much; but he had a very difficult problem before him, and it is easy to be wise after the event. If we are to judge by the results of the others when they were called upon to bowl, we cannot blame him; for not one of them could be compared with the famous pair. Blackham was as good at the wicket as ever; McDonnell hit brilliantly now and then; and Bonnor, when he made up his mind to hit, was still very effective.

There was quite as much interest displayed over county cricket as over the Australian contests; and Surrey came out far ahead of the others. Lohmann was in great form with the ball; and the batting of Messrs W. W. Read, J. Shuter, M. P. Bowden, and Abel and M. Read, who averaged over 30 runs each against the first-class counties, was also a great source of strength. Mr W. W. Read outshone himself in individual performances, scoring 338 in a single innings against Oxford University, which was the second highest ever obtained in a first-class match.

Kent and Yorkshire were next on the list, and Gloucestershire made a distinct step forward. For Gloucestershire against Yorkshire, in the return match at Clifton, I made 148 and 153, and it was the third time I scored the century twice in the same match. Nottinghamshire was lower down than it had been for years, and missed greatly the services of Shrewsbury, who was in Australia looking after the business arrangements of an English football team.

The two matches played by the Gentlemen and Players resulted in a win to each. The first, at Lord's, on the 9th and 10th of July, was finished in two days, the Gentlemen winning it in a most sensational way by 5 runs. The wicket was in favour of the bowlers, and low scoring was

Gentlemen, 1889: Mr J. A. Dixon, Mr M. P. Bowden, Mr W. Newham, Lord George Scott, Mr J. Ecclesm Mr J. Shutter, Mr W. G. Grace, Mr A. G. Steel, Mr W. W. Read, Mr S. M. L Woods, Mr C. A. Smith.

the rule on both sides. The Players were left with 78 to make to win. They scored 71 for 6 wickets, and then collapsed; Mr S. M. J. Woods, who played for the first time, doing most execution with the ball. His 10 wickets for 76 runs in the whole match was a fine performance, and clearly showed how well the Gentlemen could hold their own in these or any contests when their fine batting was backed up by good bowling. The return match, at the Oval, was won by the Players by an innings and 39 runs, and their luck in winning the toss had much to do with it. Heavy rains prevented a start until the second day; and after the Players batted the wicket played badly.

A second team of Parsees visited England that year, and displayed much better form than the first did in 1886. They played 31 matches; winning 8, losing 11, and 12 were drawn. That was a great improvement on their first visit when everything went against them. In one thing they showed excellent promise their consistent efforts in playing an uphill match. More than once, when disaster stared them in the face, and everything seemed to be going against them, they played most pluckily, and made a close match of it.

Second-class county cricket showed considerable development. In all ten counties were represented, and Leicestershire, Somersetshire, and Warwickshire were the most successful.

Two English teams visited Australia in 1887/88: one was under the leadership of Mr G. F. Vernon, who went out at the invitation of the Melbourne CC; the other was under Shrewsbury. Both teams were very successful in their contests, but came to grief financially at which no one was surprised. On one occasion the best of the two teams played against a combined eleven of Australia, and upheld the credit of the old country with marked success.

At the annual meeting of the County Cricket Council on December 10th, 1888, the following resolution was passed and added to the rules of County Cricket:

> That a man can play for his old county during the two years that he is qualifying for another.

In 1889, Shrewsbury's presence in the Nottinghamshire eleven made a great difference to that County. Gunn and Barnes were also in excellent form; and up to the end of July results pointed to their taking a very high position. But the wet wickets which prevailed the greater part of August upset more than one member of the team who had been doing exceptionally well, and their brilliant performances in the early part of the season were greatly discounted.

Surrey did not play up to its 1888 form, its batting being the weak point. Neither Mr W. W. Read, Mr J. Shuter, nor Abel did so well as he had done in the past; but, fortunately Lohmann was very effective with the ball, and he was well supported by Beaumont, Bowley, and a promising colt – Sharpe.

Lancashire came out better than it had done for a year or two. Two importations, Mold and A. Ward, had qualified by residence, and valuable additions to the eleven they proved to be; Mold as a fast bowler, and A. Ward as a batsman. Briggs was as successful as ever with both ball and bat; and Watson showed that, though he had played for nearly twenty years, his bowling had lost none of its sting.

Gloucestershire was not so successful as in the previous year; but at last it possessed a ground of its own, which was admitted to be one of the best in the world, and the Committee became hopeful of improvement at no distant date. It was still lacking in first-class bowling.

Yorkshire met with disaster after disaster, and the season was the worst the county had experienced since it was formed.

Sussex had a most disappointing year also.

An English eleven sailed from England to South Africa at the end of 1888, and played till the end of March, 1889. Australia and Canada had been visited repeatedly; but this was a new departure, and indicative of how the game spreads wherever Englishmen congregate. The arrangements were conducted by Major Warton; and the team was captained by Mr C. A. Smith, of Sussex. The team was not a representative one, but it had in it such well-known players as Abel, Ulyett, Maurice Read, and Briggs, who gave the colonists a fine illustration of all-round cricket. Abel's doings with the bat were noteworthy – 22 completed innings, 1,075 runs, average 48.19; while Briggs astonished everyone out there by his fine performance with the ball 1,220.3 overs, 628 maidens, 1,512 runs, 290 wickets, average 5.62. Two matches were played against a combined eleven of South Africa, which the English team won very easily.

The Gentlemen of Philadelphia visited us again in 1889, and gave a very fine batting display against second-class teams Three of them had an average of over 30 runs per innings, and six more of over 20. Like the majority of amateur elevens, their weak spot was bowling, and some very heavy scores were made against them. Mr W. W. Read, in particular, did very well against them for the Gentlemen of Surrey, scoring 105 and 130, and so added the feat of two centuries in a match to his great performances. Twelve matches was the total number played; of which the Philadelphians won 4, lost 3, and 5 were drawn.

Three matches were played by the Gentlemen and Players in 1889: the first, at the Oval, on the 4th, 5th, and 6th of July; the second, at Lord's, on the 8th and 9th of July; the third, at Hastings, on the 16th, lyth, and 1 8th of September. The Oval match was productive of heavy scoring – the Gentlemen making 347 and 225, to the Players' 396 and 177 second for 1 wicket. Gunn, Barnes, and Quaife did great things in batting for the Players; and Messrs O'Brien, Stoddart, Cranston, W. W. Read, Nepean and myself did best for the Gentlemen. The match at Lord's was another decisive victory for the Players, who won by ten wickets; Barnes batting in great form for 130 not out. At Hastings, the Gentlemen won by 1 wicket after a very sensational finish. It was too late in the season to expect heavy scoring throughout the match; and although the Gentlemen were only left with 73 runs to get to win, the state of the wicket rendered it rather difficult. Five wickets fell for 25 runs, Lohmann and Attewell doing what they liked with the ball; when the ninth man was out 8 runs were still wanted, and the excitement all over the ground was intense. Mr McCormick, of Sussex fame, was equal to the task, however; for, after playing carefully some time for 17 runs, he finished up the match with two hits to the boundary.

The North *v*. South matches were again overdone, as many as five being played, the North having the best of it. The most interesting of all, though it was not finished, was that played at Scarborough on the 5th, 6th, and 7th of September. The North scored 360 in its first innings, the South 197. On the last day the South had to follow on against a majority of 163. The wicket was far from perfect, and the ball had to be watched carefully; but Abel and myself put on 226 for the first wicket, after three hours and three-quarters' play; and when the stumps were drawn the total was 278 for three wickets of which Abel had scored 105 by careful and scientific cricket, while my share was 154.

Gunn and Barnes came out at the top of the batting averages, and Maurice Read was a good third. The Gentlemen were again well to the front, Mr T. C. O'Brien showing up splendidly. It will be a very long time before his magnificent display for Middlesex against Yorkshire in the second innings, at Lord's on the 22nd of June, will be forgotten. Middlesex was left to get 280 runs to win and 3 hours and 35 minutes in which to do it. At half-past five, 4 wickets were down for 129. When Mr O'Brien went in 151 runs were wanted to win, and no one dreamt for a moment that it could be done in the time. He hit as no man had hit for many a long day; but at 6.15, 83 runs were still wanted. With the help of Mr Vernon, he kept up the pace, and accomplished one of the greatest feats of batting ever performed since the game began, winning the match for his side with ten minutes to spare. The brilliancy of his hitting from first to last, the excitement over it, and the burst of enthusiasm which it produced, were worth a day's travel to witness. It was truly a great performance, and stamped him as one of the most dashing batsmen of his or any time.

Mr J. Cranston was another amateur who did exceptionally well. He had been well known for years as one of the most reliable bats in the Gloucestershire eleven, but that year saw him classed as the best left-handed batsman in England.

200 runs and over in an innings was scored by 27 players, and over 100 about a thousand times. The months of May and August were wet, but June and July enabled the batsmen to score rapidly. One very remarkable match was played at Lord's on the 9th and 10th August, for MCC and Ground *v.* Northumberland. Gunn and Mr Brodrick-Cloete began the batting for MCC Mr Brodrick-Cloete's wicket fell with the score at 9, and then Attewell took his place. The score was 325 at the end of the first day, Gunn and Attewell still in. Next day the score was increased to 428, when Attewell was caught, having made exactly 200. The innings was declared at an end, Gunn's score being 219 not out. Northumberland made 141 first innings, and 117 second.

At the third annual meeting of the County Cricket Council, on 6th December, resolutions to the following effect were passed:

1. In the interests of County Cricket it is desirable that an official classification of counties should be made annually by this Council, and that a committee of the County Council, consisting of the President, with three representatives from first-class and three from second-class counties, be appointed to recommend a scheme for this purpose; such scheme to include a scheme of promotion by merit, under which a county may rise from one class to another.
2. That all three-day matches shall begin at twelve o'clock the first day, and not later than 11.30 following days.

Two or three important changes had been made in the laws at a meeting of the MCC, held in the month of May. They were as follow:

1. That the over in future shall consist of five balls instead of four.
2. That the bowler may change ends as often as he pleases, but may not bowl two overs in succession.

3. That the Captain of the batting side may declare the innings at an
   end in a one-day match whenever he chooses to do so; but only
   on the last day of a match arranged for more than one day.

The alterations elicited a great number of opinions for and against;
but by the end of the year it was generally admitted that they had
worked satisfactorily. Declaring the innings at an end in one-day
matches caused the greatest stir; and when one comes to think of it,
it cannot be a very pleasing thing for the tail of an eleven to be told
that there is no need for them to bat, and that they must be content
with fielding for once in a way.

The seventh Australian team, which visited England in 1890, under the
leadership of Murdoch, might be classed in strength with McDonnell's,
although it did not show such good results. For the first time since
these teams came to us in 1878, they lost more matches than they won;
and I need not say the result was alike disappointing to Australian
and English cricketers. We had been led to expect one of the strongest
elevens that had ever left Australia; and for a match or two, in the early
part of the tout, it looked as if the prediction would be verified: but
afterwards they met with defeat after defeat, and finished up the tour
with 38 matches played: 13 won, 16 lost, 9 drawn. Their best wins
were against Lord Sheffield's eleven, Lord Londesborough's eleven and
Surrey; but they were defeated twice by England, twice by the Players
of England, twice by the South of England, twice by the MCC, twice
by Nottinghamshire and twice by Yorkshire: so that their claim to be
classed with a representative English eleven was completely disposed
of. A third match against England, at Manchester, had to be abandoned
owing to heavy rains, not a ball being bowled in the three days.

Murdoch showed that he had lost little of his skill with the bat,
and he was ably supported by a new player, Dr. J. E. Barrett; but with
these exceptions, the batting was weak, which indeed was the case
with all the previous teams Murdoch has always been considered a
hard-wicket bat, and it was rather unfortunate for him that the season
should have turned out a wet one; but considering he had given up
the game for years, his display was very good, and it caused general
satisfaction when he came out at the head of the averages.

Barrett, who ran him a close race for first place, confirmed the great
reputation which he had made in Australia, and did much better than

was expected. Very rarely, if ever, has any young player done so well on a first appearance; indeed, it is held very generally by the Australians themselves that young players never play up to their form the first tour, and we have only to look at the performances of Charlton, Walters, and others to see the truth of it.

His style was not very taking, but he watched the ball very carefully, and was something more than a stone wall type of batsman. His patience was untiring, and when the bowling was good there was no tempting him to hit; but immediately the bowler began to tire and sent up a loose ball, Barrett cracked it to the boundary as well as most batsmen. His fine score of 170 for once out, in the concluding match at Manchester, will be remembered for many a long day. He was a fair bowler also, and with practice will be yet heard of in that department.

Of the others, in batting, very little need be said. Lyons gave us occasional displays of lofty hitting, but he was not the equal of Bonnor in that respect; and for brilliancy, dash, cleanness and placing, was far behind McDonnell in his best days. Trott maintained his 1888 reputation, and at times did exceptionally well, but he lacked in consistency. Turner, Ferris, and Blackham, batted as well as they ever did; but the others met with only moderate success.

It is almost impossible to praise Turner and Ferris too highly for their great bowling performances. Murdoch, like McDonnell, found that they were head and shoulders above everybody else, and he must have had many an anxious quarter of an hour speculating what the team would do in the case of either breaking down. Turner, now and then, was irresistible, and carried everything before him on sticky wickets; but Ferris did better on the hard, good wickets, pegging away in his persistent, plucky way, never minding being hit, and determined at all costs to get the batsmen out Rumours had reached us before the team appeared that Ferris had gone off, but he bowled better than ever; and it was a fitting finish to their grand displays that Turner and he should have ended the season with the same number of wickets, 215, to their credit.

Equally high praise may be bestowed on Blackham's wicketkeeping. It was finer than ever, and he did more work than ever; and he is still today, as he has been any time in the last twelve years, the finest wicketkeeper who ever donned gloves. Gregory, in the field, was conspicuous for quickness, certainty, and a wonderful return, and is

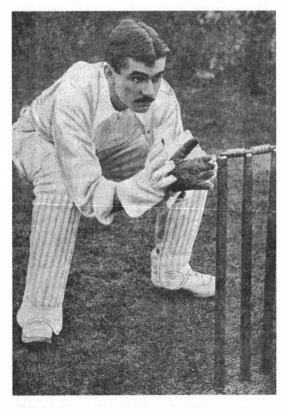

Mr G. McGregor.

worthy of a very high place among brilliant cover-points. Two or three batsmen who were ignorant of his powers had to pay the penalty of a run-out in attempting a short run.

First-class county cricket and representative matches suffered very little by the Australian visit. In the former, Surrey, as was expected, took a very decided lead in the early part of the season, and came out well ahead of the others. Ably led by Mr J. Shuter, it scored victory after victory, and it was only at the end of the year that it suffered defeat. It had a very strong batting team, nearly every member of the eleven being good for runs; while in bowling, Lohmann and Sharpe were up to the form of any bowler in England. Lohmann's performance of taking over 200 wickets in first-class cricket for the third year in succession had never before been accomplished. Turner and Ferris reached that figure in 1888 and 1890, Southerton in 1870, Peate in 1882, and Spofforth in 1884; but these are the only names I can recall.

Lancashire did very well, and took second place; and both Kent and Yorkshire came out better than in the previous year. Greater things were expected of Nottinghamshire; but, with the exception of Shrewsbury and Gunn with the bat, and Attewell with the ball, hardly a member of the team played up to his 1889 form. Gloucestershire went through rather a peculiar experience: until the latter part of July it never won a match, but after it began its Northern tour it never suffered defeat. In batting, J. Cranston, my brother E.M., Painter, and myself were most successful; and Woof bowled very well on the slow wickets. Sussex had a very disastrous season, losing 11 of the 12 matches played.

Great improvement was displayed by one or two of the second-class counties: Somersetshire in particular played grandly, and went through the season without knowing defeat.

The Gentlemen were beaten by the Players at the Oval, but had the best of a drawn match at Lord's.

In the beginning of the season Shrewsbury and Gunn attracted great attention by their wonderful batting displays; but after the wet set in, the former fell off. Their grand stand for Nottinghamshire *v.* Sussex, in which they made 398 before being parted, was a new record for longest partnership in first-class cricket; and Gunn's 228 for the Players was the highest ever made against an Australian eleven in England. Messrs A. N. Hornby, A. J. Webbe, and Hall and Ulyett, batted consistently the greater part of the season, and Abel finished up in fine form.

Mr A. E. Stoddart played two very fine innings in the earlier part of the season: one for the South *v.* North, at Lord's, when he scored 115 out of 169 without a mistake on a difficult wicket; the other for the Gentlemen *v.* Players, at the Oval, when he hit a brilliant 85 on another difficult wicket; but later on he fell woefully off, and could hardly get a run.

Three young Cambridge University players came to the front, Messrs G. McGregor, E. C. Streatfeild, and R. N. Douglas. McGregor's reputation as a wicketkeeper was made the year before, but 1890 saw him in improved form, and he was paid the very high compliment of being chosen to play for England *v*. Australia. All three played for the Gentlemen. Under the leadership of Mr S. M. J. Woods, they helped very materially by their good form to give their University a high position. The four professionals, Briggs, Lohmann, Peel, and Attewell, by their fine allround play, maintained their great reputations.

On the evening of the 11th of August, a special meeting of the County Cricket Council was held in the pavilion of the Surrey County Club. There were present delegates from Surrey, Kent, Gloucestershire, Yorkshire, Sussex, Warwickshire, Derbyshire, Leicestershire, Hampshire, Northamptonshire, Norfolk and Essex. Mr J. Shuter presided, and it was decided:

I. That for the season 1891 the counties be divided into three classes, namely:

FIRST CLASS: Notts, Kent, Yorkshire, Lancashire, Middlesex, Sussex, Surrey, Gloucestershire

SECOND CLASS: Warwickshire, Somersetshire, Staffordshire, Derbyshire, Cheshire, Hampshire, Leicestershire, Essex

THIRD CLASS: Hertfordshire, Lincolnshire, Glamorganshire, Northamptonshire, Northumberland, Devonshire, Norfolk, Durham

II. (a) That every first-class county be required to play matches with at least six other first-class counties. These to include matches with the Champion county of the previous year.
(b) That every second-class county play two matches with at least three other second-class counties, these three to include the Champion county in the second-class for the previous year.
(c) That every third-class county play two matches with at least three other third-class counties.

III. That in each of the three classes an order of merit be drawn up from the results of the season's play in 1891 and future years, and that this order be determined by the same method as that by which the Championship for the first-class counties is at present decided; viz., by subtracting wins from losses, and not counting drawn games.

IV. That in 1892 the lowest county in the first-class and the highest county in the second-class play each other home-and-home matches, these constituting a series which shall be termed the qualifying series. The same arrangement to apply to the lowest of the second-class and the highest of the thirdclass counties.

V. That if a county be, by these means, reduced in class, it shall, for the following season, be considered the highest in the class to which it has descended, and shall follow the course of procedure set forth in No. 4.

That, on the other hand, if a county, after playing in a qualifying series as the highest best of an inferior class, shall have to remain in the same class, it shall not be considered the highest for the next season unless it shall obtain such a position by virtue of its performances in that season.

The scheme of classification did not give general satisfaction, and a newspaper warfare was kept up for sometime afterwards. Later in the year delegates from the second-class counties Hampshire, Warwickshire, Staffordshire, Essex, Cheshire and Derbyshire met in the pavilion at Lord's, and passed a resolution to be submitted as an amendment by Warwickshire at the annual meeting of the County Cricket Council to be held in December.

The annual meeting was held in the pavilion at Lord's, on the 8th December, Mr M. J. Ellison presiding. It was evident that special interest was taken in the points to be considered, for there was a large attendance of delegates from the first, second, and thirdclass counties. After the minutes of the previous general meeting and the special meeting in August were read, and a statement of accounts and balancesheet were passed, Mr Ansell, of Warwickshire, moved, on behalf of the second-class counties, the following amendments to the classification scheme:

In Rule II (6) to omit the clause: 'These three to include the Champion County in the second-class for the previous year.'
To strike out IV. and V., and substitute the following:

IV. That at the end of each season, in the month of August or September, the lowest county in the first-class shall play the highest of the second-class for right of place. One game only shall be played, and upon neutral ground, to a finish, the winner being placed in the superior class and the loser in the class below for the following year.

Note (a). In the event of two counties being equal at the top or bottom of either class, the question of their superiority shall first be decided on neutral ground, played to a finish, and followed immediately by the match for right of place in the superior class for the next year.

Note (b). In the event of three counties being equal, either at the bottom of the first or top of the second class, the matter shall remain in abeyance for that year.

V. Should the trial matches fail to define the positions ot competing counties, the Cricket Council itself shall undertake the classification for the following year.

Note (c). This scheme shall apply also to the lowest of the second and the highest of the third-class counties.

The first motion, to omit II. (b), was carried with one dissentient, Gloucestershire; but when Mr Ansell brought forward his second motion, to strike out Rules IV. and V., and substitute fresh matter, it became perfectly evident that a great diversity of opinion existed. A very animated discussion arose, and, in unmistakable tones, the majority of the delegates declined to pledge themselves to any classification scheme that could compel them to play more matches than they wished to. Mr Ansell's motion that Rules IV. and V. should be struck out, was agreed to; but the meeting rejected the proposals of Warwickshire by 11 votes to 4. Mr J. B. Wostinholm then moved that the rules of the Council be suspended for further discussion of the subject; but Mr A. J. Webbe jumped up and moved as an amendment that the Council be suspended *sine die*. The voting for the amendment was 7 for and 7 against; and the

Chairman giving his casting vote in favour of it, the meeting came to an abrupt ending.

At the end of 1864 a batting average of 25 runs per innings was very exceptional, and rarely accomplished by other than a professional player. It may be explained in this way – that amateur bowling was lamentably weak, while professional bowling was very strong, and a carefully prepared ground the exception.

The year 1865 saw a slight change. Two or three of the amateurs gave evidence of marked improvement with both bat and ball; and, for the first time since 1854, the Gentlemen beat the Players. The batting averages leaped up considerably in 1866; seven amateurs had an average of 30 runs and over per innings, while only one professional reached that figure; and there were fifteen amateurs with an average of over 20 to 4 professionals. But the professionals had quite as great a monopoly of the bowling; 13 to 4 was their proportion in that department. And so it went on for twenty years; the amateurs keeping a strong lead with the bat, the professionals with the ball.

The year 1885 brought further change. The professionals not only maintained their superiority with the ball, but challenged the supremacy of the amateurs with the bat. For twenty completed innings in first-class matches, thirteen professionals had an average of over 23 runs per innings; while the number of amateurs who had it was only six. Nor was it a mere flash in the pan; for the years 1886 and 1887 saw the professionals still challenging the amateurs for first place in batting honours, while still retaining their high position with the ball. The year 1888 brought the amateurs to the front with the bat again; but 1889 and 1890 show it was again a close race between them.

Never, in any year, have the amateurs had a look-in with the professionals in bowling, so far as numbers are concerned, and only once or twice have they headed the list. Mr A. G. Steel did very well for them in 1878; while my performances in the years 1867, 1874, 1875, and 1877 might be classed with first-class professional bowling.

And so we may face the fact that the professional standard of all-round play is higher today than at any time since the game began. The professionals are now the equals of the amateurs in batting and fielding, and their superiors in bowling. And I am very much afraid it is likely to continue so for a considerable time. Amateur bowling is weaker today than it has been for many years, while the outlook for the

Thomas Verity's pavilion at Lord's at the turn of the twentieth century.

future is not particularly bright. It used to be said, some twenty years ago, that it was always safe to back the Players against the Gentlemen. After 1864 prophets were more modest in their utterances. The last two years have shown that the Players are taking their old position.

A careful reader will have noticed how, bit by bit, travelling elevens lost their attraction, and were slowly, but surely, effaced by the growing and absorbing interest taken in county matches.

The history of county cricket is worthy of a book to itself, and cannot have justice done to it here. Surrey, Sussex, Kent, Middlesex, Hampshire and Nottinghamshire have been in existence for more than one hundred years; and all of them, at one time or another, were strong enough to play an eleven of England. But county cricket pure and simple may be said to have reached its highest development in the last twenty years. Yorkshire was established in the early part of the present century, Lancashire in 1864, and Gloucestershire and Derbyshire in 1870. How those counties have fought against each other with varying success can be seen from the yearly results I have given. From 1870 to 1890 Nottinghamshire stands out preeminently among the first-class counties, having been at the head of the list seven times, while it will be seen Sussex has been at the bottom eight times.

I shall not trouble my readers by saying much about the future of the counties. Surrey and Nottinghamshire's prospects are as bright today as at any time in their history; but, then, the brightest prospects have often been shattered in cricket, and many a county that was expected to do well has done ill. It is never safe to prophesy when the unexpected happens so often. Counties in the South have greater difficulties to contend against in obtaining first-class bowlers than the counties in the North, but all of them are striving their utmost to meet the difficulty and keep their position in contests which are now looked upon as the most exciting of all: contests that have become the backbone of the game.

7

The Marylebone Club & University Cricket

My connection with the Marylebone Club dates from the 13th of May, 1869, when I was not quite 21 years of age. I have said elsewhere that I considered it a very high compliment to be thought worthy of a place in the club which has done more than any other to develop the game, and I have nothing but the very pleasantest recollections of the 22 years I have played for it. The MCC had been in existence 82 years when I joined it; there were 1,200 members, and the number of matches played during the season was something under 40. Today it is 104 years old; the list of members has swelled to 3,500, and as many as 160 matches were played last year, of which 84 were won, 40 lost, and 36 drawn. It will be of interest to touch briefly upon the growth of the old club, which is now acknowledged to be the authority on cricket, not only in England, but wherever the game is played.

About the year 1780 the White Conduit Club was the most important in London, and Thomas Lord, a kind of half-attendant, half-ground bowler, was in the habit of bowling to the members. The White Conduit Club, like most cricket clubs, had to contend against internal dissensions, and some of the members decided to go elsewhere. But the difficulty in the way was a suitable spot for a ground, for there were at most only two of any importance in London at the time. Lord was asked to look about in the neighbourhood of Marylebone, and was promised influential support if he succeeded. The Earl of Winchelsea and Col. the Hon. Lennox were the principal movers in the matter; and Lord, being a bit of an enthusiast, and realising that the speculation was likely to turn out well, at once proceeded to carry out the suggestion. By 1787 a suitable spot, now known as Dorset Square, was acquired, and Lord's Ground and the Marylebone Club became accomplished facts.

The Club must have had an influential membership even at that date, for the following year we find it revising the laws of the game. At once it began to play matches with the White Conduit and other clubs; but the first recorded is MCC *v.* White Conduit Club, on the 27th June, 1788, which the MCC won by 83 runs. Everything went smoothly for a period of twenty-two years; then Lord, owing to a dispute with his landlord about an increase of rent, had to leave Dorset Square. North Bank, Regent's Park, was next chosen, in 1810: but that was to be a very short abiding place; for in 1812 the making of Regent's Canal caused the ground to be cut up.

Neither the Club nor Lord was disheartened; for in 1814 the present site in John's Wood was secured, and there the club has played ever since. A year or two previously the Homerton Club, the next in importance, amalgamated with the MCC, and the playing eleven became a very strong one. But it should be remembered that before this some of the members of the old Hambledon Club, which broke up in 1791, had played for the MCC, and consequently strengthened it. Matches against England, London, Kent, Middlesex, Hampshire, and other clubs, had been of frequent occurrence before the end of the eighteenth century, and the fame of the MCC had gone over the land.

Lord and the club committee must have thought highly of the turf on which they played at Dorset Square; for it was taken up and relaid on the North Bank Ground, and afterwards transferred to St John's Wood Road. The earliest recorded match of the MCC on its present ground was played against Hertfordshire on the 22nd June, 1814, the MCC winning by an innings and 27 runs. In the eleven representing the winning side were four players who were well known all over the cricket world, and who maintained their reputation for many years afterwards Lord Frederick Beauclerk, Messrs E. H. Budd, G. Osbaldeston, and W. Ward.

Harrow and Winchester played against each other for the first time at Lord's on the 27th and 28th July, 1825, and the match will be remembered for the disastrous fire which took place in the pavilion during the night of the last day. Valuable records of the game which could not be replaced were destroyed, and Lord suffered rather heavily. Something like 2,600 was due to him for subscriptions; but as the books had been burnt, it was difficult for him to remember who had paid and who had not.

It is just possible that Lord was discouraged by it: anyhow, we find he desired to retire, and for the moment it looked as if the ground would fall into the hands of the builders, who had coveted it for many years. Mr Ward very generously stepped in and purchased the remainder of the lease at a very high price, and the club continued its prosperous career. The pavilion was quickly rebuilt, and two years later Oxford and Cambridge began their annual contests.

Mr Ward unfortunately could not see his way to hold the lease after 1835, and Mr J. H. Dark took it off his hands and became the proprietor in 1836. The club seems to have got on pretty smoothly under the proprietorship of Mr Dark until 1863, when he proposed to part with the remainder of his lease of 29 years for the sum of £15,000. The year after he accepted £11,000; and Mr Moses, the ground landlord, offered a renewal of the ground rent for 99 years at the rate of £550 per annum. Considering that the old rent had only been £150, the club had now to face a considerable increase in its yearly expenses. Nothing daunted, the Committee accepted: but Mr Moses came forward in 1865 with a new offer; viz., to sell the fee outright for a sum of £21,000. Eventually he accepted £18,150; and Mr W. Nicholson, a member of the committee, in a very landable spirit advanced the money on a mortgage of the premises at the rate of £5 per cent, which he afterwards reduced to £4 per cent, and conceded to the club the right to pay him off by annual instalments.

At last the club could call the ground its own, and the strides it made in the next twenty years were really remarkable. By 1878 the whole amount had been paid off, and the finances of the club established on a firm footing, which it has since maintained. In 1866, when Mr Nicholson bought up the freehold, the club numbered 980 members, and had an income slightly over £6,000; today, as I have already said, it has 3,500 members, with a total income of £30,000. It is no secret that the committee, if they desired, could double the membership in a month's time; for applications for election come from all parts of the globe. However, they have no desire to do so, for it is their aim that the club shall not exceed the limit which would affect the comfort and enjoyment of the present members; and a rule has been passed which admits only of 156 members being elected yearly, active cricketers preferred, and half of them being specially selected.

There is no need to say that the club is in a prosperous condition. If proof were wanted of it, I have only to refer to the handsome pavilion which was recently built at a cost of £20,000. The Hon. Sir Spencer Ponsonby Fane laid the first stone on the 17th September, 1889, and everything was completed by the beginning of 1890. It is capable of accommodating 3,000 people, and is a vast improvement on the old structure, which had weathered the storms of 65 years. The entire size of the ground is 12 acres; the enclosed part for playing matches, 6 acres. All round it improvements have been made and are being made yearly. Ten men are employed throughout the year to look after it, and everything in connection with it is in apple-pie order.

The Marylebone Cricket Club is the first in the world, and is held in deserved respect by everyone who plays the game. At home and abroad, every Englishman refers to it with pardonable pride, and upholds it as the chief bulwark of our national game.

The MCC is everywhere acknowledged to be the maker and preserver of the laws. It has been accused of being too conservative in some respects, and of not marching quickly enough in the interests of the game; but my experience of the club has shown me that it has been quick to act immediately a grievance has been made clear. Rarely a year has passed in which some point of law has not cropped up, and received calm and careful consideration. Unfair bowling, the selection of umpires, county qualifications, disputes between players of the North and South in fact, everything bearing on the welfare of the game have in turn been discussed and decided; and the opinion is general today that the old club has been faithful to the trust which has been placed in its hands for upwards of a hundred years.

The centenary celebration, which was held on the 13th, 14th, 15th, 16th, 17th and 18th June, 1887, was an important landmark in the history of the club. The first three days were devoted to first-class cricket, MCC and Ground *v.* England, when A. E. Stoddart and Shrewsbury batted in fine form for the latter. The last three days, the Gentlemen of the MCC played Eighteen Veterans of Over Forty, and the giants of the past could be seen batting with some of the giants of the present. The dinner which was held in the tennis court in the evening of the 15th brought together a most distinguished company of players and lovers of the game, numbering about 200. Success to the Great Army of Cricketers, the Church, the Army, the Navy, the Bench and the Bar, Medicine and the Cricket Counties was proposed in turn, and no such memorable meeting has been held since cricket was first played.

The Committee of the MCC have never lost sight of the interests of professional players. Young and promising players have always been encouraged, and the most successful have rarely failed to secure an engagement on the staff of ground bowlers. There are over 40 professional cricketers engaged at Lord's, many of them earning as much as £10 per week. The season lasts about 16 weeks. For country matches they are paid at the rate of £6 per match; for matches played at Lord's, £3 10s. if they win and £3 if they lose. The ground bowlers are paid from 30 shillings to 50 shillings per week, and they can always depend on handsome gratuities from the members. Every player selected by the Committee to play against the Gentlemen is paid at the rate of £10 per match; and after years of faithful service, nearly every first-class player can rely upon a benefit match, which may be expected to realise a goodly sum.

It will readily be understood that every player covets the position of ground bowler at Lord's, and avails himself of the first offer to play there, in the hope of creating a favourable impression. The MCC is generous in another way: the expenses of county teams playing against it at Lord's being defrayed by the club, while the expenses of MCC elevens which visit the provinces come out of the club funds only.

The club can also show a most distinguished roll of office bearers, but no trustworthy record can be given before 1826.

PRESIDENTS:

1826	Charles Barnett, Esq	1827	Henry Kingscote, Esq
1828	A. F. Greville, Esq	1829	John Barnard, Esq
1830	Hon. G. Ponsonby	1831	Wm. Deedes, Esq
1832	Henry Howard, Esq	1833	Herbert Jenner, Esq
1834	Hon. H. Ashley	1835	Lord Charles Russell
1836	Lord Suffield	1837	Viscount Grimston
1838	Marquis of Exeter	1839	Earl of Chesterfield
1840	Earl of Verulam	1841	Earl Craven
1842	Earl of March	1843	Earl of Ducie
1844	Sir John Bayley, Bart.	1845	Thos. Chamberlayne, Esq
1846	Earl of Winterton	1847	Earl of Strathmore
1848	Earl of Leicester	1849	Earl of Darnley
1850	Earl Guernsey	1851	Earl Stamford &
1852	Viscount Dupplin		Warrington

1853	Marquis of Worcester	1854	Earl Vane
1855	Earl of Uxbridge	1856	Viscount Milton
1857	Sir Frederick Bathurst,	1858	Lord Garlics
	Bart. 1890	1859	Earl of Coventry
1860	Lord Skelmersdale	1861	Earl Spencer
1862	Earl of Sefton	1863	Lord Suffield
1864	Earl of Dudley	1865	Lord Ebury
1866	Earl of Sandwich	1867	Earl of Verulam
1868	Lord Methuen	1869	Marquis of Lansdowne
1870	J. H. Scourfield, Esq	1871	Earl of Clarendon
1872	Viscount Down	1873	Earl of Cadogan
1874	Marquis of Hamilton	1875	Sir Charles Legard
1876	Lord Londesborough		Bart., M.P.
1877	Duke of Beaufort	1878	Lord Fitzhardinge
1879	W. Nicholson, Esq	1880	Sir Wm. Hart-Dyke,
1881	Lord George Hamilton		Bart., M.P.
1882	Lord Belper	1883	Hon. Robert Grimston
1884	Earl of Winterton	1885	Lord Wenloch
1886	Lord Lyttelton	1887	The Hon. E. Chandos
1888	The Duke of Buccleuch		Leigh, Q.C.
1889	Sir Henry James, Q.C.	1890	Lord W. de Eresby

Only one of them died in office, and that was the Hon. Robert Grimston in 1883, than whom no warmer supporter of the game ever lived. He closely identified himself in his later years with the I Zingari and Essex clubs; but he will be best remembered for his enthusiasm over the Eton and Harrow matches at Lord's. If you had wished to know what enthusiasm meant, you had only to keep your eye on him on these occasions. For the time being there was only one thing to him worth thinking about, and it was that particular match. He was oblivious to everything outside of it, and would listen to nothing that did not bear upon the past matches of the two schools, or the one going on. And as for cheering, coaching, and encouraging his own school, the majority of us were not to be compared with him. He desired a close, exciting match; but Harrow he would have win, and when it did, there was no happier man on earth.

The MCC has always been fortunate in the gentlemen who have filled the offices of Treasurer and Secretary.

Past Treasurers:

F. Ladbrooke, Esq	R. Kynaston, Esq
H. Kingscote, Esq	T. Burgoyne, Esq

Present Treasurer:
The Hon. Sir Spencer Ponsonby Fane, K.C. B.

Past Hon. Secretaries:
1822 to 1841 – Mr B. Aislabie.
1842 to 1857 – Mr Roger Kynaston.
1858 to 1862 – Mr Alfred Baillie.
1863 to 1867 – Mr R. A. Fitzgerald.

On the 1st January, 1868, Mr Fitzgerald became paid Secretary of the club at a salary of £400 per annum, which office he held until 1876. Mr H. Perkins was elected in 1877 at tne same salary, and is still in office.

Annual List Of Matches Played By The MCC During The Last Twenty Years

Date	Matches	Won	Lost	Drawn
1871	37	17	8	12
1872	44	21	10	13
1873	46	17	13	16
1874	50	19	18	13
1875	48	21	7	20
1876	60	23	16	21
1877	65	27	11	27
1878	77	33	18	26
1879	84	43	7	34
1880	95	42	17	36
1881	117	55	11	51
1882	123	47	24	52
1883	130	49	17	64
1884	121	59	34	28
1885	136	72	30	34
1886	128	76	26	26

1887	141	85	29	27
1888	147	75	23	49
1889	152	99	29	24
1890	160	84	40	36
Totals	1,961	964	388	609

University Cricket

It will be very naturally asked, what do I know about University Cricket Not very much, I admit; for I never was in residence at either Cambridge or Oxford. But I know something about University players, and I have made a point of watching the doings of both elevens with more than common interest; for well I know it is from them the Gentlemen must expect to improve in bowling strength to enable them to ccntend at all successfully against the Players. It may safely be said that, with two or three exceptions, the great amateur bowlers of the last 50 years have belonged to either Cambridge or Oxford, and, quoting from memory, I cannot remember a year in which the Gentlemen had not two or more players in their eleven from one or the other. And, speaking from my twenty-five years' experience of first-class cricket, I fail to see that it is likely to be otherwise in the future.

I know that good bowlers and batsmen are made long before the age at which public school boys usually go to Oxford or Cambridge, and that Eton, Harrow, Rugby, and one or two others ought to have the credit of having trained the eminent University players who have stirred the cricket world. Still there can be very little doubt that it is the hard discipline which comes after 17 or 18 years of age that develops the promising boy into a first-class player.

Cambridge has the credit of having produced more first-class bowlers than Oxford, and the names of the most prominent will come readily to the mind of every cricketer Messrs A. G. Steel and C. T. Studd in the past, and S. M. J. Woods and E. C. Streatfeild of today. Of course, if we go back farther, such great names as M. Kempson, C. D. Marsham, E. L. Fellowes, W. F. Maitland, R. Lang, H. M. Plowden, Hon. F. G. Pelham, W. N. Powys, D. Buchanan, S. E. Butler (who took all 10 wickets of Cambridge for 38 runs, in 1871), and others will be remembered. A still larger number might be mentioned; but those I have given are sufficient to prove what I have said that the great amateur bowlers have mostly come from Oxford or Cambridge.

And the same may be said of our crack batsmen, though in a lesser degree. Such great names as J. Makinson, C. G. Lane, Hon. C. G. Lyttelton, R. A. H. Mitchell, C. E. Green, W. Yardley, C. I. Thornton, W. H. Hadow, C. J. Ottaway, E. F. S. Tylecote, Lord Harris, A. J. Webbe, A. P. Lucas, Hon. A. Lyttelton, W. S. Patterson, Hon. E. Lyttelton, F. H. Buckland, A. G. Steel, C. T. Studd, Hon. Ivo Bligh, W. H. Patterson, Lord Hawke, J. H. Brain, T. C. O'Brien, K. J. Key, W. Rashleigh, Lord George Scott, H. J. Mordaunt, and others will be easily remembered: but they are by no means the only eminent batsmen who have helped materially to make cricket history during the last 25 years; for opposite them can be placed the names of a great many players of equal reputation who never belonged to either University. Nor is the reason for this far to seek; batting has always been the most popular branch of the game to the amateur, and it must be borne in mind that County Clubs, with their ground bowlers, have enabled him to keep up his form without drawing too much upon his time. Half an hour's practice twice a week is sufficient to keep most batsmen in form, and there are very few so placed who cannot obtain it.

Keeping up one's bowling form requires rather more attention. I know it is generally accepted that a really good bowler is born, not made; but that does not mean that he can trust to his natural talents alone to perform great feats. Nothing short of hard work, and plenty of it, will make a good bowler, however natural or exceptional his style; and, unfortunately, very few except University players seem to be able to give the necessary time. About the best illustration I can remember at the moment is Mr M. Kempson, with whom I have had many an interesting chat. His great desire was to play for the Gentlemen against the Players some day; and at Cambridge he used to bowl to the professionals, as well as have them bowl to him. In 1853, he bowled two hours a day for six weeks in preparation for the match; and it is now a matter of history how well he bowled, and, with Sir F. Bathurst, won the match for the Gentlemen. His careful preparation enabled him to do more with the ball than he ever did before or afterwards; and in that particular match he could almost do what he liked with it. And I remember he told me how smartly he got rid of Box, one of the most dangerous batsmen in the Players' eleven. Box's favourite hit was a smart cut between the slips, when he gpt the right ball. Mr Kempson arranged with Mr Nicholson, who was keeping wicket, to motion short-leg to third man as soon as he gave the signal. He did so before he delivered the last ball of the first over: bowled exactly the right ball, and Box cut it straight into Sir F. Bathurst's hands. Box's astonishment was something to be seen, not described.

The Universities have also given us some of the most brilliant of our amateur fieldsmen. Their name is legion; and I need not specify them, unless in the case of great wicketkeepers. The Hon. Alfred Lyttelton I have already referred to; but two others have since appeared who may claim the same excellence, Messrs Philipson and McGregor. McGregor, in my estimation, is above the form of any amateur wicketkeeper who has yet represented his University, or played in any of the great contests.

The Oxford and Cambridge contests were begun in 1827, and except five have all been played at Lord's. The closest fights were in 1841, 1870, and 1875, when the victories were gained by the narrow majorities of 8, 2, and 6 runs. On five occasions Oxford has won by an innings, while Cambridge has done the same thing thrice.

Not until 1870 did any player score 100 runs in an innings; but it has been done thirteen times since. They are as follow:

Mr K. J. Key (Oxford)	143 in 1886
Mr W. Yardley (Cambridge)	130 in 1872
Mr H. J. Mordaunt (Cambridge)	127 in 1889
Mr G. B. Studd (Cambridge)	120 in 1882
Mr F. H. Buckland (Oxford)	*117 in 1877
Mr W. H. Game (Oxford)	109 in 1876
Mr W. H. Patterson (Oxford)	*107 in 1881
Mr W. Rashleigh (Oxford)	107 in 1886
Mr W. S. Patterson (Cambridge)	*105 in 1876
Mr E. Crawley (Cambridge)	*103 in 1887
Mr C. W. Wright (Cambridge)	102 in 1883
Mr H. W. Bainbridge (Cambridge)	101 in 1885
Mr W. Yardley (Cambridge)	100 in 1870
Lord George Scott (Oxford)	100 in 1887

Eight of them go to the credit of Cambridge, six to Oxford.

The highest innings yet made in these matches have been:

Cambridge	388 in 1872, 302 in 1876 and 300 in 1889
Oxford	313 in 1887, 306 in 1881 and 304 in 1886

The Cambridge eleven of 1878, under the captaincy of the Hon. E. Lyttelton, is considered to have, been the strongest that ever played, and almost up to the form of an English representative eleven. Their defeat of the first Australian eleven by an innings and 72 runs was the heaviest inflicted upon that team during the whole tour.

OXFORD *v.* CAMBRIDGE CONTESTS

1827 Played at Lord's, 4th June, drawn.

1829 Played at Oxford, 8th June Oxford won by 115 runs.

1836 Played at Lord's, 23rd June Oxford won by 121 runs.

1838 Played at Lord's, 6th July Oxford won by 98 runs.

1839 Played at Lord's, 17th June Cambridge won by an innings and 125 runs.

1840 Played at Lord's, 8th July Cambridge won by 63 runs.

1841 Played at Lord's, 14th July Cambridge won by 8 runs.

1842 Played at Lord's, 9th June Cambridge won by 162 runs.

1843 Played at Oxford, 8th June Cambridge won by 54 runs.

1844 Played at Lord's, 4th July Drawn.

1845 Played at Lord's, 12th June Cambridge won by 6 wickets.

1846 Played at Oxford, 11th June Oxford won by 3 wickets.

1847 Played at Lord's, 17th June Cambridge won by 138 runs.

1848 Played at Oxford, 15th June Oxford won by 23 runs.

1849 Played at Lord's, 21st June Cambridge won by 3 wickets.

1850 Played at Oxford, 6th June Oxford won by 127 runs.

1851 Played at Lord's, 3rd July Cambridge won by an innings and 4 runs.

1852 Played at Lord's, 8th July Oxford won by an innings and 77 runs.

1853 Played at Lord's, 14th June Oxford won by an innings and 19 runs.

1854 Played at Lord's, 3rd July Oxford won by an innings and 8 runs.

1855 Played at Lord's, 21st June Oxford won 3 wickets.

1856 Played at Lord's, 16th June Cambridge won by 3 wickets.

1857 Played at Lord's, 25th June Oxford won by 81 runs.

1858 Played at Lord's, 21st June Oxford won by an innings and 38 runs.

1859 Played at Lord's, 23rd June Cambridge won by 28 runs.

1860 Played at Lord's, 25th June Cambridge won by 3 wickets.

1861 Played at Lord's, 17th June Cambridge won by 133 runs.

1862 Played at Lord's, 23rd June Cambridge won by 8 wickets.

1863 Played at Lord's, 22nd June Oxford won by 8 wickets.

1864 Played at Lord's, 13th June Oxford won by 4 wickets.

1865 Played at Lord's, 26th June Oxford won by 114 runs.

1866 Played at Lord's, 18th June Oxford won by 12 runs.

1867 Played at Lord's, 1st July Cambridge won by 5 wickets.

1868 Played at Lord's, 22nd June Cambridge won by 168 runs.

1869 Played at Lord's, 21st June Cambridge won by 58 runs.

1870 Played at Lord's, 27th June Cambridge won by 2 runs.

1871 Played at Lord's, 26th June Oxford won by 8 wickets.

1872 Played at Lord's, 24th June Cambridge won by an innings and 166 runs.

1873 Played at Lord's, 23rd June Oxford won by 3 wickets.

1874 Played at Lord's, 29th June Oxford won by an innings and 92 runs.

1875 Played at Lord's, 28th June Oxford won by 6 runs.

1876 Played at Lord's, 26th June Cambridge won by 9 wickets.

1877 Played at Lord's, 25th JuneOxford won by 10 wickets.

1878 Played at Lord's, 1st July Cambridge won by 238 runs.

1879 Played at Lord's, 1st July Cambridge won by 9 wickets.

1880 Played at Lord's, 28th June Cambridge won by 115 runs.

1881 Played at Lord's, 27th June Oxford won by 135 runs.

1882 Played at Lord's, 26th June Cambridge won by 7wickets.

1883 Played at Lord's, 25th June Cambridge won by 7 wickets.

1884 Played at Lord's, 30th June Oxford won by 7 wickets.

1885 Played at Lord's, 29th JuneCambridge won by 7 wickets.

1886 Played at Lord's, 5th July Oxford won by 133runs.

1887 Played at Lord's, 4th July Oxford won by 7wickets.

1888 Played at Lord's, 28th June Drawn.

1889 Played at Lord's, 1st July Cambridge won by an innings and 105 runs.

1890 Played at Lord's, 30th June Cambridge won by 7 wickets.

Matches played 56: Cambridge won 28, Oxford won 25, drawn 3.

8

Batting

I should like to say that good batsmen are born, not made; but my long experience comes up before me, and tells me that it is not so. There are gifts of eye and wrist which nearly all good batsmen possess in a greater or lesser degree that enable them to play certain strokes with great effect; but, to acquire all-round proficiency, I am strongly convinced that constant practice and sound coaching have all to do with it. I try to remember the time when I first handled a bat, and I can recall nothing but the advice that was drilled into me – stand well up to the wicket; keep your left shoulder well forward; practise constantly and put your whole heart into it.

Opinions vary as to the qualifications a player must possess to be classed as a first-class batsman, and I fear always will vary. Some of the players I have met possessed a beautifully free style, and gave the impression of being able to score largely; but somehow the runs never came. Some had a cramped and ungainly style, which provoked severe comments; but nevertheless the runs did come. Then there were others who kept up their wickets for hours for very small scores; while opposite them were free-hitters who made more runs in a tenth part of the time.

Now it will not do to say that all of them may not be described as first-class batsmen. To score 50 runs off one's own bat in an hour is a very fast rate of scoring, and if it be done in a free, hard-hitting style always commands our admiration. To score the same number in two or three hours by patient defence and quiet placing may not receive the same amount of praise, but under certain conditions it may be a more valuable innings to one's side. I do not sympathise with the batsman who plays only to keep up his wicket, and does not try to hit; but I do sympathise with those who, not possessing great hitting powers, keep adding quietly, though slowly, to the score as best they can.

I am now speaking to the young player, and will touch upon details that are too often neglected when he begins to play.

It may be safely laid down that the duty of a batsman is to make runs, and that he who can make them quickly or slowly as occasion requires belongs to the very highest class.

First let me urge upon him to practise in earnest from the outset, and if possible to get his first lesson from an experienced player. He need not have it from one who in his time made his hundreds against the finest bowling in England, and who talks about the glories of the past; a humbler individual, who has a real love for the game, will often be of more use, and will not be averse to showing how it is done. He has, in all likelihood, been through the mill himself, and knows that nothing short of patient practice will lead to success. That is the teacher worth listening to; but the pupil should not be content with his help alone. He should seek for every opportunity to witness the great players of the day, and watch their styles attentively, so that he may have both example and precept.

One of the first essentials to the making of a good batsman is a good wicket. There are very few schools of any importance now without a cricket ground, and the pitch is generally well looked after; but there are hundreds of beginners living in the country who are not so favoured, and who have to look after the pitch themselves. Let me impress on them the great need of doing so. I have said elsewhere that I cannot remember when we had not a good pitch at home; but let me say also that its condition was entirely owing to our own efforts. Many an hour we spent rolling it; and we had our reward. Once you have played on a good wicket, you will never be satisfied with an indifferent one.

You will be singularly fortunate if you have a piece of ground of any size at your home; but it is not absolutely necessary that it should be very large. 30 to 40 yards long, by 15 to 20 broad, with stop-nets, will serve your purpose; and it will not be a disadvantage at that stage of your progress to be told that, for other than cricket reasons, you must keep the ball down when you hit. And you need not worry if the whole of the ground is not turfed over. As long as you have 10 yards in good condition, carefully rolled in front of the wicket you are batting at, you have all that is needed for satisfactory practice.

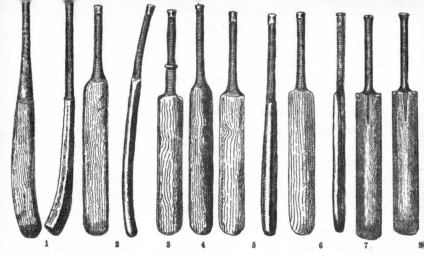

The drawings of bats 1 to 6 are taken by permission from *Echoes from Old Cricket Fields* by Mr F. Gale. The approximate dates are as follows: No. 1, 1743; No. 2, weighing 5lbs, 1771; No. 3, 1790 – This is a double-handed bat and belonged to Robinson, a man with a crippled hand who wore an iron strapped to his wrist; No. 4, marked on the back *1792*, and named 'Little Joey', belonged to Ring of Dartford, an old hambledon man, to whose style of play is attributed the origin of the law l. b.-w.; No. 5, weighing about 2¾ lbs, 1800; No. 6, marked on back with brass bands 1827 – belonged to John Bowyer, and weighed about 2¾ lbs; Nos 7 and 8 are in my possession, and are of present date: they weigh 2 lbs, 5½ ozs, and illustrate the plan of splicing, No. 7 in addition showing the whale-bone. Figures 1, 2, 5, 6 and 8, show the front and edge of bat, and figures 3, 4, and 7, front only.

Always play with a bat suited to your strength and height. Every boy longs for a full-sized bat, and thinks it a reproach to practise with anything else. I can assure you that you are going the wrong way to acquire a correct style if your wish be gratified, and may get into faulty habits that will stick to you all your life. Youth is the impressionable time for both mental and physical training, and in the majority of cases it is more difficult to unlearn than learn.

You may not always be able to get a bat the weight you desire, and very little mischief may result from playing with 1, 2 or 3 ounces too heavy, for weight does not affect your playing straight or driving properly; but it is better to err on the side of having one too light, for with a heavy one you cannot cut or time the ball correctly. A full-sized bat in the hands of a boy who is not very tall is an unwieldy weapon, and destructive of a free, sound style; and it is impossible to play straight with it. Is there any need for me to say that playing with a straight bat is more likely to protect your wicket than playing with a cross bat? If you have any doubt about it, get some one to hold a bat both ways in front of a wicket, and see for yourself which style covers it most.

As a rule, you will find that a bat is about the proper length for your height when you can ground it properly, and play perfectly straight while holding it about the middle of the handle, which is considered the best place to grip both for defensive and offensive purposes. A few stone wall players and some others play with the right hand close to the shoulder; but this, while admittedly good for defence, will undoubtedly cramp your hitting. E. F. S. Tylecote was the best first-class player I ever met who held the bat in that way. Going to the other extreme of holding it at the top of the handle will admit of loftier and more vigorous hitting, but it will weaken your defence. I believe in holding it with the right hand about half way up, and the left just above it. With the hands in that position you are able to defend your wicket against all kinds of bowling and still hit freely.

While you are waiting for the ball, make sure that the hands are in the right position; grip the handle firmly, and keep the left shoulder well forward, or you will never play with a straight bat. But try to get some one to show you how to hold the bat and place the hands, and you will in 5 minutes get a better idea of the right and wrong ways of doing it than you would get in an hour from the most elaborate treatise ever written on batting. Indeed, this advice might be applied to many other details, as it is difficult to give a clear idea without drawings.

The next point is a very important one where and how to stand at the wicket. It makes very little difference whether you take guard to cover middle stump or middle and leg; but the position of the feet cannot be too carefully studied and practised. Place the right foot just inside the crease, and make sure that the toes are clear of the wicket. The left foot should be outside the crease, clear of the wicket, at a distance to enable you to stand easily and move it backward or forward comfortably. Some players, and good players too, place the foot in front of the wicket; but that I am certain is a mistake, and with a bad umpire at the bowler's end may cause you to lose your wicket. The players themselves will be the first to tell you it is a bad

habit; but it was one they acquired in their boyhood, and it has stuck
to them since.

You must not go to the other extreme of standing too wide of the
wicket, or you will give the bowler an opening to bowl you off your
pads. I have always tried to keep my feet clear of the wicket, but so close
that it was impossible for a ball to get past between the pads and the
wicket. Sometimes I have drawn a line from the leg stump to the crease,
so that I might see at a glance if my feet were clear, and it is not a bad
habit for a young player to cultivate. Once he has got into the habit of
standing correctly, he may drop doing it in a match, although I believe
in taking every precaution whether practising or playing in a match.

Take your block a little more than a length of the bat from the
wicket, and be sure to make a good mark so that you will not lose
sight of it. If after playing for a little while it gets worn and dim, do
not hesitate to ask the umpire to give it to you again.

You are now ready to play the ball, and will ground your bat in the
block hole when the bowler begins his run. One or two writers say:
'Stand with your weight equally balanced on both legs.' That I believe
to be a grave mistake. The weight should be chiefly on the right leg,
and kept there when you raise your bat to play the ball. For want
of that being constantly drilled into the learner's head, he too often
moves the right foot, which is opposed to all good play. Anything that
will cause you to move the right foot when defending your wicket
should be avoided, and I am inclined to think that standing with your
weight equally balanced on both legs has a tendency that way. In fact,
I believe it to be good advice that the beginner's right foot should be
pegged down for some time, until he acquire ease and confidence in
playing back and forward.

Another mistake committed is twirling or flourishing the bat after
you have raised it from the block hole, preparatory to hitting or
playing the ball. It serves no practical purpose, unless it be to cover
your nervousness, and it is decidedly bad form. You have all your
work cut out to keep your eye on the bowler's arm, and flourishing the
bat does not help you; besides, I very much question if you can come
down so quickly on a shooter with the bat constantly on the move, as
you can holding it quietly a few inches from the ground.

And now we come to the first and important stage in the art of
batting how to keep up your wicket. That must be the aim of the

beginner; for no one will ever score largely and consistently who cannot do it. It is better a thousand times to be able to keep your wicket up for an hour, even if you only score 10 runs, than to make the same number of runs in the first over and be bowled the next. I admit that the addition to the total score is the same; but 10 runs in an hour, if made by the first or fifth man of your side, are worth double that number made in a couple of overs; for in all probability you will have taken the sting out of the bowling, and paved the way for the batsmen who follow.

The art of defence may be summed up thus: the power to play both forward and back. It was not an uncommon thing years ago to hear it said of this and that player, 'Oh, he plays everything back, and is wonderfully strong and patient in his defence.' If you had asked, 'Cannot he play forward also?' you would very likely have been told that he did not trouble about it, and that the wicket was too rough and bumpy to attempt it; besides, he had such a long reach that the balls he could not play back to he could invariably hit. Now if anyone were to make that statement today, he might escape ridicule, but believe me he would be very quickly classed as a second-rate batsman. The wickets are now too good to be used as an excuse, while so accurate has become the bowling, that a batsman who could only play back would very quickly get stuck up, and be caught at point or short-slip.

Both styles of play must be cultivated, and until the beginner has acquired proficiency in them his defence will be very imperfect. The grand essential is to keep the right foot firm and play with a straight bat. If you are compelled to play back, you will have to draw back the left foot; but on no account must you move the right. That you must keep as firm as if it were riveted to the ground, or you will very likely be driven on to your wicket. And do not forget to keep your left shoulder well forward and come down on the ball with firmness.

The great secret of good back play is a quick eye and watching the ball. Perhaps the bowler is bowling round the wicket, and you have taken guard for middle-stump. He may bowl on the off stump a ball not far enough up to play forward to, but with sufficient break to hit the leg stump; you will then have to change quickly to protect it. Or the ball may have break enough to hit the pads and cannon on to the wicket, if you are not quick enough with eye and wrist to meet it. Be sure to grip the bat firmly, and have the handle sloping slightly

Mr W. G. Grace.
(*Batting position
as the bowler starts
to bowl.*)

forward, and be on the look-out for an occasional shooter. They do not come so often as they used to, but that makes them all the more dangerous when they do come.

Whatever you do, do not get in front of the wicket when you play the ball. There is no need to give that bit of advice as long as you keep the right foot firm and in the position I have already advised you to place it when standing at the wicket; but unfortunately there are a few of our very finest batsmen today who step right in front to most balls, whose example you may be tempted to follow. You cannot be too much on your guard against it; for, sooner or later, a bowler with a good head on his shoulders will get a ball past your bat, and you will have to pay the penalty of lbw. There are others who get in front when the ball is pitched just outside the leg stump in trying to play it hard to square-leg. My experience has shown me that it is unnecessary even then, and that by keeping your right foot firmly in its place and drawing back the left until the heels are almost touching, you can resort to what is called the glide stroke and place the ball to leg.

To play forward, you must advance the left leg; but must take care not to over-reach yourself, or you will move the right foot. Keeping the right foot on the ground is even more important in playing forward than playing back; for you have to remember that it is just on the edge of the crease, and the slightest movement may cause you to lift it, and if you miss the ball a smart wicketkeeper will stump you before you can recover yourself. You can find out for yourself, by practising at a wicket without a bowler, how far you can reach with safety without dragging the right foot.

Another very important thing to remember in playing forward is, never to place the bat further forward than the level of the left foot, and to be sure to have the handle of it slanting, so that the top of it is nearer than the blade to the bowler. Upon that will depend whether you meet the ball firmly and correctly. Try to have the bat as close to the left leg as you can with safety, so that if the ball should break slightly back, it will not pass between the bat and the pads.

Forward and back play are the two strokes you must rely on to protect your wicket, and you must practise them diligently. Occasionally you will get a ball which puts you in two minds, and, for want of decision to play one way or the other, it may either beat you altogether, or cause you to play it in a half-hearted way and be caught. I have invariably found that when that occurred with me I had either been careless in watching the bowler's arm, or that he had deceived me by altering his pace without a change of action. Spofforth and Lohmann are good at that, and have taken in many batsmen the first time they bowled against them.

When that experience comes, you will have to be quick to get out of the difficulty; there is only one way that I know of, and that is, to meet it with the half-cock stroke. You have made up your mind to play forward, and taken the initial step; but at the last moment you find that the ball is going to pitch shorter than you at first thought. You must rely on your arms to extricate you from the difficulty by drawing back the bat until it is just over the popping-crease, a few inches from the ground. Drawing back the left foot alone will not help you; therefore concentrate upon a rapid use of the arms

I shall now enumerate the wickets upon which I have found forward play and back play most effective.

1. A fast, dry and true wicket.
2. A fast, good wet wicket.
3. A slow, good wicket after rain.
4. A drying sticky wicket.

On a fast, dry and true wicket I never hesitate to play forward; for the bowler can get little or no work on the ball, and, what is more, the further it is pitched up and the faster it comes along the easier it is to play forward to it. My scores of 344 for MCC *v.* Kent, and 318 not out for Gloucestershire *v.* Yorkshire, in 1876, were made on wickets of that kind, and I played forward to nearly every good-length ball.

I carry out the same principle on a fast, good wet wicket; for the bowler has much difficulty in getting work on the ball, owing to its wet, slippery state: but I watch the ball more carefully, for I know it will occasionally keep low and travel faster after it pitches, while shooters occur more frequently than on a dry wicket.

On a slow, good wicket after rain the bowler can get more work on the ball than on a good, fast wicket; but the ball does not come so quickly off the pitch, and it rarely rises higher than the bails. You can play either back or forward on a wicket of that kind, according to the pitch of the ball; but in playing forward you must not play too quickly, as the ball sometimes hangs a bit, and you may play it back to the bowler. Turner beat me with his second ball in that way in the first innings of the England *v.* Australia match at Lord's on the 21st July, 1890; and I candidly confess I felt, and I daresay looked, particularly foolish over it. Playing a little too soon at the ball, which got up and hung, I met it on the shoulder of the bat, and an easy catch to Turner followed. In the second innings the wicket was much faster, and I felt quite at home and played forward with perfect confidence.

Back play is most effective on a drying sticky wicket. That is about the worst you can play on; for the ball not only gets up high, but the bowler can get a great amount of work on it, and you have no course but to watch it until the last moment and play back to it. Keep your eye on the bowler; watch how he holds the ball and runs up to the wicket before delivering it, and you may be able to detect any alteration in length and pace. And never get flurried whatever his action may be; for if you take your eyes off his arm or lose your head for a second, he has you at a disadvantage.

And now I come to a point which is fast becoming a characteristic of all good batsmen; and that is, playing the ball with the bat, and not allowing the ball to hit the bat. Your forward play and back play may be perfect; but if you can only stop the ball, you will never belong to the ranks of first-class batsmen. Make an effort to play the ball away from you with some force, and with practice you will do it as readily as merely stopping it and allowing it to roll a yard or two away. In Chapter III I pointed out that it was years before I gained sufficient command of the bat to enable me to place the ball where I wished. At first I was content to be able to play it away anywhere; but with constant practice I gained the power of placing it between the fieldsmen.

I firmly believe most players can do the same if they only try hard enough. Eye and wrist will respond when the brain commands; but here and there you may find a batsman who seems to be able to do better than another. Timing the ball is the secret of all good play; and timing, as far as I can make out, means the harmonious working of eye, wrist, arms, legs, and shoulders, which can only be acquired by constant practice.

It may be said that keeping up one's wicket is all very well, but what about hitting and the making of runs? Well, let me tell you that if you can keep up your wicket and play the ball hard away from you, runs will come. There is a variety of hits that ought to be touched upon, such as the cut, the leg-hit, the drive, etc.; but they almost demand a treatise to themselves.

Of the cut, the most charming of all strokes, because it seems to be made with very little effort, I may say that it depends entirely on the perfect timing of the ball. The right foot should be moved to the front of the off stump, and the stroke should be made with the wrist when the ball is about a foot in front of the wicket. Half the secret of good cutting consists in hitting slightly over the ball, which will cause it to touch the ground at a short distance from the wicket without affecting its speed. The batsman should not be satisfied that it is a genuine cut unless the ball travels more in the direction of longslip than point; of course, I am speaking of a fast good-length ball, a little outside the off stump. A longhop should be hit hard between point and mid-off with a horizontal bat, and the batsman should advance the left leg in front of the wicket in doing it; or if the ball is not very wide, he should draw back the right foot: that is one of Mr W. W. Read's best strokes.

There is very little leg-hitting nowadays, owing to the wonderful accuracy of the bowling. The bowler, as a rule, has eight men on the off side of the wicket, and very seldom bowls to leg. Occasionally you may get a half-volley on the pads, or slightly inside of them; but that should be driven between short-leg and mid-on, instead of pulled to leg. When you get a good-length ball, or one a little over-pitched, just outside of the pads, the proper way to treat it is to throw out the left leg and hit as near to the pitch as possible with a horizontal bat, but be careful not to get under the ball; if it is a long-hop, then you should draw back the left leg and hit or play it to leg.

In driving, you should aim at getting well over the ball and playing with a straight bat, and not be satisfied unless you keep the ball well down. Of course you will notice if the fieldsmen are too close in, or if the boundaries are short, and may risk something in lofty hitting instead of driving. It used to be considered by some very good players bad cricket to hit a straight ball, whatever the length of it. On the faith of it, Wootton and Grundy, two of the very best bowlers of their time, placed all their fieldsmen, with the exception of long-leg, close in, and treated the batsmen to an occasional long-hop or half-volley with perfect complacence. I believe my brother E. M. was the first to upset that theory by hitting the ball as hard as he could over the bowler's head, or to longon, and not troubling about the flight of it. I considered the example a good one and followed in his footsteps, and I do the same thing today under similar circumstances; but you very seldom have the chance now, as all bowlers have one or two men in the long field.

The great thing in hitting is, not to be half-hearted about it; but when you make up your mind to hit, to do it as if the whole match depended upon that particular stroke. That applies especially to slow round-arm or lob bowling. The fear of being stumped has deterred many a man from running out far enough, and a weak hit, followed by a catch, is the result. You may as well be hanged for a sheep as a lamb; so go out with a will, hit hard, and forget there is a wicketkeeper or fieldsman within a mile of you.

It is a mistake to hit at the pitch of slow round or underhand bowling. There is generally sufficient twist on the ball to beat you, and if you do not miss it altogether, you will most likely get caught at coverpoint. And the same may be said of a mediumpace good-length ball on the off stump, breaking slightly away from you. In my younger days, when I was quicker of foot than now, I often ran out to slow round and underhand bowling, and hit the ball full pitch, or waited and got it long-hop. I still consider it good play, and there is no doubt it has a demoralising effect on some bowlers.

There are two or three other hits that I might allude to; but those I have touched on are the principal ones, and the beginner should practise them as often as he can. He should also make a point of watching every first-class batsman, and make a note of his characteristic strokes. Very rarely will he find two batsmen hit in the same way, and it is always of interest to note where they differ. I also think it useful in practice to indulge in an occasional burst of hard hitting, but always try to keep the ball well down.

Judgment as to how and when to run is one of the characteristics of a good batsman. You should always back up 2 or 3 yards, but not before the ball is delivered, or the bowler may put down the wicket and run you out. Remember that it is the striker's duty to call if the ball is hit in front of the wicket, and the non-striker's, as a rule, if hit behind the wicket. When you call for a run, shout in a decided manner. Run hard directly your partner calls you, if you intend to go; if not, stop him at once. The great thing is to make up your mind instantly, and you will then be seldom run out. Do not run up the centre of the pitch, as you will cut it up; and to avoid collisions you and your partner should each, if possible, run on his own side, and certainly not cross more than once.

'Always run for a catch' is an old adage, and very good advice if the run is an easy one; but if there is any chance of a run-out, you should never do so. Never fail to run your bat along the ground for a yard or two before you reach the popping-crease. Many a batsman would have saved his wicket had he taken this precaution; for want of it, many have been run out. The first run should always be at your top speed: but do not rush past the wicket as some do; turn quickly, and be ready for another. When a ball is hit to the long field, and both batsmen are on the 'lookout,' a second run can often be obtained if the fieldsman fumbles the ball or throws it in slowly. It is astonishing what a sharp run can be made with safety by two good men who understand each other; when it is repeated two or three times, the field often becomes demoralised, and by mistakes and reckless throwing-in adds many runs to the score. A good example of this was shown last year by S. M. J. Woods and G. McGregor, who, for Lord Londesborough's eleven *v.* Australians, almost played tip-and-run for a few overs, and put on 24 runs for the last wicket.

There are many other points to be considered, such as knowing when to play a slow, patient game, or a forcing game; but these are the growth of time, and an experienced captain considers it a part of his duties to point them out to you. Just let me say that the prominent characteristic of all first-class batsmen is consistency in scoring. They display the same carefulness after having made a hundred runs as they do after scoring ten. Try to follow in their footsteps; for that is the only way to score largely. And never grumble if you have a run of ill-luck and fail to score heavily for weeks in succession. It is an experience which comes to us all at some time or other, and he is made of sterling stuff, and a real lover of our grand old game, who accepts it cheerfully. And always be modest in the hour of success.

I ought to have said something about the young batsman's outfit. Too little attention is paid to that by fairly good coaches; but, believe me, bad-fitting boots, or boots without proper spikes, may make all the difference in your play. No good cricketer is careless on that point; for he knows well that he must feel at ease, if he hopes to be at all successful. Pads that do not fit comfortably will tire you as much as hard hitting, and you should make sure before you begin your innings that they are carefully strapped, and not likely to get loose.

Gloves are even more important, and if they do not fit nicely, will affect your hitting. No player of any eminence now bats without a right-hand glove at least; but I strongly advocate both right and left being used. And you cannot be too careful about the quality of the rubber; for a blow on the back of the hand or fingers when imperfectly covered, will play sad havoc with your scoring, and may stop your cricket for some time. You should also make sure that the fastenings are all right, as carelessness there will make the hands uncomfortable; and a loose, flapping glove may be the cause of your losing your wicket, as the ball is more likely to hit a glove of that description than one firmly fastened.

And a belt instead of a scarf is sometimes an element of danger. The handle of the bat may come in contact with the buckle, and the noise be mistaken by the umpire for a snick off the bat. In fact, I once saw a man given out in that way. The ball passed so close to the bat, that the umpire, hearing a snick, thought it must have touched it; and, on being appealed to, unhesitatingly gave him out.

9

Bowling

The majority of cricket writers whose opinions are worth reading are agreed that a first-class bowler is born, not made, and my experience of cricket has confirmed the truth of it. I have met but few bowlers in the first flight who did not possess the natural gift of making the ball come more quickly off the pitch than one would expect; but not one can tell how he does this. Mr M. Kempson, whose bowling helped the Gentlemen to beat the Players in 1853, is of opinion that the secret of bowling is incommunicable, but a gift improvable by practice to any degree of perfection. I am not going to cry down perseverance and energy, for I owe too much to them; but I repeat, a first-class bowler must have the inestimable something which enables him to begin bowling as naturally as a duck takes to water. Afterwards it depends entirely on himself whether he is to make a great name or not. There is only one way of doing that, and it is by sheer hard work with muscle and brain.

Physical strength alone will not do on the perfect wickets we have nowadays: it must be accompanied with a good head. How often have we heard it said of this and the other bowler that he has not come up to the promise of his youth, although he has been a most diligent and exemplary worker! We have no need to go far for an explanation: it all lies in the not uncommon experience that he has the misfortune to be lacking in brain power, and will never be other than a member of the ding-dong 'stuff-em-in' type if he were to practise for a hundred years. He can do what he is told, bowl straight and keep a good length; but he has not the power to read the batsman's thoughts, or the ingenuity to find out his weakness. He will always be a good change bowler, but will never reach the first class.

Several things should be impressed on the young bowler when he begins, but the following in particular:

1. Bowl straight.
2. Bowl a good length.
3. Vary your pace and pitch.
4. Try to get some break on the ball.
5. Learn something about the nature and condition of the wicket on which you are bowling.
6. Seek for the weak spots in the batsman's defence.

Anybody can bowl fairly straight is a truism; but how many can do it without tiring quickly? The young bowler should be taught to begin at 18 or 20 yards, a distance at which he can bowl without overextending himself, and not be satisfied unless he can hit the stumps pretty often. The length of run he must find out for himself; but one great point he must observe not to stop for a second when he reaches the crease before he delivers the ball. I have seen a good many bowlers do that, who could only account for it by the fact that they had been taught badly and could not help doing it. Well, it is a very bad habit, for half the benefit of the run is lost. The young bowler should be corrected every time he does it. Years ago I rather fancied a short run, believing it tired the bowler less; but I have changed my opinion, and would advise something between 6 and 10 yards or more. Nearly all the good bowlers we have today, no matter their pace, take a longish run, and the giants of the past did the same thing. Mr S. M. J. Woods, Lohmann, Briggs, Peel and Attewell are the most prominent of our English bowlers at present, and all take a good run; and the Australians, Messrs Spofforth, Boyle, Turner and Ferris, do the same.

The young player cannot do better than watch first-class bowlers carefully, make a note of their styles, and mark their points of difference.

Another point that used to be urged strongly was to present a full front to the batsman at the moment the ball left the hand. That has been considerably modified of late years, and there are now more advocates for a side position. Presenting a full front means that the bowler's arm can be seen plainly before the ball leaves the hand a point in favour of the batsman; a side position means that arm and hand are hidden until the last moment a point in favour of the bowler. I could mention the names of half a dozen bowlers, of whom it has been said that their delivery was a most puzzling one, and that it was pretty much owing to their being able to keep their arm out of sight. Of others, again, it has been said: 'We have no difficulty with them we can see them all the way.'

I am not advocating the cultivation of a style merely for the purpose of distracting the attention of the batsman; but I would point out the great success that has attended such bowlers as Messrs C. A. Smith, Spofforth, Giffen and Ferris, who have peculiar deliveries. When Smith begins his run he is behind the umpire and out of sight of the batsman; and I can assure you it is rather startling when he suddenly appears at the bowling crease. Spofforth goes to the other extreme, starting some yards on the off-side of the batsman, and giving the impression that he is aiming at a point nearer short-leg than the wicket. G. Giffen is even more tantalising; for, just before the ball leaves his hand, his arm is completely hidden, and there is more of his back than his face to be seen. Ferris, the left-hander, starts his long run with his bowling-hand close to his leg; when he has got over 3 or 4 yards he brings both hands together almost on a level with his chin, and looks as if he were kissing the tips of his fingers to the crowd. Down goes the hand again, another trot of 4 yards and he brings his hands together above his head; and just as you get a little bit excited and wonder when he is really going to bowl, his arm disappears behind, to reappear with startling rapidity to deliver the ball. J. C. Shaw, the famous left-hander, also puzzled most batsmen the first over or two. He brought his arm from behind his back, and caused me a lot of trouble in the early part of most innings I played against him. I could name many others who want careful watching; but those I have given are sufficient to prove what I say that the bowler who delivers the ball sideways is more difficult to watch than the bowler who delivers it with a full front.

The next point to be considered is the height of the arm in delivering the ball. It may now be safely accepted that above the shoulder is more effective than under it; in fact, the higher the better. If the wicket be at all fast, the ball invariably comes quicker off the pitch, rises higher, and is more likely to lead to a catch. However, care must be taken to bowl with a free arm, or there will be very little sting or 'devil' as it is called in the ball. Most of the great fast bowlers of the past had a beautiful arm action, and have not been surpassed in that respect by Lohmann, Turner, or Sharpe three of the most prominent bowlers we have at the present time.

George Freeman, the best fast bowler I ever played against, had a lovely free action, though he did not raise his arm much above the shoulder. He did not appear so fast as he really was; but he made the ball come quickly off the pitch, and he took many wickets with balls that kept low. John Jackson was slightly before my time, but his arm action delighted me the little I saw of it. Tarrant, with his long run all over the place, was another: then there was Allen Hill, whose beautiful delivery was a model for all time. Martin McIntyre, with his head-over-heels action, though not in the same bowling class as Freeman and Jackson, got up his pace entirely owing to his freedom of arm; and Mold and Sharpe, of the present time, are worthy of being watched. And among the amateurs may be mentioned, Messrs C. D. Marsham, Foord-Kelcey, Christopherson, A. H. Evans, R. Lipscomb, and S. M. J. Woods.

The young bowler must not think because he can bowl straight that he is worthy of taking his place among good bowlers. He is still in the very elementary stage and not out of the alphabet of the game. A good length is the next thing to be studied, and though I have put it second on the list, it is really the key-note to all good bowling. Delivery, break, and pace are much to be desired, but without length they are utterly useless. There are some bowlers who, by their wonderful accuracy of length, stick up the batsmen and get wickets on the most perfect grounds, and I need only mention Attewell, who is without a superior today, as a fine example of what I refer to. Good wickets reduce most bowlers to a level, and it is only the good-length and head bowlers who can do anything on them. Willsher was past his best when I met him; but though he had lost much of his break and pace, he still kept a grand length, and was successful up to the last day he played. Break and pace may go, and very often do go earlier than one could wish, but as long as a bowler preserves his length he can do good work in most elevens.

A good-length ball may be described as one which very often finds the batsmen in two minds. He is in doubt whether to play forward or back to it, and while he is deciding, either the ball beats him altogether, or he spoons it to a fieldsman close in. It is difficult to say exactly the distance it should pitch from the batsman's wicket, but the opinion of very good and experienced players is, that for slow bowling it should pitch about 4 yards from the wicket; for medium pace, 4½ yards to 5; for fast, from 5 to 7. Of course the quality of the batsman will always have to be considered; for what may be a good-length ball to a batsman with a short reach, will be almost a half-volley to a tall player possessing an exceptionally long reach. The beginner cannot do better, however, than to put a mark, say a feather or a piece of paper, at either of the distances I have mentioned, according to his pace, and practise diligently. Anything pitched within a foot of it will be a good-length ball, and will test the defence of any batsman.

I said that the young bowler should begin at a distance suited to his strength. Let me now press upon him the greater need not to exceed his strength when he is able to bowl the full length. Promising bowlers have been ruined for want of that caution, especially among the amateurs. The temptation to bowl just a little faster ought to be repressed rather than encouraged, for it is fatal to success and not unlikely to lead to a breakdown. Find out exactly what you can do in practice without tiring, and stick to it. It is a rule that cannot be too strongly taken to heart in learning; for on our vastly improved wickets today the innings are of longer duration, and the physical strain demanded of a first-class bowler is greater than at any time since the game began. I need only allude to the exceptionally hard work which Turner and Ferris went through for the Australian elevens which came to us in 1888 and 1890. It would not have surprised anyone if either had broken down. Every player aiming at becoming a really good bowler for his county must face the fact that he may have to bowl for hours and days at a time, and that bowling above his strength will wear him out and lead to short-length balls which the most indifferent batsman can play with ease.

Vary your pace is my next bit of advice. That does not mean you are to bowl a lot of balls faster than you are in the habit of doing, but rather that you are to resort to slower ones. Of course you will indulge in a fast one occasionally; but remember that you will find it easier to keep your good length in attempting a slower one. You must try to hide a change of action in your delivery, or an acute batsman will at once perceive it, and be on his guard. The great Australian bowlers are very good at bowling a slower or faster ball without a perceptible change of action.

Spofforth, in particular, was a master of the art, and I question if anyone has surpassed him since. He was most successful with his medium-pace balls, which were rather slower than his usual deliveries. There was the same run, the same action, the same elevation; and so completely was the batsman deceived that he played seconds too soon and was completely beaten. Palmer was another who was very successful in the same way; and Alfred Shaw was for years the chief among English bowlers in that respect. Shaw was a model of beautiful style and accurate length, and, at his best, could stick up the best batsmen in England. His change of pace was generally to a slower ball; and now and then he changed his elevation, a device which put the batsman in two minds.

Lohmann today is equally effective; and it is simply ludicrous to watch batsman after batsman walk into the trap. After the trick was done one could not help saying, 'What an absurdly simple ball to have been bowled by!' but, all the same, it was a triumph of the bowler's art.

Try to get some break on the ball. That is the next stage for the young bowler, and must be acquired if he desires to reach the first class. There are times when the wicket is perfection, and straight good-length balls have little effect against a first-rate batsman. He keeps playing them with a straight bat, hoping to tire the bowler out, when loose ones will come and the runs with them. Professional batting is improved all round; but its strongest point is the unwearied patience and strong defence of its finest representatives. If the young bowler thinks he will tire out a Shrewsbury, a Gunn – I shall not say a Scotton – he is hugely mistaken; and if he has nothing but straight good-length balls in his attack, he may make up his mind for a long day's work.

As soon as he has mastered length, he must try to add to his skill the power of breaking the ball, and then he may safely believe that he is within measurable distance of becoming first class. The amount of break he can get on the ball will depend very much on his pace. Should he be fast he must not hope for too much, for the two rarely go together. Slow and medium-pace bowlers do most at that, and get from one inch to two feet on a favourable wicket. A very important point is, whatever amount one does put on, to try to have sufficient command of the ball so that if it beat the batsman it will hit the wicket. It is a confession of weakness trying to put on 6 inches and find it breaking 12, beating the batsman and yet missing the wicket.

I have seen Spofforth, time after time, vary his break from 3 to 12 inches the same over, and every time the ball got past the batsman it hit the wicket. No greater compliment can be paid to any bowler, for his ability to do it shows that he has perfect command of the ball. If the bowler be right-handed, he breaks, as a rule, from the off; if left-handed, generally from leg. Here and there you may find a phenomenon who can do it both ways; but then he is a phenomenon, and one does not write for that class of bowler.

The state of the wicket has much to do with the amount of break to be obtained. When it is dry and hard you must be content with very little indeed; but after heavy rains, with a strong sun drying it, you may be able to perform wonders. A. G. Steel and Spofforth among the amateurs, Peate, Alfred Shaw and J. C. Shaw among the professionals, used to perform great things then, the amount of curl they got on being simply astonishing. Mr D. Buchanan, Jimmy Southerton and Barratt belonged to that school; and Messrs Turner and Ferris, and Peel and Briggs, of our own time, are very effective also.

The next point to be considered is: learn something about the nature and condition of the wicket on which you are bowling. Nothing shows the experienced captain so much as the thought he exercises before a match. Before he has tossed for choice of innings, he has examined the wicket carefully, taken into consideration the changes which are likely to occur during the next hour or two, and deliberated whether they will be in favour of the batsman or the bowler. Surely it is not too much to expect the bowler, upon whom so much depends, to give the same thought.

Remember it is a very old saying that 'a match well made is half won'. There are very few grounds on which a bowler may not find one end more helpful than the other. Perhaps there is a slight slope which will enable him to get a great deal of twist on the ball, or a spot that will cause it to kick and rise quickly off the pitch. Not to find that out before the match begins means that the bowler has failed to do his duty to his side, and lacks one of the characteristics of a first-class player.

Old Nyren says in his treatise of the game: 'Contrive, if fortune so favour you, that your bowler shall bowl his first ball *when a cloud is passing over.*' I have never been able to have the cloud passing when I bowled my first ball – indeed, I have rarely noticed the cloud passing at all – but on more than one occasion I have observed a distracting glare or leafy tree behind one of the wickets, and I always took particular care to put my most deadly bowler on at that end. Now, if a captain can notice these among the multitude of things he has to consider, surely a bowler ought to. Then there are some grounds on which the ball bounds higher than others, and a short-pitched one cannot be pulled very easily. That is something to know when you put in a faster one occasionally and cannot be so sure of your length. Lord's Ground was of that nature not so many years ago, and Wootton and Grundy, who knew every foot of it, never hesitated to bowl a little bit short. There are many other points of detail which a bowler ought to know, but I need not enumerate them. I have said sufficient to make the bowler think for himself, if he possess the thinking faculties; if he does not, he may as well give up the hope of ever becoming first-class.

And that brings me to my last point – seek for the weak spot in the batsman's defence. There are very few batsmen without one, and the sooner you find it out the better for your side and yourself. No one plays the first over or two with the same confidence he shows after he has been batting for a quarter of an hour, and if you can only spot his weakness and lay siege to it, then you have an excellent chance of getting him out. It used to be considered a very good plan to bowl a yorker to a batsman immediately he came in, on the assumption, I believe, that he would not be ready for it. A straight half-volley was also thought likely to find him half-hearted in hitting, and a catch sure to follow. Now most batsmen have made up their minds to get either of those balls early in their innings, and you must not be disappointed if you fail to succeed with it. One thing I can tell you: it is a huge mistake to give him a short one. It is the one ball which he can see best of all, and he rarely fails to play it. Repeat it, and you have given him a favourable start, and will have some difficulty in finding his weak spot and getting him out.

It is better a thousand times to bowl an over-pitched ball than a short one at any time of his innings. You cannot do better than begin in your usual way, aiming at a good-length straight ball, and not attempting too much. If you find that he is playing confidently, then you may change your tactics and tempt him to hit. You need not be disheartened because your good balls have been played so easily, for there are more ways of getting a batsman out than bowling him. The mistake is too often made of pegging straight at the wicket to keep down the runs, trusting that the batsman will sooner or later allow one to pass him. Maiden overs are useful in their way, and serve a good purpose when they are bowled by a change bowler to give the principal bowler of his side a rest, but a really first-class bowler has something else to think about. He is played to get men out, and by hook or crook he means to do it.

Messrs Spofforth, Boyle and Ferris, of the Australians, and Mr A. G. Steel, Freeman, A. Shaw, Southerton, and Tom Emmett, were a treat to witness in that respect. They gave the batsman no rest, and tried him with every conceivable kind of ball until he made a mistake. If he had a particular hit they humoured him, but they took care to have a safe pair of hands waiting for it: if they failed to beat him with a break-back, they tried a simple straight one, or tossed a full-pitch at him; in short, did everything to prevent him from feeling at home. I remember once at Cheltenham, when playing for Gloucestershire *v.* Nottinghamshire, placing an extra man at long-leg and bowling entirely for catches, and it was amusing to find how one after another fell into the trap and were caught out. Of course I could depend on my fieldsmen, and that is a point slow and medium-pace bowlers must always consider.

Fast bowlers depend on their pace and length to beat the batsmen, slow bowlers depend principally on their fieldsmen. I am sorry to say there are exceptions here and there. More than once I have seen a medium-pace bowler deliver a goodly number of balls, all of them a good length, who thought he had done particularly well because no runs had been scored. He felt slightly hurt when it was pointed out to him that there were ten men in the field who would not mind attempting a catch and be glad to have a little more exercise than the mere promenade at the end of each over. Most big hitters lift the ball occasionally when they are given a straight half-volley, or one slightly to leg. And remember that though the old trap of bowling outside the off-stump and causing the ball to break away from the batsman is well known, very few can resist having a smack at it some time in their innings.

An article on bowling would not be complete without some reference to slow underhand, or, to use the familiar word, 'lobs'. Fast underhand and daisy-cutters are seldom seen nowadays, and would have little chance on our perfect wickets; but lobs are still as effective as ever, and there are two or three first-class batsmen who, after playing all kinds of round-arm bowling with confidence, lose their heads entirely at the sight of lobs.

The lob bowler, like the slow round-arm bowler, must depend on his field, especially on his wicketkeeper, and not mind being hit. Good men have been and will continue to be clean bowled by a ball of that kind, but for one clean bowled the lob bowler may expect half a dozen caught out or stumped. The bowler should guard against being too slow, or a quick-footed batsman will hit him full pitch; but whatever mistake he makes, he must not bowl too short. And the elevation should not be too high, or he will get hit all over the ground; although there are some batsmen who spoon a ball which is bowled straight at them before touching the ground. Of course the more break a lob bowler can get on the better, and he must be very accurate in his length. That was the great characteristic of old Clarke's lobs, the finest lob bowler we have ever had; but he also possessed the gift of making the ball come quickly off the pitch. I have it on good authority that at his best he could pitch a ball half a dozen times in succession on a spot not more than three inches in diameter; and I firmly believe that if we had a lob bowler of his quality at the present time, he would get good batsmen out even on our perfect wickets.

From what I have said the young player will gather that there is a large amount of thought required to make a first-class bowler, and that he must not expect to do brilliant things at first, even if he possess the perfection of style. Style is the foundation of a good bowler; but hard thought and constant practice are necessary to make him first-class.

10

Fielding

It has been said that anyone can field well if he looks out for every ball and tries his hardest. I do not altogether agree with that, for I have seen more than one cricketer do his very best and yet fall short of what is considered first-class form; but I am strongly of opinion that perseverance and attention are the essential points which every young fieldsman must keep in mind. In fielding, as in batting and bowling, success can only be achieved after long practice and experience. I sometimes think that our representative teams are chosen without sufficient consideration of the fitness of some of the players for the positions in the field where they are almost sure to be placed; for more than once I have noticed a man who was known to be good close in compelled to go out to the long-field, because there was no one else who could do better. Not being accustomed to that position, he could not do himself justice.

It may be safely taken for granted, then, that for one player who can go anywhere in the field with credit to himself there are a dozen, if not more, who are only fit for one position. Messrs V. E. Walker, A. N. Hornby, Geo. Strachan, and Ulyett in their best days, and Messrs A. E. Stoddart, S. M. J. Woods, and Peel and Maurice Read at the present time, may be quoted as fine illustrations of first-class all-round fieldsmen. Activity, dash and throwing-in are the qualities which are indispensable to enable a fieldsman to go anywhere. Speed and being able to throw-in well are, more or less, gifts which belong to the few; but dash and certainty are the fruits of long practice, which most players can acquire if they give their mind to them. The most of those I have named are always on the look-out and seem to know when the ball is coming their way, and pick it up and return in one action.

A lazy or indifferent fieldsman has a demoralising effect on the rest of the eleven, and is an eyesore to every lover of the game: a very bad one will, probably, lose more runs than he makes, and is better out of the team altogether. A good man may not always bat or bowl up to his best form; but, if he tries, can always save runs in the field. The young player should keep that before him, if he desires to play in good matches; for every Committee and Captain know and consider it in the selection of a team.

Before touching upon the different positions in the field, I shall mention a few points which every beginner should carry in his mind:

I.   Always be on the look-out; and use two hands, if possible.

II.   Keep your legs together when the ball is hit straight to you.

III. Do not dash in too quickly.

IV.   Pick up the ball and throw it in with one action.

V.   Throw at the wicketkeeper's head, or so that the ball will bound to the bails.

VI.   Always back up when the ball is thrown in; but do not go too near to the wicketkeeper or bowler, or you will miss it: about 8 yards is the best distance to be from each other in backing up.

VII. Always try for a catch. Impossible things are not expected of you; but you never know what you can reach until you try.

VIII. Keep your hands out of your pockets, and never wear a jacket or coat in the field. A sweater will interfere very little with your movements and keep you warm enough under all circumstances.

IX.   Do not go into the field with a cigarette or a pipe in your mouth.

X.   Go cheerfully and promptly. to whatever position the bowler or captain sends you.

XI.   If you make a mistake, do your best to rectify it.

These are golden maxims, which every player should consider carefully; but the whole secret of success lies in his trying all he can. My brother Fred and Jupp used to go after everything and try for every catch, as if the match depended on their individual efforts; and the extraordinary results which followed surprised themselves as well as others. There is no finer sight in the cricket field than a brilliant fieldsman doing his utmost; and every feat he performs meets with quick and hearty recognition by the spectators. Grounds generally are now as near as can be to perfection, and fine fielding has become comparatively easy.

The grounds of the past were not to be compared with those of today. The best pitches were, as a rule, treacherous and kicked a good deal. I do not know what might not be said of the out-fielding. It is told of Clarke's All-England eleven that, on one occasion when they played in Cornwall, one of the players flushed a covey of partridges in the long-field, so excellent was the cover. As a contrast to this it might today be said of every important ground that a wicket could be pitched on any part of it, and that a false bound in the field is the exception rather than the rule. I shall now refer to the different positions in the field, and begin with the:

Wicketkeeper

He is worthy of the first place; for there is little doubt that his is the most important and responsible position of all. He should stand so that he can take the ball immediately it passes the wicket, and at once knock the bails off if necessary.

I would refer my readers to the illustration of G. McGregor on page 146. He (as well as Blackham, the prince of wicketkeepers) stands so close that the fingers almost touch the bails. Their hands are touching each other unless the ball is wide of the wicket, and catching or stumping is done without any show or fuss. They always stand with a full front to the bowler, and seldom move the feet unless the ball is very wide.

The wicketkeeper should be always on the alert, and if he has a doubt as to whether the foot is over the crease should whip off the bails, especially when the ball is on the leg side; for he cannot always see with certainty. But should he knock the bails off when he knows the batsman is in his ground, he should replace them quietly without appealing. Nothing looks so bad in a wicketkeeper as fussiness and appealing without reason.

Until late years our amateur wicketkeepers have never been up to the form of the professional; and by good judges it has been considered owing to their habit of standing too far back, and snapping at the ball instead of taking it quietly.

The wicketkeeper should be quick to go after a ball when it is near the wicket, or when it is played to leg where there is no fieldsman, and try to save the run. He should always be behind the wicket when the ball is thrown in to him. He must not mind hard knocks; and ought to accustom himself to all kinds of bowling.

As far as hard knocks go, wicketkeepers today have reason to be thankful for improved grounds; and perhaps that may, in a degree, account for the better form shown by them.

The best amateur wicketkeepers I have met were J. Round, E. F. S. Tylecote, J. A. Bush, G. A. B. Leatham, A. Lyttelton, H. Philipson, J. McC. Blackham, G. McGregor, and A. T. Kemble. The best professionals were Lockyer, Biddulph, Finder, Plumb, Pooley, Phillips, Pilling, and Sherwin. Some took slow bowling best, some fast. Blackham, McGregor, and Lyttelton might be placed as the best of the amateurs; while Pilling was, undoubtedly, the best of the professionals. With the exception of Blackham and McGregor no amateur has been up to the form of the professionals.

Long-Stop

Long-stopping is fast becoming a thing of the past; owing to the improvement in grounds and in wicketkeeping, and bowling. A good man was wanted for that post to such fast bowlers as Sir Frederick Bathurst and Messrs Mynn, Marcon and Fellowes, especially on rough, bumpy wickets, when most of the balls kept kicking and twisting; but today the bowling is straighter, and a ball rarely gets past both batsman and wicketkeeper. I am speaking of first-class cricket: in second-class matches the wicketkeeper is not always efficient and a long-stop may be necessary. He should stand rather deep, but close enough to save a bye; and he must be a quick and accurate thrower, and never get bustled or lose his head when a sharp run is attempted. He must be quick to decide at which wicket to throw. The Revd C. H. Ridding, Mr H. Perkins, Mr H. M. Marshall and Mortlock, were the most expert long-stoppers at the time when long-stop was even of more importance than the wicketkeeper. The first-named had a wonderfully good return, and knew, as if by instinct, at which end there was the greater chance of a run-out. He stood rather on the leg side, and was very quick to back up sharp returns to the wicketkeeper.

'Hows that?'
(*From drawing by N. Felix, 1853.*)

Short-Slip

The qualities required to make a good short-slip are judgment, quickness and a safe pair of hands. He must have sound judgment to know how far to stand from the wicket according to the pace of the bowling, for the bowler does not always know. He must be quick to get to a ball coming low down or going over his head at lightning pace; and he must have a safe pair of hands, and be able to hold the ball even if he loses his balance and stumbles in reaching it. He should stand slightly stooping, with his eyes on the ball and the batsman; but not so near that he cannot see the ball properly, or he will miss all the quick snicks. The state of the wicket will always be a guide to a great extent, and he must be on the look-out for every change in the pace and flight of the ball.

The position used to be filled by the bowler when not bowling, to save him from running and over-exertion; but nowadays the post is one which gives plenty of exercise, as he has to run after most of the snicks which pass the wicketkeeper. He must back up the wicketkeeper to save overthrows, take his place when he leaves the wicket, and be able to throw smartly and accurately.

Alfred Shaw was very successful in that position, and Watson and Abel are exceptionally good at it today. Lohmann is a marvel: he seems to be able to get to everything within 6 feet of him; and anything he can reach, he can hold. Time after time I have seen him go head over heels in trying for an almost impossible catch; but rarely, if ever, did he lose hold of the ball. The young player should watch him; for he is a fine illustration of quickness and safety, and is continually bringing off remarkable catches.

Third Man

This position can only be filled by a really good man, for it is one in which temper and judgment will be tried to the utmost. He is expected to stop everything that comes to him, for, if he miss it, it may mean a boundary hit, and if he is too far away, the batsman will steal a sharp run. Whatever the state of the ground, but particularly if at all rough, the ball, after it pitches, comes twisting and kicking; and if he is standing too square, he will have to try for it with his left hand. The slightest mistake, and the batsman is off; and the fraction of a second makes all the difference between a run and a run-out. The fieldsman must never get flurried, must be quick to decide the wicket to be thrown at, and not forget to throw the ball straight at the wicketkeeper or bowler's head, or so that it will fall into his hands about the height of his chest after first bound.

Sharp runs have a most demoralising effect on some fieldsmen; and I remember, on more than one occasion, in an important match third man losing his head completely and mistakes and overthrows were the result.

Third man must ask the bowler whether he should stand rather fine or square; he should also find out whether the batsmen are quick or slow in running, so that he may go close in or deep as the case may

Field placed for slow round-arm bowling.

be. Four of the best men in this position at the present time are Messrs A. E. Stoddart, P. J. de Paravicini, and Gunn and Maurice Read.

Point

A good point must have perfect eyesight, a pair of very safe hands, and the activity of a cat; but even with these it will take many years before he becomes first-class. It is essential for him to know something of the style of every batsman; for upon that depends whether he will do brilliant things, or simply stop the balls that come straight to him. It is a matter of opinion whether he should watch the ball or the batsman, but everyone is agreed that he should not stand perfectly still in one position. His original position should be in a line with the wicket, or a little in front of it, according to the pace of the bowling and condition of the ground. The left foot should be a little in advance, the body slightly stooping, and the hands ready to receive the ball.

Nerve goes a great length in that position; and those who have it most perform the greatest feats. My brother E. M., was the finest point I have ever seen; for not only did he bring off some extraordinary catches that came at a terrific pace straight to him, but he could tell, almost by intuition, where the batsman meant to put the ball; and no matter how close he stood, never failed to hold it. With a poky batsman he took the most outrageous liberties, and times without number he has taken the ball within an inch or two of the bat. He exercised a magnetic influence upon certain batsmen. No matter how hard they tried they could not keep the ball away from him, and Jupp in his later days got fairly stuck up by his restless activity and catlike quickness. He was equally certain with either hand whether the ball was hit at his feet or a foot or two above his head.

V. E. Walker, T. S. Pearson and Carpenter were excellent points also, and W. W. Read and Shrewsbury are quite as good. All of them stand much further back than my brother. Mr Walker was the quickest of the five, and was very good at finding out in an over or so the batsman's strength and weakness.

Cover-Point

Cover-point affords plenty of opportunities for a brilliant fieldsman to distinguish himself. He gets plenty of work; for if he is unable to get to the ball when it is hit anywhere near to him, he has to go after it at his best pace, in the hope of stopping it before it reaches the boundary. Pick-up and return must be one action, or the batsman will steal a sharp run; and he must be quick and accurate in his return, or overthrows will occur pretty often. To fast bowling he may stand rather deep and wait for the ball, but to medium pace and slow he must dart in if he wants to save the run. He has to gauge to a yard the exact position to stand, and he must be constantly on the look-out; for, as a rule, he gets twice as much work as any two other fieldsmen. He must be prepared for an occasional curly one breaking away from him, which he will do well to stop. If, when dashing in to save the run, he cannot get into position to throw in his usual way, an underhand return can be utilised.

Messrs Halifax Wyatt, G. Strachan, W. W. Read, Revd Vernon Royle, and John Smith, of Cambridge, were brilliant in that position, and worked untiringly. Messrs Gregory and J. Shuter, Briggs, and Peel, are just as good today. Mr Gregory's fine exhibition was one of the features of the fielding of the 1890 Australian team.

Short-Leg

It is not so very many years ago that the weakest fieldsman in the eleven was invariably placed at short-leg. A complete change has taken place with respect to that position, and a quick eye and a safe pair of hands are now as much needed there as in any part of the field. Leghitting is very little resorted to now, for the reason that a first-class bowler rarely bowls one on that side; but the batsman tries hard to play away to leg everything bowled on the leg-stumps and pads, and the fieldsman has to be as nimble as a cat to save the run. He has also to go as close in as he can with safety, so as to get hold of a catch. Very often when it comes to him there is a fair amount of spin on it, and if he is not very careful he will miss it altogether.

Short-leg must keep his wits about him, for the ball is on him instantly; and should it pass, will most probably travel for two or three runs. He must be quick to detect the intention of the batsman, whether he means to play it fine, square, or more in the direction of mid-on; but he must be guided by the wish of the bowler as to where he should stand. He should stand slightly stooping, with his hands ready for the ball to drop into them; and be quick to save overthrows from cover-point and mid-off. Against a poky batsman, on a sticky wicket, he has often as many opportunities as point of bringing off a smart catch. He must keep his head under all circumstances, but especially when a sharp run is attempted: the slightest indecision then, and the run-out is lost. A bad thrower should never be placed there, or overthrows will be of common occurrence, and many a run-out lost.

Long-Leg

Owing to the accuracy of the bowling, very few balls are now hit to long-leg. Fast bowling without length in the old days was not uncommon, and one never was surprised to see a ball hit to leg as often as anywhere else; but I have seen many a long innings played in the last year or two with only a few hits to leg in it. To medium-pace bowling so accurate as we have now, there is no need for a long-leg, and a man can be better utilised on the off-side; indeed, most bowlers would rather have an extra man there, and take the chance of an occasional one being pulled or hit to leg.

My brother Fred, and J. Smith of Cambridgeshire were the best in that position of all the cricketers I have known. They had the four things required to fill it: a safe pair of hands, dash, speed, and good throwing. Rarely did they fail to bring off a catch they could get to, and I have seen batsman after batsman afraid to hit out when either was in that part of the field. They could tell to a yard whether they had to move forward or go back, and never thought anything out of their reach; but it was in their dash they shone conspicuously over others. They did not expect to save the first run, but they considered it bad fielding if a second were obtained. Immediately the batsman hit they were on move, and they covered the first 10 yards at top speed, and had the ball into the wicketkeepers' hands almost as soon as the first run was finished. If they could use both hands, they invariably did it; but if time did not permit, they were equally certain with right or left, and they did not forget to allow for the spin which is more or less on every ball hit to leg. Their throw-in was as straight as an arrow, and invariably fell into the wicketkeeper's hands first-bound a foot above the wicket. They rarely stopped a ball with their foot; for they were strongly of opinion that a good fieldsman in that position could stop anything possible more effectually with his hand, and that upon the quick pick-up and return depended the saving of the second run.

Another good quality of theirs was their judgment in knowing whether to stand fine or square. Very rarely do you meet two batsmen who hit exactly alike to leg. My brother and Smith generally thought of that, and could tell exactly where to go without being told to nearly every batsman they played against.

Mid-On

Mid-on is one of the easiest places in the field; for there is no twist on the ball, and the fieldsman has plenty of time to see it coming to him. His position depends entirely on the bowling, and he is placed close in or deep according to the wish of the bowler. Boyle fielding close in to Spofforth's bowling was a fine illustration of what can be done against certain batsmen when fieldsman and bowler have perfect faith in each other; but the fact of it not being generally adopted shows that it will not do for everyday use. On a line with the bowler's wicket is the position usually taken, but a great deal will depend on the activity of the batsmen. If they are very quick runners, the fieldsman should go as near as he can with safety, and he should practise picking-up and throwing-in underhand. The state of the ground must always be remembered: when it is dry and fast, he should not be too near; but when it is soft and slow, he should go closer in.

Mid-Off

The position of mid-off is rather more difficult to fill than that of mid-on, especially to a slow left-hand bowler.. The ball has a slight twist on it; and often when it is. hit, it rises at a peculiar and trying angle. It is just the distance when the ball is at its greatest velocity, and a catch that, at first sight, looks as if it could be taken breast-high has often to be taken above the head. There is rather a peculiar sensation for a second when the ball comes that way, and it requires a good man to catch it.

Messrs I. D. Walker, A. J. Webbe, and F. Townsend are very good in that position. I have seen them bring off catch after catch at all conceivable altitudes sometimes with one hand, sometimes with both. Now it would be at a foot from the ground, then breast high, and occasionally with hand fully extended over the head. Messrs W. J. Ford and A. N. Hornby used to be difficult men to field to in that position, their hitting being exceptionally hard and low. The ball came like a flash of lightning sometimes actually humming and required a very quick eye and hand to stop it. More than once the fieldsman has been seen to draw away from it altogether. Against good batsmen who play hard from the wicket and place the ball, mid-off has plenty of work to save the run. He must be constantly on the watch, and dash in immediately the ball leaves the bat; in fact, he should be able to tell from the nature of the ball bowled whether it is likely to come his way, and should be on the move as soon as it is hit. If the bowling is round the wicket, he should not go quite so far out as he would when it is over; for the bowler cannot cover so much ground on his side when bowling that way.

Long-Field

No one who is not accustomed to the position of long-field should be placed there, whether it be on the on-side, the off-side, or over the bowler's head. Close in, remarkable catches are brought off, but no one is surprised when one is missed now and then. In the long-field the fieldsman has plenty of time to see the ball coming; but a lofty catch, and one that has to be waited for, is more difficult to bring off than one that comes quickly and is all over in a second or two. While the ball is travelling to long-field there is time for many thoughts to flash through his mind: chief of which are, that the players and spectators have all turned their eyes upon him, and that he will get no sympathy should he fail to bring off the catch.

I question if there is any position in the field that the beginner should practice so much as that of longfield. He should begin with having the ball thrown low and straight at him at a distance of 70 yards; afterwards he should go back further, and have it thrown higher into the air; and then at a distance away from him that he can reach at full speed. He will find that in each case making the catch is slightly different, but waiting for and bringing off a very lofty one most difficult of all. When the ball is dropping into his hands, he should allow them to give a little to it, or it will rebound out of them. A brilliant out-fieldsman is worth his place in any eleven for the work he can do there alone. Upon him will depend whether the hit is to count 1, 2, or 4 runs: a mistake there means, in most cases, a boundary hit.

One sterling cricketer comes to my mind who is a grand example of what I mean: Mr P. J. de Paravicini. From the time Mr Paravicini captained the Eton XI in '80 and '81 down to the present time, no player has shown more clearly what a quick pair of legs, a safe pair of hands, and a sound head can do in the long-field. He is dashing and safe, equally good with both hands, and does not know what an impossible catch means. Some of his feats for Middlesex have been quite phenomenal.

Many a match has been lost by bad generalship; so it may be safely said that an eleven in the field is of little use without a good captain at the head of it. The ideal captain should possess sound judgment, enthusiasm, firmness and good temper, and have plenty of patience; for his duties are numerous, and he is certain to have these qualities severely tried during a long or close match. I have said elsewhere that an experienced captain before tossing takes into consideration the light and state of the ground. There are other things as well that make or mar a match: the time for drawing stumps and interval allowed for luncheon. These, though seemingly small points, should always be decided before tossing, or unpleasantness may follow.

If the toss falls in his favour, the captain should, as a rule, decide for his side to bat first; for the wicket is generally better, and every batsman is more likely to score when he is fresh than when tired: besides, the light is invariably better in the morning than in the evening, and it is easier to save runs than make them at a pinch.

It used to be thought bad judgment to put two quick scorers in together, the reason given being that they would run each other off his legs in consequence. I do not think it matters much today when nearly every hit of any force goes to the boundary and there is little occasion to run more than one run. Twenty-five years ago it was different; for a hit for six one ball, and seven the next, occurred now and then, and, as there were no boundaries, two free-hitters very soon tired themselves out.

A captain, once he has decided upon the order of his men going in, should stick to it, unless exceptional circumstances arise which, according to his judgment, demand a change – such as keeping back a good man a few minutes before time for drawing stumps, or a sudden change in the light. He should also impress on his men the importance of going promptly to the wicket when their turn comes. Carelessness in that respect shows ignorance of the laws, is annoying to the other side, and not likely to improve the form of the batsman who is waiting.

If his bowlers are fair bats he should not put them down very low on the list; for it is now pretty well known that if a bowler makes runs, he cannot bowl well without a short rest. Lohmann never bowls up to his proper form if he has made a score just before he begins. The hitting has cramped his fingers, and he cannot feel the ball properly for an over or two. His is not a solitary case.

A captain has now the power of closing his innings anytime on the last day of a match; but great judgment is required to do it at the right moment. If he be halfhearted or timid, he will decide to do so when it is absolutely certain that he cannot lose; but it is just as likely that his delay of half an hour, or even a quarter, has made it impossible for him to win. If he have pluck and dash, and does not mind risking a little, he may snatch a brilliant victory a few minutes before time. Personally I side with a forward policy, and would rather any day have an exciting finish than one in which players and spectators have lost all interest.

Between the innings, and on each morning when his side is going to bat, the captain should see that the pitch is carefully and thoroughly rolled. I am glad to say that there is little need of this on our leading and best county grounds; still, it should not be neglected.

A captain has greater responsibility on his shoulders when his eleven is in the field. His hardest task is to make the best use of the bowling under his command. Occasionally when the wicket is difficult the first two bowlers may get the batsmen out without a change being necessary; and the captain may have little to do but see that his fieldsmen are always in their proper places. But when the wicket is an easy one a long innings is oftener the case, and he is sure to have his skill and resources tried to the utmost. He should always begin with what he considers his two best bowlers, and never forget that a difference in pace and style is likely to prove most effective. A fast right-hand bowler at one end and a slow left-hand at the other is a powerful combination.

Should these fail to come off, the captain should. not hesitate to make a change, if only for a few overs. Any change is better than none. A very good plan is to make it after 20 runs have been scored, if no wicket has fallen. A change should also be made after a series of maiden-overs without a wicket falling. Of course, there are times when a bowler is out of luck. He keeps beating the batsman ball after ball, but the wicket does not fall, or perhaps catches are missed off him. In that case, the captain will do right to keep him on a little longer.

The bowler should be allowed to place his own field. At the same time, the captain should make suggestions now and again about having another man in the longfield, an extra short-leg or cover-point; anything, in fact, that would tend to get the batsmen out. The captain should keep his eye on all the field, and notice at the beginning of each over whether they are in their right places. Some fieldsmen cannot stand in the same place two overs in succession, and it is very annoying to the bowler to see runs scored off him on account of it. The captain should also notice whether the field back up properly, and set them a good example in that respect. He should also field, if possible, somewhere near the wicket, so that he may be able to watch the bowling. In that position, he will have better command of the team than anywhere in the long-field. When a ball is skied and two men go for it, he should immediately shout the name of the fieldsman who has the better chance of bringing off the catch. Quick decision then will save them from colliding, and often prevent an easy catch from being missed.

In conclusion, let me say that, whether in the field or out of it, the captain should not openly reprimand any of his eleven for a mistake. A word or two spoken quietly will have more effect; and he should remember, above all things, to set a good example and always practise what he preaches.

11

The Laws of Cricket

As Revised by the Committee of the Marylebone Cricket Club, 1884 and 1889.

1. The Game.

A match is played between two sides of eleven players The Game, each, unless otherwise agreed to; each side has two innings, taken alternately, except in the case provided for in Law 53. The choice of innings shall be decided by tossing.

2. Runs.

The score shall be reckoned by runs. A run is scored:

1st. So often as the batsmen after a hit, or at any time while the ball is in play, shall have crossed and made good their ground from end to end.

2nd. For penalties under Laws 16, 34, 41, and allowances under 44.

Any run or runs so scored shall be duly recorded by scorers appointed for the purpose.

The side which scores the greatest number of runs wins the match. No match is won unless played out or given up, except in the case provided in Law 45.

3. Appointment of Umpires.

Before the commencement of the match two Umpires shall be appointed, one for each end.

4. The Ball.

The Ball shall weigh not less than five ounces and a half, nor more than five ounces and three-quarters. It shall measure not less than nine inches, nor more than nine inches and one-quarter in circumference. At the beginning of each innings either side may demand a new ball.

5. The Bat.

The Bat shall not exceed four inches and one-quarter in the widest part; it shall not be more than thirty-eight inches in length.

6. The Wickets.

The Wickets shall be pitched opposite and parallel to each other at a distance of 22 yards. Each wicket shall be eight inches in width, and consist of three stumps, with two bails upon the top. The stumps shall be of equal and sufficient size to prevent the ball from passing through, twenty-seven inches out of the ground. The bails shall be each four inches in length, and when in position on the top of the stumps, shall not project more than half an inch above them. The wickets shall not be changed during a match, unless the ground between them become unfit for play; and then only by consent of both sides.

7. The Bowling Crease.

The Bowling Crease shall be in a line with the stumps, six feet eight inches in length the stumps in the centre, with a return crease at each end, at right angles behind the wicket.

8. The Popping Crease.

The Popping Crease shall be marked four feet from the wicket, parallel to it, and be deemed unlimited in length.

9. The Ground.

The Ground shall not be rolled, watered, covered, mown, or beaten during a match, except before the commencement of each innings and of each day's play; when, unless the in-side object, the ground shall be swept and rolled for not more than ten minutes. This shall not prevent the batsman from beating the ground with his bat, nor the batsman nor bowler using sawdust in order to obtain a proper foothold.

10. The Bowler.

The ball must be bowled; if thrown or jerked the umpire shall call 'No Ball.'

11. No Ball.

The Bowler shall deliver the ball with one foot on the ground behind the bowling crease, and within the return crease, otherwise the umpire shall call 'No Ball.'

12. Wide Ball.

If the bowler shall bowl the ball so high over or so wide of the wicket that, in the opinion of the umpire, it is not within reach of the striker, the umpire shall call 'Wide Ball.'

13. The Over.

The ball shall be bowled in Overs of five balls from each wicket alternately. When five balls have been bowled, and the ball is finally settled in the bowler's or wicketkeeper's hands, the umpire shall call 'Over.' Neither a 'no ball' nor a 'wide ball' shall be reckoned as one of the 'over.'

14. The bowler shall be allowed to change ends as often as he pleases, provided only that he does not bowl two overs consecutively in one innings.

15. The bowler may require the batsman at the wicket from which he is bowling to stand on that side of it which he may direct.

16. Scoring off No Balls and Wide Balls.

The striker may hit a 'No Ball,' and whatever runs result shall be added to his score; but he shall not be out from a 'no ball,' unless he be run out or break Laws 26, 27, 29, 30. All runs made from a 'no ball,' otherwise than from the bat, shall be scored 'no balls,' and if no run be made one run shall be added to that score. From a 'Wide Ball' as many runs as are run shall be added to the score as 'wide balls,' and if no run be otherwise obtained one run shall be so added.

17. Bye.

If the ball, not having been called 'wide' or 'no ball', pass the striker without touching his bat or person, and any runs be obtained, the umpire shall call 'Bye'; but if the ball touch any part of the striker's person (hand excepted), and any run be obtained, the umpire shall call 'Leg-bye', such runs to be scored' byes' and 'leg-byes' respectively.

18. Play.

At the beginning of the match, and of each innings, the umpire at the bowler's wicket shall call 'Play'. From that time no trial ball shall be allowed to any bowler on the ground between the wickets; and when one of the batsmen is out, the use of the bat shall not be allowed to any person until the next batsman shall come in.

19. Definitions.

A batsman shall be held to be 'out of his ground', unless his bat in hand or some part of his person be grounded within the line of the popping crease.

20. The wicket shall be held to be 'down' when either of the bails is struck off, or if both bails be off, when a stump is struck out of the ground.

21. The Striker.

The striker is out if the wicket be bowled down, even if the ball first touch the striker's bat or person; 'Bowled.'

22. Or, if the ball, from a stroke of the bat or hand, but not the wrist, be held before it touch the ground, although it be hugged to the body of the catcher; 'Caught.'

23. Or, if in playing at the ball, provided it be not touched by the bat or hand, the striker be out of his ground, and the wicket be put down by the wicketkeeper with the ball or with hand or arm, with ball in hand; 'Stumped.'

24. Or, if with any part of his person he stop the ball which, in the opinion of the umpire at the bowler's wicket, shall have been pitched in a straight line from it to the striker's wicket and would have hit it; 'Leg before wicket.'

25. Or, if in playing at the ball he hit down his wicket with his bat or any part of his person or dress; 'Hit wicket'.

26. Or, if under pretence of running, or otherwise, either of the batsmen wilfully prevent a ball from being caught; 'Obstructing the field.'

27. Or, if the ball be struck, or be stopped by any part of his person, and he wilfully strike it again, except it be done for the purpose of guarding his wicket, which he may do with his bat, or any part of his person except his hands; 'Hit the ball twice.'

28. The Batsman.
Either batsman is out if in running, or at any other time, while the ball is in play, he be out of his ground, and his wicket be struck down by the ball after touching any fieldsman, or by the hand or arm, with ball in hand, of any fieldsman; 'Run out.'

29. Or, if he touch with his hands or take up the ball while in play, unless at the request of the opposite side; 'Handled the ball.'

30. Or, if he wilfully obstruct any fieldsman; 'Obstructing the field.'

31. If the batsmen have crossed each other, he that runs for the wicket which is put down is out; if they have not crossed, he that has left the wicket which is put down is out.

32. The striker being caught no run shall be scored. A batsman being run out, that run which was being attempted shall not be scored.

33. A batsman being out from any cause, the ball shall be 'Dead.'

34. Lost Ball.
If a ball in play cannot be found or recovered, any fieldsman may call 'Lost Ball,' when the ball shall be 'dead'; six runs shall be added to the score; but if more than six runs have been run before

'lost ball' has been called, as many runs as have been run shall be scored.

35. After the ball shall have been finally settled in the wicketkeeper's or bowler's hand, it shall be 'dead'; but when the bowler is about to deliver the ball, if the batsman at his wicket be out of his ground before actual delivery, the said bowler may run him out; but if the bowler throw at that wicket and any run result, it shall be scored 'no ball.'

36. A batsman shall not retire from his wicket and return to it to complete his innings after another has been in, without the consent of the opposite side.

37. Substitute.
A Substitute shall be allowed to field or run between wickets for any player who may, during the match, be incapacitated from illness or injury, but for no other reason, except with the consent of the opposite side.

38. In all cases where a substitute shall be allowed, the consent of the opposite side shall be obtained as to the person to act as substitute, and the place in the field which he shall take.

39. In case any substitute shall be allowed to run between wickets, the striker may be run out if either he or his substitute be out of his ground. If the striker be out of his ground while the ball is in play, the wicket which he has left may be put down and the striker given out, although the other batsman may have made good the ground at that end, and the striker and his substitute at the other end.

40. A batsman is liable to be out for any infringement of the Laws by his substitute.

41. The Fieldsman.
The Fieldsman may stop the ball with any part of his The Fieldsman person; but if he wilfully stop it otherwise, the ball shall be 'dead,' and five runs added to the score; whatever runs may have been made, five only shall be added.

42. Wicketkeeper.

The Wicketkeeper shall stand behind the wicket. If he shall take the ball, for the purpose of stumping, before it has passed the wicket, or, if he shall incommode the striker by any noise or motion, or, if any part of his person be over or before the wicket, the striker shall not be out, excepting under Laws 26, 27, 28, 29, and 30.

43. Duties of Umpires.

The Umpires are the sole judges of fair or unfair play, of the fitness of the ground, the weather, and the light for play. All disputes shall be determined by them, and if they disagree, the actual state of things shall continue.

44. They shall pitch fair wickets, arrange boundaries where necessary, and the allowances to be made for them, and change ends after each side has had one innings.

45. They shall allow two minutes for each striker to come in, and ten minutes between each innings. When they shall call 'Play', the side refusing to play shall lose the match.

46. They shall not order a batsman out unless appealed to by the other side.

47. The umpire at the bowler's wicket shall be appealed to before the other umpire in all cases, except those of stumping, hit wicket, run out at the striker's wicket, or, arising out of Law 42; but in any case in which an umpire is unable to give a decision, he shall appeal to the other umpire, whose decision shall be final.

48. If the umpire at the bowler's end be not satisfied of the absolute fairness of the delivery of any ball, he shall call 'No Ball'.

48a. The Umpire shall take especial care to call 'No Ball' instantly upon delivery; 'Wide Ball' as soon as it shall have passed the striker.

49. If either batsman run a short run, the Umpire shall call 'One Short', and the run shall not be scored.

50. After the Umpire has called 'Over', the ball is 'dead', but an appeal may be made as to whether either batsman is out; such appeal shall not be made after the delivery of the next ball, nor after cessation of play.

51. No umpire shall be allowed to bet.

52. No umpire shall be changed during a match, unless with the consent of both sides, except in case of violation of Law 51; then either side may dismiss him.

53. Following Innings.
The side which goes in second shall follow their innings, if they have scored eighty runs less than the opposite side.

54. On the last day of a match, and in a one-day match at any time, the in-side may declare their innings at an end.

One-Day Matches

1. The side which goes in second shall follow their innings, if they have scored sixty runs less than the opposite side.

2. The match, unless played out, shall be decided by the first innings. Prior to the commencement of a match it may be agreed that the over consist of five or six balls.

Single Wicket

The Laws are, where they apply, the same as the above, with the following alterations and additions.

1. 1 wicket shall be pitched, as in Law 6, with a bowling stump opposite to it at a distance of 22 yards. The bowling crease shall be in a line with the bowling stump, and drawn according to Law 7.

2. When there shall be less than five players on a side, bounds shall be placed 22 yards each in a line from the off and leg-stump.

3. The ball must be hit before the bounds to entitle the striker to a run, which run cannot be obtained unless he touch the bowling stump or crease in a line with his bat, or some part of his person, or go beyond them, and return to the popping crease.

4. When the striker shall hit the ball, one of his feet must be on the ground behind the popping crease, otherwise the umpire shall call 'No Hit' and no run shall be scored.

5. When there shall be less than five players on a side, neither byes, leg-byes, nor overthrows shall be allowed; nor shall the striker be caught out behind the wicket, nor stumped.

6. The fieldsman must return the ball so that it shall cross the ground between the wicket and the bowling stump, or between the bowling stump and the bounds; the striker may run till the ball be so returned.

7. After the striker shall have made one run, if he start again, he must touch the bowling stump or crease and turn before the ball cross the ground to entitle him to another.

8. The striker shall be entitled to three runs for lost ball, and the same number for ball wilfully stopped by a fieldsman otherwise than with any part of his person.

9. When there shall be more than four players on a side, there shall be no bounds. All hits, byes, leg-byes, and overthrows shall then be allowed.

10. There shall be no restriction as to the ball being bowled in overs; but no more than one minute shall be allowed between each ball.

Rules of County Cricket

1. That no cricketer, whether amateur or professional, shall play for more than one county during the same season.

2. Every cricketer born in one county and residing in another shall be free to choose at the commencement of each season for which of those counties he will play, and shall, during that season, play for that county only.

3. A cricketer shall be qualified to play for any county in which he is residing and has resided for the previous two years; or a cricketer may elect to play for the county in which his family home is, so long as it remains open to him as an occasional residence. A man can play for his old county during the two years that he is qualifying for another.

4. That, should any question arise as to the residential qualification, the same should be left to the decision of the committee of the Marylebone Club.

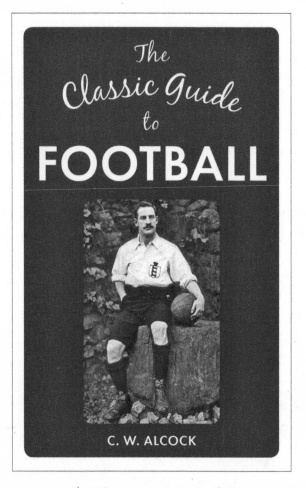

The Classic Guide to Football
C. W. Alcock

Charles William Alcock, one of the fathers of modern football, sets down much of the history and knowledge he accumulated over his long career in this, one of the very first 'manuals' of the sport.

978 1 4456 4016 7
160 pages

Available from all good bookshops or order direct
from our website www.amberleybooks.com

The Classic Guide to Tennis
John Moyer Heathcote

Among the committee that devised the original rules of lawn rennis, John Moyer Heathcote's classic guide to tennis instructs the budding tennis player in how to become a master of the game.

978 1 4456 4118 8
224 pages

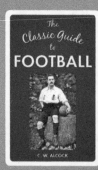